Border Crossing

Border Crossing

True Stories of the RUC Special Branch,
the Garda Special Branch and the IRA Moles

George Clarke

Gill & Macmillan

Gill & Macmillan Ltd
Hume Avenue, Park West, Dublin 12
with associated companies throughout the world
www.gillmacmillan.ie

© George Clarke 2009
978 07171 4568 3

Typography design by Make Communication
Print origination by Síofra Murphy
Printed by ColourBooks Ltd, Dublin

This book is typeset in Linotype Minion and Neue Helvetica.

The paper used in this book comes from the wood pulp of
managed forests. For every tree felled, at least one tree is
planted, thereby renewing natural resources.

A CIP catalogue record for this book is available
from the British Library.

5 4 3 2

*This book is dedicated to those members of
An Garda Síochána and the RUC who lost their
lives whilst performing their duty of protecting the
people from terrorism, and to my wife and family,
especially my eldest son, who had a less than
normal life as a boy monitoring my personal
safety on a daily basis.*

Do all the good you can
By all the means you can
In all the ways you can
In all the places you can
At all the times you can
To all the people you can
As long as ever you can

JOHN WESLEY 1703–1791

Contents

PREFACE   XI

1.   London Bombs   1
2.   Meeting with McMahon in County
     Louth   17
3.   Ultimatum to London from McMahon   32
4.   Myself   40
5.   Pre-Internment Source   62
6.   Special Branch Intelligence-Gathering   77
7.   Criminal Injury Claims   85
8.   Proposed Bombing of Newry RUC
     Station   89
9.   Bridge Vehicle Checkpoint Incident   95
10. Proposed Bomb to Kevin Street   98
11. Robert Nairac and the SAS   105
12. Internment   116
13. Further Meet with McMahon   127
14. Dublin Trip with MIO   135
15. Further Meet of the Triangle re:
     Rogue Members of RUC/Gardaí   140
16. The Cherry Blossom Kid   147
17. Bomb at Forkhill   153
18. Meeting with Source and with Garda
     Special Branch   158
19. Meeting with Garvin   163
20. Ending of Customs Checks at Border
     Posts   167
21. Enoch Powell   172

22.	Michael McVerry	174
23.	Further Meet of Triangle	180
24.	Too Many Cooks	186
25.	Family Flee to London	194
26.	Murder Trial and Sequel	199
27.	Port Laoise Jail	208
28.	Catholic Peace Association	213
29.	Charlie Haughey and the Bugging Devices	216
30.	Visit to Chief Constable	223
31.	The Night I Joined the Clergy	229
32.	Ice Skating	234
33.	Brush with Royalty	238
34.	Move from the Border	241

Preface

It requires many years of slow, dedicated work by the intelligence services of a country to infiltrate a terrorist organisation and to maintain a continuous progress. The difficulties tend to multiply when this organisation is in its infancy. Every avenue of contact has to be explored. Nothing is in, nothing is out. So it was in Ulster from 1970. The Provisional IRA was finding its feet, having broken away from the mainstream movement, which was to be known in the future as the Official IRA. The latter had been dormant since the abortive '56 campaign, and had been re-grouping since the 1969 civil rights marches. The new Provisional movement began to pull out all the stops to obtain up-to-date weaponry. There was a hectic period of recruitment in 1970–71. This was going to be a long-haul campaign. Seán Mac Stíofáin was appointed chief-of-staff, and soon developed a ruthless reputation.

The RUC Special Branch was the only intelligence agency in the Province, and they had the task of infiltrating the Provos. I covered South Armagh/South Down, and as the violence increased and the North slid towards anarchy, more and more young PIRA members went on the run to the Republic, especially around the Dundalk area. At this time there was absolutely no contact between the police forces North and South, in any way whatsoever. When I made unofficial contact with my Garda Special Branch counterparts in early 1971 and started a priceless liaison—which developed into the co-operation between the two forces we see today—many, many lives were saved. We had many successes, some of which can be told, some that probably cannot, ever. This was a dangerous liaison, dangerous for me in visiting the Republic almost daily and dangerous for Garda Special Branch, who were operating in an unofficial role, unknown to their government, or indeed their colleagues. We were never going to stop the bombings and shootings, but we certainly slowed PIRA down on many occasions, with seizures of weapons and explosives. This book is dedicated to those members of Garda Special Branch who, both before and after internment, had a liaison with me, preferring to stop murder and destruction than turn a blind eye to a republican all-Ireland agenda. They were the real heroes.

This book is written without malice towards any government, organisation, or any person. I must stress that the chapters are not in chronological order, and that I have chosen days in my working life at random. Some names and places have been changed to respect the wishes of those living. Some are now deceased.

Chapter 1
London Bombs

It was early spring 1973. I hadn't long finished my evening meal and the children were getting ready for bed when the phone rang. Eileen looked at me. 'Are you in then?'

I nodded. It had been the usual eventful day. I had visited Dublin early in the morning. I had made contact with a young Provisional IRA volunteer, whom I had recruited as an informant about a year previously. I was surprised that he was still active in the movement. He was a bit of a rough diamond, but he was producing first-rate intelligence. I had recently turned a blind eye, and had not put pen to paper when he was involved in IRA operations. I had made sure the military were in other places during these operations so they wouldn't be killed or injured. A high-grade source couldn't be handled any other way. He had to take part, be active, or he would be useless. A cell system was being developed by the Provisionals and things would never be the same again. I picked up the phone. 'Hello?'

'Hello, Ops room here, the military checkpoint on the Newry to Dundalk road at the border are requesting a Special Branch officer.'

'Do you know what's up?'

'I haven't all the facts, but it seems an unknown male who refuses to identify himself has approached them at the permanent vehicle checkpoint. All he will say is that he wants to talk to Special Branch only.'

'Okay, I'll come to the office shortly.'

'The Military Intelligence officer has intimated he will transport you to the checkpoint by chopper. The weather is just about flyable.'

'Thanks, I'll call him when I get in.'

Trust the MIO to stick his nose in, I thought to myself, always on the lookout for any bits of stray intelligence wafting around. Having the MIO present made things simple at military checkpoints or establishments. Then you had to explain nothing, but I wasn't too happy with the MIO at present. A young casual contact I was grooming as an informant in Provisional Sinn Féin was probably going to be invited into the Provos. That is, until a week ago, when the military detained him on suspicion, for four hours, as they could do. He had to report this to the Sinn Féin Cumann, and was immediately suspended for six months in case he had been recruited by Military Intelligence.

I had been in the office when the lad was detained, and had been given the names for comment. I had two choices: declare an interest and have him released immediately, with the military recognising a source, or say nothing and hope that after six months things would be okay again. I chose the latter. I would forget about him for a year maybe, unless the source contacted me first. I had to be wary; sometimes the Provos would put a tail on those lifted for 'screening', as the army called it, in case they were tainted. It was better to leave them alone for some time.

I drove the ten-minute journey to the office. It was raining heavily and visibility was not good. Not good helicopter weather, of which I was glad. I lifted the internal phone. 'Special Branch here, any further messages?' I said.

'Yes, the MIO is on his way from Bessbrook.'

'Thanks, Jimmy.'

I decided that I didn't want the MIO involved, so I grabbed my coat and hat and headed down the stairs. Something told me this was a job for me alone. I was soaked covering the forty yards back to my car, and cursed the weather. The sentry at the gate waved me out and I set off for the border checkpoint. I didn't like travelling the border roads after dark; anything could happen. There had been many IRA checkpoints recently and I didn't believe in taking too many chances. Although I crossed the border two or three times weekly to make contact with Provo sources 'on the run' from the security forces in the North, many of whom were now living in Dundalk in the Republic, I did go in daylight hours where possible. It was quite easy to meet in supermarkets, chapels, or outside Garda stations.

Fifteen minutes later and I was at the border checkpoint. My car was stopped.

'You sent for Special Branch. Can I see the officer in charge?' I asked.

'Have you identification, sir?'

I showed the soldier my warrant card.

'Lieutenant Smith is in charge, he's in the armoured carrier with the gentleman. If you park here I will take you over.'

We approached the vehicle and the soldier knocked on the rear door. The door opened and the lieutenant jumped out, a tall, fair-haired young man. He introduced himself and we shook hands. He told me a bit more about the man they had.

'He just appeared, walking out of the mist and rain, and asked that he be allowed to speak to Special Branch. He will not give his name, but by his accent he's from the South. He was soaked. I have put a blanket around him.'

The officer shone his torch into the rear of the vehicle. A figure sat huddled in one of the seats. I climbed in and asked the lieutenant, who was coming in after me, to remain outside. He didn't appear to be too happy with this.

'Special Branch?' asked the figure in the blanket.

'Yes, and you are?'

'Look, I have something for you. Can we go to your base?'

'Who are you?'

'I helped you guys in the last campaign in 1956. I have something urgent. I know Billy Jones—has he retired yet?'

The name he had just dropped was that of a senior officer at Special Branch Headquarters.

'Is everything okay?' shouted the lieutenant from outside. He opened the door.

'Yes, I'm taking this gentleman to the police station.'

The lieutenant stuttered slightly. 'But sir, the MIO is on his way here, he has been on the radio. I think you should wait. I cannot let you go. Who is this man?'

'Call the MIO now, and tell him that I am taking the gentleman to my office. He can contact me there.'

The lieutenant did as requested and I heard him ask permission of the MIO to search and detain the gentleman. I also heard the MIO, Captain Robert Laycock, order him to do all that Special Branch required. I helped the man down from the personnel carrier and handed the blanket to one of the soldiers. Together we got into my car and drove off.

We hadn't gone a hundred yards when I asked him, 'Were you searched?'

'No.'

'Are you carrying a weapon?'

'No, do you think I'm a fool?'

I smelt a funny smell from him and I realised it was peat. The man must have burned peat in his abode.

I was about to start with a few basic questions when the stranger asked, 'Are there any other checkpoints on this road?'

'Why?'

'Just for my own information.'

He then asked if I had ever been to Port Laoise in the Republic. I said that I had.

'Do you know the prison?'

'Yes.'

'There will be a break-out there soon.'

'Is this your information?'

'No. It's where I shop on occasions or visit the jail. I have to arrange for a heavy-duty chainsaw.'

'For what?'

'A prison break has been discussed.'

We talked as if we had known each other for years, and I didn't realise it then, but this was the start of an extraordinary relationship.

We reached the office and I opened the door. The place was in darkness; it was good that no one was around. I turned on the lights and offered the man a chair. He sat down and removed his woollen hat and glasses.

'Now you see the real me,' he said.

Before me sat a middle-aged man, he was thick-set with short, greying hair, round-faced with a three-day growth of beard. He offered his hand and as I shook it I felt enormous strength in his fingers.

I looked at him and said, 'Look, I've got to check you out. I must know who you are.'

'I know that. Telephone Billy Jones and tell him you're with someone who loves De Kuypers gin.'

I studied him for a moment, looked at my telephone list and dialled a number.

'Sir, it's George Clarke. I have a fellow in the office who tells me he loves De Kuypers gin.'

There was silence for a moment. 'Jesus, is he a Southerner?'

I replied in the affirmative and he continued, 'I know him well. Get what he has, and promise him anything he wants.'

'Tell him it's London,' interrupted the man.

'He says it's London.'

'Say nothing else on this line. Get the information up to me at HQ as quickly as you can. If he doesn't offer to identify himself don't question him on it.'

I put down the phone, looked at him and said, 'Well, let's have it.'

'There are four car bombs on the way to London at this moment. They are to detonate tomorrow at noon.'

He went on to name the IRA team involved and who was in charge of the operation. I listened intently. This was hot stuff. It would be the first time the Provos had attempted any serious outrage in London.

I noted all the intelligence and said, 'Look, I really do need to know who you are because I must grade this information.'

'Okay, we must be honest. I'll give you my true name, and you give me your name. I think we could be involved a lot in the future, but I'm looking for serious money.'

'What do you mean by serious?'

'Fifteen thousand for starters.'

'I have to report this, because it's out of my league.'

'You do that, and tell them the well will run dry if they fuck me about, and I'll tell you now that my name is Séamus McMahon.'

I breathed deeply and looked at him closely. I had heard of him, a senior member of the Provos and one of the so-called godfathers. My mind raced. I had to get him out of the office quickly before the MIO or any of my colleagues arrived.

I formally introduced myself to him, and said, 'I've got to get you out of the office now.'

I gave him his hat, coat and glasses and almost pulled him out of the office, down the stairs and back to the car. I had to get this intelligence to HQ for transmission to Special Branch in London. I looked at my watch. It was 10 p.m., only fourteen hours until the bombs were due to go off.

'My car is a mile over the border. Can you take me to it?' he asked.

I drove like hell and dropped him at his car, having first exchanged code names and a means of contact. McMahon had been insistent that we use the same code name, 'Seán'. I agreed. My home was en route to Belfast and I called in for a couple of minutes to put on a cardigan, it was cold. Eileen was already in bed; the children had an early rise for school.

'I'm going to HQ at Knock in Belfast,' I said.

'At this time of night? Well, at least it's North and not South. I'll sleep easier,' she replied.

As I drove into the security entrance to Headquarters, it was still raining. I showed my ID to the young constable on duty and pitied his job on such a dirty night. The car park in the precinct was almost full. Armoured personnel vehicles were moving out of the gates in a line. A bomb had been detonated in the city centre, with fatalities, earlier in the night. I had heard the radio transmissions from the hidden car radio under my seat as I approached the city. I had chosen my route to Headquarters at Knock carefully, coming in from the south-east. There were quite a few people about, even though the past few days in Belfast had been like a war zone. Nothing really mattered except keeping out of trouble.

My mind flashed back to 1941 in Belfast when, as a child living in the north of the city, I had fled with my mother and sisters to the slopes of the Cavehill overlooking Belfast when the siren had sounded and German bombers were attempting to drop bombs on the shipyard and Shorts aircraft factory. On that particular night their aim was off target and whole streets of houses were flattened instead. I remember looking down and thinking that the entire city was on fire. We lay in the fields until the 'all clear' siren sounded, and joined the long lines of people, mostly women and children, heading home and wondering if they still had homes to go to. Most able-bodied men in Ulster had gone to fight the Nazi menace, and the fact was noticed when moving around the city. The buses and shops were full of women and children. In the Republic it was different. I remember going on a field trip to Dublin during rationing with my mother to buy and smuggle essentials like eggs, meal and butter north to Belfast. How unusual it was to see so many men; but they didn't have to fight Hitler, did they?

———

I climbed the stairs at HQ and nodded at various officers on my way to the third floor. As I entered the double doors to the Special Branch/Security Services corridor, I met one of the 'Republican Desk Officers' whose job it was to grade and collate all intelligence on the republican side.

'Hiya, George, how's things at the border? I see you are being as successful as ever. The boss is waiting for you in his office. I've just taken him a cup of tea, grab a cup. See you in a while.'

My boss was the assistant chief constable, Special Branch.

'Right, Joe, thanks. I don't hope to be here long.'

I knocked on the boss's door.

'Come in,' a voice yelled. I entered and was taken aback to see the chief constable sitting on an easy chair.

'You know George from the southern region?' asked my boss.

'Yes I do. How are you, George?' the chief asked.

'I'm fine, thank you,' I replied.

I had served with the chief constable when he had been a district inspector in a once peaceful Belfast. While he had studied and gone on to greater things, I had been content with my happily married lot. Promotion meant moving to country areas, at that time, and I wasn't ambitious in any way whatsoever.

'Well, George, give us the facts. Did our friend identify himself?'

'Yes, sir, he did.'

'I knew him years ago,' said the boss, 'he gave me some good intelligence once in the 1956 campaign, but disappeared from the scene and it was only last year that we learned he was involved again.'

'Did you ever consider contacting him again?' I asked.

'Sure I did, but things were quiet and it would have been difficult contacting him, and he just appeared to melt away.'

'Well, sir, he states that at twelve noon tomorrow four car bombs will go off in London. He is only sure of two targets, the Old Bailey and New Scotland Yard. He has named some of the bombing team of men and women. Gerry Kelly of the Belfast Brigade would appear to be in charge of the operation. There are also two sisters named Price taking part. The cars were driven over with the bombs built into the car boots. They had a training camp in the South from where the operation was planned. I have no makes of cars or registration numbers but they have Northern Ireland plates, he's sure of that, although they may be changed on arrival in England.'

I gave all the intelligence. The boss grabbed the phone and dialled a number.

'Hello J. Sorry, did I get you up? Can you go to a secure phone immediately?' He replaced the receiver. 'You've had a long day, George. Didn't you say earlier you were in Dublin this morning?'

'Yes, I have been over the border twice today.'

'I don't want to hear this,' smiled the chief constable. 'For God's sake watch yourself. If anything happened to you we would deny you were operating in the Republic. You know how bolshie the Garda Síochána and the Free State government are.'

I laughed. 'Liaison at your level may be nil, but I see a couple of my own rank regularly. They provide good stuff.'

'What do you give in return?'

I laughed again. 'Friendship. After all, the war is on this side, isn't it?'

The phone rang and the deputy answered. 'Right J., go secure.' He pressed the secure button on the phone. 'Hello J., I've got some high-grade stuff for you. It looks like the war is going to spread to the mainland.'

He relayed all the facts and at the end of the call mentioned that a sizeable sum of money was being asked for the information. J. must have asked how much, as he then said: 'Fifteen thousand for starters but the source is high-grade, very high-grade, and this may be only for starters. I'm sure you have a lot to organise at your end in London, the best of luck. I'll phone you again at 10 a.m.'

He set the phone down. The chief constable, who had listened intently to the phone call, said, 'Things are not getting any better, are they? I've got a meeting with the secretary of state at 9 a.m. How much can I say to him?'

Billy Jones thought for a moment. 'You can say that Special Branch has told you that something is cooking in London, nothing else. No names, and you certainly know nothing of the source of the intelligence. I am sure the secretary of state will be getting a feedback from the other end in London anyway.'

'Right, Bill, I know the score. I'll see you later.' He rose from his chair. 'Well done George', he said. 'Keep up the good work,' and he left the office.

'What arrangements have you made with McMahon, George?' asked my boss.

'He is phoning my extension in a few days' time. It was the only arrangement open to me at short notice, and I have arranged a code name.'

'Right, something tells me we'll have trouble over the cash because if things don't go well over there, I can smell problems. But it's their pigeon really.'

I looked at my watch—it was approaching 1.30 a.m.

'Right sir, I'll head home.'

'I'll give you a call later, George. Thanks, and keep your head down.'

As I left the office Bill Jones picked up the phone. I drove home and looked forward to bed, I really did feel tired, but I knew I might not sleep well, thinking of noon in London, only a few hours away.

The noise of the alarm clock sounded far away and I felt Eileen clamber out of bed. I heard the children being awakened and the commotion in the bathroom, then blackness and quiet.

'It's half past eight, George. Are you in work this morning?' Eileen said.

I jumped out of bed and into the shower. As I dressed I could smell the frying bacon wafting up the stairs. 'Good girl Eileen,' I thought, 'this is just what I need.' I felt really hungry.

'The children need shoes', said Eileen at the breakfast table.

'Right,' I replied.

'Does that mean we can go shopping after school?'

'I don't know yet, I'll let you know at lunchtime.'

She looked annoyed but said nothing.

———

I drove into work wondering what I should tell the local uniform commander. Nothing much if I could help it. The intelligence referred to London, so I had no obligation to even mention it. A certain tension existed between the anti-terrorist Special Branch and the other departments within the force. This is probably because unless you are a member of the Branch, you cannot have much idea about how they operate. A sort of mystique builds up and jealousy erupts, sometimes openly. It could be said that on entering the Special Branch, you leave the job at least as you knew it. The main gripe of the other departments is that they are given very little inside information.

They cannot understand the 'need to know' principle, on which all good Special Branch operatives set their foundations. It's difficult listening to a uniform officer telling you of his suspicions regarding a certain character when you know more than he does about the subject. It's hard not to give a nod and a wink when all that's normal within you tells you to. It's hard to get information regarding a suspect from a member of another department when you don't want them to know what you require. It's hard to remain passive when the CID sergeant innocently tells you of impending arrests for crime and asks you if any on the list are of interest to Special Branch, and you see a source or a potential source staring at you from a page. It's hard to remain silent.

I knew I would tell the local uniform commander nothing of the events of the previous night. He was a good commander who wisely let Special Branch carry on with their work. He knew he would be put in the picture regarding anything to do with his division. Usually he got on well with me and knew of the dangerous work I performed. Lives were being saved daily by good intelligence, which was used both ways: to protect the community and to protect the source. He knew that rules were bent continuously but with the greater good in mind.

I entered the office and was immediately confronted by my chief inspector, Jack Bishop. He was sitting at the typist desk talking to the Military Intelligence officer, Robert Laycock.

'What on earth happened last night? Robert here says you vanished with an unnamed gentleman from the border vehicle checkpoint?'

The MIO chipped in, 'Where did you go? I drove all the way to the checkpoint, missed you, returned here and missed you again.'

'Sorry about that, Robert, but the man was a complete screwball. He ranted that the Irish Army was going to invade Northern Ireland and drive out the British. I got rid of him as quickly as I could.'

'Who was he?' said Bishop.

'A fellow named Seán Lynch from Dundalk, or that is where he said he was from anyway. I got rid of him quick.'

The MIO looked at me quizzically. 'Where did you leave him?'

'I gave him his fare, and left him at the bus station.'

The chief appeared to accept my version of events and went into his own office to answer the phone. The MIO looked at me and smiled. Laycock certainly didn't believe me!

The typist, Jean, arrived into the office with a tray of coffee mugs. I grabbed one gratefully. 'Are you growing a moustache again, George?' she asked.

I laughed. 'Trying to.'

I had a habit of growing a moustache for six months, and then being clean-shaven for another six months. I needed the change of appearance now and again; everyone was now growing their hair long and I could not let my appearance be against the trend. I didn't like it much.

There were now so many terrorist incidents on the border that extra battalions of troops were being stationed at Armagh and Newry. The police were becoming heavily dependent on the military for assistance in everyday work. They couldn't even go to a road accident without the military accompanying them, or at least making the surrounding area secure. Most areas in the two RUC divisions were considered a 'no-go' along the border and many roads were out of bounds to security force traffic. Border stations like Forkhill and Crossmaglen were used as helicopter bases, and all personnel, whether police or military, were flown in and out. To travel by road invited the risk of land-mines.

As part and parcel of this extra military activity, it had been agreed that it was necessary to have a Military Intelligence officer in each police division. Laycock had been assigned to my division. He was an Intelligence Corp captain, exceptionally well trained in intelligence matters, and was that very day moving to a desk in the Special Branch office. Not only that, he was also bringing a corporal clerk, who would attend to all his needs and take care of his paperwork.

The five members of Special Branch attached to the office had mixed feelings about all this. So far, the military officers encountered in our day-to-day work were upper-class twits, living in another world. Each unit had a four-month stint and all they really wanted were 'kills' or 'trophies'. I had always been invited to the arrival cocktail party of each new unit in the officers' mess, and knew full well that I myself was considered to be an Indian too, albeit a friendly one. I rarely went to these functions because they turned into a brain-picking exercise, although I took great delight sometimes in dropping a name and steering the new arrivals in the wrong direction.

It was still early days with the military in my area, but already they were attempting to recruit informants and offering large sums of money. This was getting under my skin, and breaking established ground rules. I was aware that the new unit was building a dossier on every man, woman and child in the division, including their photos. This was not a hard task. The military could detain someone they suspected of a terrorist connection for four hours. This was called 'screening', and before they were released, they were all photographed after their personal details had been taken. The military carried cameras in their vehicles and anywhere people congregated—Gaelic matches, shopping centres, parades—provided a lot of material. Photos were taken and put into albums, enlarged and left in police stations for identification. It wouldn't be long before practically every civilian in the area would be known, and although I was keeping an open mind since the MIO had arrived, I knew in my heart that I could use him to Special Branch advantage. Would there be trust between us? I had a feeling there would be because Laycock was a professional. Could he be trusted not to pass intelligence up the military pipeline? Only time would tell.

———

I sat at my desk drafting my intelligence report on the events of the previous night. When the MIO left the office a short time later, I went into the office of the chief inspector, Jack Bishop, and set the draft on his desk. The report contained everything except the name of the source.

The chief read it and said, 'What's going on, George? What was that shit story a while ago?'

'That was for Laycock's benefit.'

'Ah, right. You've been to Belfast to the boss, I see. Do you think it's good stuff?'

'Well, we'll know at twelve o'clock or thereabouts.'

'Am I going to know his name?'

I looked at him in the eye and smiled. He knew the look.

'Chief, I would tell you, but the deputy's put a stop on me.'

'You could tell me, you know.'

'I can't. Sorry, Chief.'

The phone rang and the chief answered. 'Yes, sir, he has just put me in the picture. Hold on.'

He handed me the phone.

'Hello, George, Bill here. Any further contact?'

'No, sir.'

'Well, we'll soon know, the boys in London are putting everything into locating the bombers. They've put hundreds of uniformed men into plain clothes in the search.'

'Right, sir, I've completed my paperwork, it will be going up to you today, secure internal post.'

'Right, George. See you.'

I busied myself in the office and before I knew it, it was almost noon. The chief looked in from his office.

'Fancy some army grub?'

'Ugh,' I said. 'I suppose it will save us going out for something.'

The military who were based at the police station had their own canteen, but the food was bland. Baked beans with everything, but on the odd occasion one could get a piece of fresh fish deep-fried with a baked potato. We decided to chance it and in the corridor, Captain Laycock joined us. He first invited us to lunch in the officers' mess, an offer we declined. We had just eaten a lunch of pork chop and cauliflower when two young soldiers entered the room and shouted to one of the staff, 'They've just blown up half of London; it's on the radio newsflash.'

I tried not to look in Laycock's direction but said, 'Jesus, would it be the Arabs or the IRA?'

Laycock looked at me quizzically. 'No doubt it's the Provos. Let's go to the office and see what's going on.'

We walked along the corridor and up the stairs to the first floor. The office clerk met us.

'George, there's an urgent call for you.'

She knew not to say who the caller was. I entered the general office.

'I'll take the call in the chief's office.'

I shut the door and although I could see the chief and Laycock through the glass door, they couldn't hear me, but I could feel Laycock's eyes on me as I lifted the phone.

'George.'

'Yes, sir.' It was my boss, Bill Jones.

'Have you heard the news?'

I said I was only aware of explosions in London.

'There's death and injury. The bombing team have made good their escape, and London want to know if there's anything you can add to your intelligence?'

I had to make a split-second decision.

'Well, sir, the whole team are returning after the operation on the next Belfast plane from Heathrow.'

'Jesus Christ man, how long have you known this?'

'I pass on that, sir, having promised the source that this information would only be used if necessary.'

'Source protection, shit!' shouted Bill. 'Your responsibility is to report everything, and I mean everything, not to disseminate the intelligence.'

'I had a problem, sir, and I'll explain when I see you.'

'I must let London know immediately.'

'Sir, can I ask you something?'

'Be quick about it.'

'If the police are arresting the team at Heathrow, it must appear routine and accidental good fortune. They must not know we are looking for anyone in particular, or that we knew they were leaving Heathrow for Belfast.'

'Right, I'll pass on your concerns!'

I put the phone down. The chief inspector had guessed that it was Special Branch HQ on the phone and had kept Laycock in conversation during the call. I spoke to the clerk.

'That was the vetting department at HQ on the phone, Jean. We are behind with quite a few. Would you check my desk in-tray.'

Jean never lifted her head from her work. She knew it had been the chief on the phone from Belfast, not the vetting department.

I would have some explaining to do with the deputy in Belfast. When I had taken the intelligence from McMahon, he had told me that the team would return on the plane from Heathrow after the bombings.

'I'm giving you this and I don't want you to use it,' he had said. 'If some inexperienced Special Branch member at the airport or member of the investigation interviewers mentioned our knowledge of the plane, I would be sunk because there were few others who knew of the operation,' he had told me.

I had promised not to use it and had hoped that the bombers would be caught in other ways. Now, unfortunately, I had been forced to pass on this information. The deputy would understand, but I wondered if I would live to regret my decision.

However, my fears were groundless. Detective Chief Inspector John Hewson was heading up the enquiry in London, he was an experienced Special Branch member for some years and was attached to the Irish Desk at Special Branch Scotland Yard.

When the call came through to the London office about the bombings, Hewson had immediately ordered a check of all known safe houses and houses belonging to IRA sympathisers in the forlorn hope of seeing something out of the ordinary. The Irish Desk was the high-profile department of Special Branch in London. He had travelled to Ulster many times and was on first-name terms with all of the officers on the Republican Desk at Special Branch HQ at Knock. He had been expecting the Provisionals to start spectacular actions in England for some time, although intelligence available was scant. He was a tall, fit man in his mid-forties and a keen golfer.

———

They had drawn a blank with the safe houses. Although the operation had been covert, when news of the first explosion came through he had felt like rushing to the scene, as he told me later. He didn't do this, as the scene was now a job for the CID. His job in Special Branch was best utilising the intelligence. Once the event occurred it became someone else's pigeon, and he would be the first to admit that he had learned a great deal from the RUC Special Branch in this aspect of his work. They were real professionals and from what he could learn from backchannels they even outshone MI5 and MI6, who had offices in RUC Headquarters, 'Paddy the Irishman proving to be the best intelligence gatherer of the lot.' Even the British director of intelligence, a man of long-standing experience in intelligence-gathering worldwide, acknowledged that he was learning new tricks from the RUC. Ulstermen have tactical brains and are renowned for their shrewdness. After all, they have provided a dozen presidents of the USA, and it is a well-known fact that Ulster field marshalls and generals spearheaded victory in two world wars for Britain.

In the aftermath of the explosions Hewson received an urgent phone call from RUC HQ. He listened intently.

'Roger on that, I will handle it personally. Thanks, I'll call you later.'

I later learned that Hewson had indeed played the game right. When they switched their hunt for the bombers to Heathrow, he made sure the bombing team was not aware of Special Branch knowledge of their route back to Ulster. He made it appear that they were detained by chance on follow-up operations after the explosions.

The source later told me that he had worried like hell but in the end he was happy about the way things had turned out. He was sad that Dolours and Marion Price had destroyed their lives, but was happy that Gerry Kelly was detained. He described him as ruthless and an important officer in the Belfast Provisional IRA hierarchy.

'If he hadn't been caught in London he might have done damage elsewhere, you are lucky to have him locked up.'

Who would have thought that on his release from prison Kelly would continue his deep association with Provisional Sinn Féin, and after the ceasefires, would eventually become an MLA at Stormont.

Chapter 2

Meeting with McMahon in County Louth

Two weeks later I went to Knock Headquarters to see Bill Jones as he had requested. He was on the phone and waved me to a chair. When the phone call ended he looked at me for a moment. 'George,' he said, 'John Hewson is arriving from London to see you and I want to talk to you about McMahon before he arrives. By the way, has there been any further contact?'

'No, sir, nothing at all.'

'Oh, he'll be on the phone soon. I've no doubt that he'll be looking for his £15,000.'

He went on to brief me that London wanted to 'handle' McMahon: to make him their informant. If they were going to be paying the £15,000, 'he who pays the piper . . .'

'As you know, George,' he explained, 'the GB director of intelligence, Security Services, is the boss. He has overall control over Special Branch, Military Intelligence and everything else. I have been ordered to arrange the handover of the source to Hewson, who will be his new handler.'

I could only nod my consent, but enquired, 'Will the source agree?'

'If he wants paid, he'll have to,' said Jones.

I had time to think about the matter as Jones embarked on another long telephone call. I had thought that the source was probably waiting to be able to produce further intelligence before asking for payment for the London arrests. This would make it less painful for his handlers to remunerate him. I had been really busy these last two weeks and had been wondering why there had been no further contact.

Jones finished his telephone call. 'When Hewson arrives you can use my office. I'm going to see the director at Stormont.'

'Thanks, sir,' I replied.

I had half an hour or so before Hewson arrived and I headed for the Headquarters canteen for a welcome coffee.

When Hewson turned up he held out his hand, 'George, nice to see you.'

I shook his hand.

Hewson thanked me for my input regarding the London bomb. 'It was great to get the whole IRA team.'

I nodded. 'I've been told how you handled the intelligence regarding Heathrow.'

Hewson related the events up to handing the suspects over to CID for interview and eventual prosecution. 'Between ourselves, only one of them would talk to us and no useful information was obtained. They were a ruthless lot, especially Kelly.'

I took all this with a pinch of salt. If he had gained any useful intelligence he would never have revealed it to me.

We spoke in general terms for a few minutes and then Hewson enquired, 'Has the chief superintendent put you in the picture about McMahon?'

'He has. You are to handle him on your own.'

'That's right,' replied Hewson, 'I wish he would make contact with you as I have two London numbers I want to give him when he calls.'

By now I was feeling rather annoyed and fed up with the whole business. 'If he calls!' I exclaimed.

'He'll call alright, he'll not miss his payment,' said Hewson.

I looked hard at him.

'You'll find it rather awkward handling a source in the Republic of Ireland, you being in London. It's not like me phoning you on a secure line. He'll probably be in a call box, and call boxes in the south of Ireland are anything but private.'

'I know,' said Hewson. 'I'll probably fly into Dublin for meets unless he comes up with a more subtle solution.'

He gave me his phone numbers. 'Call me as soon as he makes contact.'

I thought a moment and replied, 'I'll have to explain all to him . . .'

Hewson interrupted. 'No, I'd rather you didn't. Just give him the two numbers and no further conversation, or explanation. Okay?'

I was on the verge of raising other possible problems but decided against it. After all, I was being relieved of a very high-grade source.

Hewson had been well briefed by his superiors in London, who no doubt were hopeful of supplying HM Government with intelligence at PIRA Army Council level. This could turn things in their favour. The English public didn't like bombs exploding in their country. Things couldn't go on like this. Where would it all end?

———

I had recently supplied the military with some good intelligence which led to arrests and the seizure of a quantity of explosives in South Down. The pace of the job at this time was really hectic. My wife Eileen, and my two sons and daughter, only saw me in the mornings at breakfast and occasionally for evening meals.

It was difficult for the children of policemen attending school in a nationalist republican area. They had to tell lies. When asked, they said their father worked in an office or that he worked in Belfast. The children's ages ranged from twelve years down to eight, but amazingly the pressure didn't seem to get to them. They heard at school and on the news about policemen being shot dead almost on a daily basis. They must have worried a hell of a lot. I tried not to let them hear my telephone conversations. But it was impossible to hide some aspects of police work from them.

At least I had been in plain clothes as far back as they could remember, although my old uniforms still hung in the closet. My wife Eileen worried about my safety and I would phone her as much as I could to reassure her of my whereabouts, although I didn't always tell the truth in this respect.

The problems arose when sources, people she knew in her heart were members of a terrorist organisation, would phone when I wasn't at home. She knew most of the voices; they knew hers. They treated her with respect once they realised she could take an important garbled message quietly and with no fuss and with as little conversation as possible.

I did worry once when my eldest son, then twelve years old, had answered the phone when his mother was in the garden. The caller was in a hurry and once he knew who had answered he gave the boy an urgent message for his mother. He passed it to his mother exactly as given.

'The white Mini will be two or three cars behind a brown Audi, it has a box of tomatoes for sale, 7.30 main Dundalk to Newry road.'

The message led to the seizure of two rifles and a pistol. I was worried about my son but made no mention of it the next day.

———

I usually looked into the office most evenings after seven. I had found, more often than not, with the current level of terrorist activity that I would be called in anyway. It was two days after the meeting with Hewson when 'Seán' made contact again. He left a phone message at my office that he would call back at 8 p.m., but I was in for a surprise. I unlocked the office door and found the Military Intelligence officer, Laycock, at his desk.

'Hello, Robert,' I said, 'I didn't realise anyone was in the office.'

'Just in ahead of you, George. By the way, the colonel was really chuffed about the seizure of the weapons. He knows the info came from Special Branch, but not you specifically, of course.'

I nodded. I couldn't get used to the idea of a military officer, albeit an intelligence officer, having keys to the Special Branch office and all the secure filing cabinets. But this was the way it had to be. At least Laycock was proving useful, and I was learning quite a lot from him. I had read a Military Intsum, short for intelligence summary, which Laycock had used at a briefing. Laycock had asked me my views on the document. It was very professionally set out. Indeed, it was set out in such a manner that it could have gone to any level in the intelligence network, police, army or MI5. Laycock intimated that with the assistance of his clerk, he would issue one fortnightly: a copy to his headquarters, and a copy retained locally. It would contain a summary of all terrorist-related incidents during that fortnight. All seizures of weapons and explosives, all arrests and an outline of the current terrorist threat as gleaned from intelligence sources local and otherwise. Although I tried not to show it, I was very happy with the arrangement. Special Branch officers were notorious for their lack of records and indeed until a year previously, some office systems were very much still in the 1940s. I had one reservation, though; I wasn't happy to outline the full current threat in a military document as I couldn't monitor who would read it. I was worried about source protection, and was about to discuss the problem with Laycock when the phone rang. It was Operations.

'Phone call for you, George.'

'Hello,' said a voice, 'This is Seán.'

'Hello, Seán, how're things?' I said.

'Not too bad. I need to see you.'

I explained that there had been a change of plan and that I had two telephone numbers for him.

'What numbers?' he queried.

I thought for a moment. 'Across the water.'

'Look, I don't like this messing about,' Seán remonstrated. 'I want to see you tonight.'

'You can talk to me then, but already I have a feeling I won't like what you are going to tell me.'

I wasn't going to argue or worry about Hewson for the moment.

'Right, Seán, where to?'

I listened intently and set the phone down.

I said to Laycock, 'I'll see you tomorrow, Robert, I've got to go.'

Laycock stood up. 'Do you want company?'

I shook my head. 'Not this time.'

'I'm sitting here not doing much. I thought we had agreed to share,' said Laycock.

'I can't. Not this one. I'll explain soon.'

I let myself out of the office and headed for the car park. I had wanted to bring Laycock with me, and was on the verge of going back to the office and telling him he could come, but something inside me said 'No.' Something told me that this was strictly a loner job. And anyway the source wouldn't have been happy with a strange Englishman who would know who, and what, he was. I was sure of that. I drove across the border at Crossmaglen and along the concession road into Dundalk, named such because it crossed and re-crossed the border again in a short distance. It was not manned by Customs and Excise, as it would be logistically unsuitable to do so. For a change the weather was good and I headed south through Dundalk to a little town on the main road to Dublin called Castlebellingham.

This was no more than a small village beside a large estate, with a half-mile private road leading to the Bellingham Castle Hotel.

At the end of the nineteenth century and into the early part of the twentieth century it was the British Army Garrison, before the land border was created. I knew the history because I had a silver teapot at home with '1898 Bellingham Castle' engraved on it. It had belonged to a great uncle who had been a young army lieutenant in the garrison. This officer had gone on to serve in India and I had other valuable belongings which I had intended to offer to a military museum.

I drove to the car park adjacent to the hotel and parked. I had only been waiting about five minutes when an old dilapidated Ford Cortina, bottle green colour, arrived and parked beside me. It was McMahon. He jumped into my car and said, 'Drive.'

I did as ordered.

On the main road from the hotel McMahon said, 'Left.'

I turned left and had only gone a few hundred yards when I was told to turn left again. I did so and drove along a narrow road for about a mile. I was then directed into a laneway. About 100 yards along was a small farm cottage. Next to this was a red corrugated barn. A man smoking a pipe and wearing an old cloth cap appeared at the cottage doorway. It was hard to tell his age, but he looked elderly, certainly over sixty years of age. McMahon waved to him. The man waved back and re-entered the cottage.

'Come on,' said McMahon as he got out of the car.

I followed him into the barn and saw that it was used to store farm machinery, including an old Ferguson tractor. A stack of peat was piled just inside the door. McMahon sat on a bale of straw and I followed suit. It was dark but an outside light over the main door of the cottage shone into the barn and I could see McMahon quite clearly.

'Well, George, the first thing is, the guy in the cottage here is okay. He was involved in the Fifties campaign, a good lad.'

I nodded. 'Who am I?' I enquired, wanting 'cover' if anyone else turned up.

'You are Seán, one of the boys from Belfast down to see me on army business.'

'What about my car registration number?' I asked.

'Is it genuine?' asked McMahon.

I smiled. 'No, it's not.'

'Well then, no problem,' said McMahon.

'Anyway, he wouldn't even tell his own family we were here,' he said of the old guy.

McMahon lit a cigarette. 'I'm not supposed to use these,' he said, adding, 'What's this about two telephone numbers?'

I explained that London was insisting that they handled him as they were paying big money.

McMahon listened intently.

'Look, this is all bullshit. Are you telling me that if I know about a load of explosives going from Dundalk to Belfast that I must phone London to pass on the information? This is bullshit. God knows when I'll have anything good again regarding London. At least, anything I'm prepared to enlighten them on. What do you think?'

I shook my head. 'I've been given orders that I'm not to see you again. I shouldn't be here. Faceless men in soft shoes in London will be very annoyed. They see you as the great new saviour.'

'Fuck them,' exploded Séamus. 'I want my £15,000, and as I have told them there will be more in the future. Any hassle and I'll vanish. God help them.'

'Your prospective handler said he would fly to Dublin to meet you,' I replied, trying to calm him down.

'He must be joking. Who is he anyway?'

'Can't say. He may never be in the picture, something might happen. He will introduce himself.'

'Look,' said McMahon, 'I like the way I can meet you at short notice, certainly within two hours. And as I can trust you more and we converse more on the phone, we can use codes, which I will give you shortly. The way I'm going to play it is like this, you are the only one I will be contacting.'

'Look, I know how you feel, but I will be in deep trouble. They won't believe me and they'll demand the contact number you gave me and, more importantly, they'll renege on your money.'

But he was adamant, and angry. 'I'm not going to phone the London numbers, they can go and jump. I'll tell you what we'll do. You tell them that we are going to London to see them next week to collect my cash. Then I can operate as I like and they'll pay in advance in future.'

I laughed. 'You must be joking. I can't go to London with you. They don't want me involved,' I stressed.

'Look,' said McMahon, 'I'm not entering London by plane or train from Ireland. Jesus Christ, the only way I'm going is with you, by car.'

'They won't wear it,' I replied.

'Well if they don't, they'll rue the day.' McMahon stood up. 'We'll go on Thursday afternoon coming. You tell them it's how I want it. I don't want any of them coming to Dublin or even to Belfast to see me. I don't fucking want it,' he spat.

He told me to be in the Townsend Thoresen Irish Sea Ferry lounge at the County Antrim port of Larne at one o'clock the following Thursday afternoon. When I asked him how he would get there, he shrugged. 'Don't worry, I'll get there.'

We left the barn and McMahon shouted to the occupant of the house, who appeared at the door and waved. As we drove down the lane he asked me if I could find the house again. I said I thought I could.

'Good,' said McMahon, 'we were sitting on a hundred weight of explosives in the barn!'

I felt my muscles stiffen. I was speechless for a moment. 'Where is it destined for?' I demanded.

'Belfast,' he replied, 'but I can't let you do anything about it. There are only about five of us who are aware of this stuff and I won't know when it leaves. The Belfast IRA quartermaster will be told to come and collect. My chances of knowing when are fifty-fifty, and even then if the stuff was touched en route it would leave a bad smell—an informer at work.'

'Even a lucky vehicle checkpoint?' I cheekily enquired.

'Especially a lucky VCP,' said McMahon. 'We all know what that means and it certainly isn't luck, is it? There are other reasons I don't want this stuff touched, reasons that sometime in the future I may be able to divulge to you.'

We were back at the hotel car park in a few minutes. He jumped out quickly.

'Do you like my car?' he grinned, as he got into the battered old Cortina.

'Well, it's seen better days.'

'It was nicked in Dublin yesterday by one of the lads for a job which fell through. I'm dumping it for him when I'm finished with it tonight.'

He closed the car door and drove off. I waited a couple of minutes, then drove north towards Dundalk and home. I wondered what I was letting myself in for, and what a bloody character to be involved with. Even though I knew I liked him, I certainly wouldn't want to make an enemy of him. If I was finding it unbelievable that a senior member of the IRA was supplying me with high-level intelligence, what would the ordinary man in the street think? It was hard to believe. I wondered again if the ending would be happy: or would there be an ending? Meeting this man was fraught with real danger. He could eliminate me at any time he chose, just by issuing a simple order. It would suffice that I was a member of RUC Special Branch. And I would be considered a great coup by PIRA. I tried to put the thoughts out of my mind, instead thinking of being home in time for the late TV news and supper with Eileen.

———

The next day I entered the Special Branch office at 9 a.m., as I tried to do most days. I felt I had to be there at nine no matter how late I had worked the previous evening, even if I had been out all night. It was a habit I had been taught early in my police service.

'Good morning, Jean,' I said to the clerk typist.

'Good morning,' she replied, 'The Deputy rang just a minute ago. You have to phone him as soon as possible.'

I went into the chief inspector's office, closed the connecting door, and phoned HQ.

'Good morning, sir,' I said to Bill Jones.

'Hello, George, can you press the secure button?'

I pressed the red 'scrambler' button on the top of the phone, meant to stop police phones being bugged by terrorists or anyone else.

'Hello?' I enquired.

'Okay, George, I can hear you fine. London are pestering me about our mutual friend,' he said.

'I was just about to contact you on that, sir. He was in touch with me last night.'

'Good,' replied Jones. 'Did you give him the London numbers?'

'I tried to, sir, but he wouldn't wear it. He's adamant that he wants nothing to do with London and would prefer to work through me, and, sir, before you say it, I really did try to convince him of the new arrangements but . . .'

Jones interrupted. 'Listen, George, we—you and I—are only small players in the big game. I have been ordered. He must be handed over.'

'There was no talking to him, sir, he really is stubborn and I really hate to say this, but there's more.'

Jones was silent for about five seconds. 'Go on, go on . . .' he said.

'Well, sir, he wants me to take him to London next Thursday to collect his money.'

I went on to relate my conversation with McMahon in full. When I had finished Jones considered this for a moment, then said, 'Listen George, there'll be hell to pay over this, and I'll bet if they can't run him, they'll make changes in the financial arrangements.'

'I told him my fear on that score, but he says they would be foolish to cross him.'

'When is he contacting you again?'

'At Larne harbour on Thursday.'

'Well, you may carry on with your travel arrangements. I'll tell them they can do the persuading when they get him to London. Let them talk to him. I'll phone them with the news.'

'Would you enquire of them a rendezvous point, preferably just outside the city on the northern side and please, not in a motorway café,' I poignantly pleaded.

I caught up on my office work that morning. Just before lunch the phone rang.

'Are you coming home for lunch?' my wife asked. 'I have a dentist appointment at 3.30 p.m. Can you collect the children at school?'

I told her I would see her at one o'clock. I also made a mental note to tell her of my impending trip to London.

The following morning Chief Supt Jones phoned from HQ to give me the address of a hotel on the outskirts of London. I made my travel arrangements for Thursday. Larne is a small town north-east of Belfast, on the Antrim coast. Two ferry companies operate daily crossings to Scotland for vehicular and passenger traffic. The sea crossing takes about two and a half hours and the North Channel could provide as rough a sea crossing as anywhere in the world in inclement weather. The port of Larne became famous in the seventeenth century as the arrival destination of Scots to Plantation Ulster. Many of them had settled in the town itself and it is still considered a Protestant town to this day. It wasn't an appealing town to visit, especially for a member of the IRA, and contained little of interest to the tourist. People only passed through Larne going to or coming from the terminal.

When I arrived at Larne harbour I found the traffic using the ferry particularly heavy. I didn't join the queue of vehicles waiting to board the ferry but parked in the car park and entered the Townsend Thoresen building. I bought a Coke and watched out the window, waiting for McMahon to arrive. It was 12.30 p.m.

About five minutes later a voice behind me said, 'Hiya.'

I looked around and there he was, wearing a fawn gabardine raincoat and carrying a little suitcase. I didn't have to look too closely to see it was a real leather case.

I stood up. 'Right, let's go.'

We walked to the car and joined the queue to board the ferry. We agreed to separate on board. We would join up again at the car deck before disembarking. We had an uneventful crossing and set off for London from the terminal at Cairnryan a couple of miles along the Loch from Stranraer. As we drove McMahon was quite talkative. He spoke of making a sort of living cutting peat from a small bog he owned and selling it in bags in County Meath towns. He was also an amateur car repairer and very handy with paint spray. He had served in the Irish Free State Army for five years, until being medically discharged. A malignant tumour had been found in his stomach, and on his demob he had been operated on with success in Manchester, where he went to reside with a friend on his discharge from hospital. A year after the operation he was in remission.

His entry into the IRA was as amusing as it was tragic. He had been to Dublin in late 1956 and was walking along O'Connell Street, near the General Post Office, a rallying point for the republican cause down the years. A Sinn Féin meeting and collection was taking place. He stopped to listen for a moment, when he was approached by an unknown man who said, 'I think I know you, you are in the army, aren't you?'

He replied, 'I used to be, not anymore.'

'Where are you from?' the man probed.

'Meath,' McMahon replied.

'Great,' said the man. 'Can you give two of our lads a lift?'

McMahon mumbled something about shopping and this and that.

'Look,' said the man, 'you were in the army, we just want you to help us out.'

McMahon eventually agreed, and later that day ferried the two youths to Navan. A month later one of the youths was shot dead at the border by the RUC and McMahon realised that the man in O'Connell

Street had meant the Irish Republican Army, and not the Free State Army. From then on he had callers at various times and his house became an important safe house. Having been a corporal arms instructor during his military service, he knew about weapons, and would examine those carried by his guests. He then ended up storing weapons in the bog for them, and eventually giving instruction in handling and firing. This was how he drifted into the IRA. He found it all rather amusing. I found his life story very interesting and the time flew as we travelled. We stopped once or twice en route at service stations on the M6 motorway, had coffee at the first, and a meal at the second. As we neared London I tried to remember the directions to the hotel and after a few wrong turns we eventually arrived in the Islington area and found the hotel.

We entered the foyer together, and I spoke to the receptionist. 'Reservations for Mr Brown and Mr Smith,' I said.

The receptionist looked a little too long in the eye and I had certain feelings that other eyes were on us. 'Yes, sir, I have your reservations, rooms 268 and 278.'

She handed me the keys. I cancelled her call to the hotel porter. 'It's okay,' I said, 'we only have small cases and can manage ourselves.'

'That's fine,' she said. 'The lift is at the end of the hall and you are on the second floor.'

I thanked her and we went to our rooms. I had looked into the hotel lounge on the way to the lift and the place looked pretty full. I thought I would go and have a beer before I showered, but then changed my mind. I lay down on the bed and relaxed. I was awakened by a knock on the door. I jumped off the bed unaware of how long I had been asleep, and called out, 'Just a minute.'

I straightened my tie and went and opened the door. It was John Hewson of New Scotland Yard (NSY).

Hewson smiled. 'Welcome to London, George, did you have a good journey?'

'No problems,' I replied. 'I fell asleep. What time is it?'

'It's nearly eleven o'clock, I'll take it you haven't had a meal?'

'No, we had a good meal at the M6 services on the way and neither of us were hungry when we arrived.'

'We're going to leave it until the morning,' said Hewson, 'but I thought I needed a chat with you before I talked to McMahon. I need to know what his feelings are.'

'Well, John,' I replied, 'as you are aware, he won't wear being run from London. Doesn't think it's a good idea. Perhaps you can make him understand your point of view. At least when you talk to him you'll see the problems I experienced.'

'Did he say anything on the way?'

I explained that McMahon had slept for the first two hours of the car trip and had been fairly quiet the rest of the journey. I said nothing about McMahon's self-confessed recruitment into, and role in the IRA. A bond was growing between McMahon and myself and I felt at this time I couldn't share anything with Hewson even though some of the intelligence concerned Manchester. During my conversations with McMahon, he had no hesitation about answering my questions. He would sometimes say 'you can use that,' or 'you can't use that, ever.' He knew I required to know the whole picture and was confident it would be played in a way which wouldn't leave him worrying about a visit from his organisation.

'Have you seen him since you arrived, or has he gone to bed?' asked Hewson.

'I haven't seen him,' I replied. 'He thinks we are seeing you in the morning.'

'Right, just leave things, no point in crowding him.'

In fact McMahon had left the hotel and was sitting in a pub a couple of hundred yards from the hotel. He was drinking a De Kuypers gin, and contemplating.

The next morning I woke with the sun shining through the hotel window. It was 7.30 a.m. I quickly showered and crossed the hall to knock on McMahon's door. He was up and waiting. We went to the dining room and ate a leisurely breakfast. We then went to my room and waited. At about 9.45 a.m., Hewson arrived with a man I didn't recognise, whom he introduced as his commander. He was a slim individual, about 5'11" tall with dark hair.

'Just call me Jack,' he said as we were introduced.

Jack then addressed McMahon. 'Thanks for your intelligence regarding the bombs. We want you to work for us. We know you must have a lot to offer, and we are experts who will look after you.'

'Have you brought my cash?' McMahon asked.

The commander nodded towards a large briefcase, which he had set on the bed. 'We'll discuss the money in due course. We need to have a long chat first. Could you leave us for an hour, George?'

I got up to go.

'He stays!' commanded McMahon.

There was a silence for a moment. McMahon spoke again. 'Before we go any further, I want my money.'

Again, there was silence for the best part of ten seconds. I watched the eye contact between Hewson and the commander.

'Right,' said Jack, opening the briefcase. 'Here's an advance on your payment.' He set a bundle of notes on the bed.

McMahon gave a nervous laugh. 'Where's my £15,000 as arranged?'

'There was no agreed arrangement with us,' Hewson replied.

'The £15,000 was agreed. You got your bombing team, didn't you?'

'We did, but we almost didn't. The last piece of intelligence was only given under pressure when we failed to make arrests in the city,' countered Hewson.

'You got your info, didn't you, and I've no doubt some of you will get a medal. I want my money, now!'

The commander raised his voice. 'Look, we will decide the financial arrangements, and you'll take the advance now, and then by results from further intelligence you will get the rest. We will determine the value. This is how it will be.'

McMahon stood up and without another word opened the door to the corridor and crossed to his room. He hadn't closed his door half a minute when he reappeared with his little leather case and headed quickly towards the stairs.

Hewson ran forward. 'Look, Séamus, it's only a misunderstanding. Can we talk about it?'

McMahon carried on walking down the stairs and out of sight.

Hewson returned to the room, looking a bit flushed. 'What do you think, sir?' he enquired of his boss.

'I think he'll cool off,' said Jack. 'He has to go back to Ireland with George. Follow after him and see where he goes.' He returned the money to the briefcase. 'We had a day's sightseeing planned for you, George, but I think you should now wait here until he returns. Then phone us on this number.'

He gave me a plain card with a telephone number written on it in ink.

'Okay, sir,' I replied, 'I'll wait here and see what happens.'

As the commander left the room I could see that he was shaking with rage. His hand had trembled when returning the cash to the briefcase. The blood had drained from his face, making him look very pale.

I hung around the hotel until almost two in the afternoon, and then had a late lunch. I had spent most of the latter part of the morning sitting in the lounge or in the foyer. I enjoyed watching people coming and going, and trying to fit occupations and nationalities to faces, a skill I was quite good at. I had almost finished my meal when Hewson appeared at my table.

'He's gone. He caught the 2 p.m. flight to Dublin.'

I didn't speak.

'What do you think of the situation?' asked Hewson.

'Can I pass on that, John?' was my dry-as-sawdust riposte.

Hewson stared at me for a moment. 'Would you like to come to Scotland Yard for a chat about this? We'll have to do something. They're going daft.'

'With due respect to you, John, I didn't want to come to London and I'm leaving now, right now. I'm driving straight to Scotland, and I'll get a crossing booked when I get there.'

'If that's how you feel, I can't stop you. Your hotel bill has been taken care of, by the way. We'll have to try and rectify the situation. It will be hard for a while.'

I nodded, but didn't reply. I packed my case and Hewson walked me to the car park. We shook hands.

'Now, at least you know he's hard to get on with,' I said.

'London will still want to run him, if they're paying the cash,' replied Hewson.

I smiled, started the engine, waved at Hewson and headed for the motorway, and home.

Chapter 3
Ultimatum to London from McMahon

It was a complete surprise when McMahon phoned. Two weeks had passed since London and I hadn't really expected any further contact from him.

'Can you come and see me?' he asked.

'Look, I'm forbidden to have any contact with you apart from giving you a London telephone number.'

'Don't mention those bastards to me. I have something for you. Do you not bloody want it?'

I made a quick decision. I looked at my watch—4.30 p.m.

'I'll see you at 6.30, same place as last time.'

'No,' said McMahon, 'go to Ardee, a small town about twenty minutes south-west of Dundalk. Do you know where it is?'

'Yes.'

'Park in the main street, I will find you there, make it 7 p.m.' He hung up.

I crossed the border and at 7 p.m. parked up on Ardee's main street. It was a quaint little town with a long wide street and not much else except the ruin of an old stone tower halfway along the street, near the turn-off to Kells. A sleepy little Irish town was the classic description. I got out of the car and spent ten minutes walking up and down looking in shop windows: better than sitting in the car being conspicuous. I was about to open the car door when McMahon pulled up alongside, beckoning me to the passenger door of the old red Lada he was driving. I jumped in and McMahon drove along the main street towards Kells.

'I'm just going to drive along a couple of miles,' he said.

I looked around the interior of his Lada. It was a complete mess, littered with empty cigarette packets, sweet and crisp papers, everything bar the kitchen sink! On the back seat were two empty beer kegs. I immediately thought of bombs, as beer kegs were being used more and more to hold explosive mix.

McMahon sensed me looking at them in the rear. 'They're only two empty beer kegs. The car is owned by a friend who is a barman,' he said, laughing.

We pulled into the yard of a deserted-looking farmhouse.

'Right, we're here.' He jumped out and I followed.

Suddenly a figure wearing a balaclava and carrying a rifle appeared from behind a wall. The hair rose on my neck and my pulse was racing as I thought inwardly to myself: 'I'm fucked.' My hands wanted to immediately draw my own weapon but my brain screamed 'No.'

Sensing my distress, McMahon said to the gunman, 'Good man, Mick. This is one of the boys from Belfast down to see me. Forget his face.'

'Right, Séamus, two of the lads are behind the hedge,' replied Mick.

'Good,' said McMahon.

We entered the cottage and closed the door.

'What the fuck is going on?' I said, my mind racing. 'What are you playing at?'

'This is my local unit commanding officer—it keeps them on their toes. They will never dare ask who you are. If we are seen together, it gives me good cover.'

'Fuck you.' My instinct was to draw and shoot. 'You could be setting me up.'

'I knew you wouldn't pull a gun. You're not a fool,' McMahon coolly replied.

But he still bristled like a Kilkenny cat about his treatment across the water.

'I make no apologies for London. They cannot fuck me about. It's not only the money, you know,' he bluntly hissed.

'You could have played it differently,' I said. 'I was left in an awkward situation. They would love to have blamed me. And I am forbidden to have any dealings with you!'

'Well, I won't deal with anyone else. But they will produce my money in due course when they start to receive intelligence that further explosions are in store for London and England generally. I am quite sure that I am not their only source. I would be naive to believe that. But I want you to tell them I phoned you and gave you seven days to produce my £15,000 or the well dries up forever, with no re-opening for communication. Don't say that we met tonight. You could whet their appetite by telling them that I have good stuff concerning Manchester, which I will give them in receipt for some cash.'

'You're testing my loyalty. I feel bound to put this into the pipeline,' I said.

'You won't, as I have something for you, too.'

He handed me an envelope and I was amazed by its contents. I was still not back to normal after seeing the gunman. I scolded him, 'You are stupid carrying things like this around on paper, what happens if you lost them?'

'I won't. You can study the contents of the envelope when you get home. I must leave now to get back to Ardee. I am behind time and am giving a training session on the Armalite tonight.'

There was no sign of the gunman when we left the farmyard.

'Are they gone?' I enquired.

'No, they're still here,' said McMahon.

We reached the road again, passing between two round stone gate pillars. McMahon said, 'If we ever need a dead letter-box, use the opening behind the right-hand pillar as you enter.'

I nodded. 'Who owns this place?' I asked.

'A cousin,' laughed McMahon.

He drove me back to the main street in Ardee. I got into my car and had an uneventful trip home.

——

A few weeks later, I received a telephone call from McMahon. It was a Friday evening about nine. I had showered and was ready for bed, looking forward to a long-awaited game of golf near Belfast the next day.

'Hello,' said McMahon, 'I need to see you.'

'When?' I asked.

'Now,' he replied.

'I paused. 'Is it really necessary?'

'Yes,' he replied with an air of urgency.

'Where?'

'Go to the place we met last and travel another four miles on that road. You will come to a junction, turn left and head towards Kells. As you approach the town you'll see a petrol garage. I'll see you there.'

I followed his directions and sure enough McMahon was standing near the garage, which had closed down for the night. It was eleven o'clock.

He jumped into the passenger seat. 'How are you doing?' he asked.

As we talked, he directed me along a maze of country roads which appeared to get narrower and narrower. We finally reached a dirt road, and after about half a mile we reached a white cottage.

'Park here,' McMahon instructed, pointing to a small white wall about thirty yards past the cottage.

We got out of the car.

'This is where I live,' said McMahon.

I didn't reply. I was worried about a car sitting about fifty yards from where I had parked. I followed McMahon up a small path to the front door. I could smell the peat fire and I felt the heat on my face when the door was opened. A woman stood inside the door.

'This is Kate, a friend who does some baking for me. This is Seán,' said McMahon to her.

'Hello,' she said, shaking my hand. I nodded and she went out the front door, closing it behind her.

An oil lamp cast an eerie glow over the room and before I had time to take stock of the layout, McMahon said, 'Come on through, Seán, there's someone I want you to meet.'

I froze and my eyes followed McMahon towards the long kitchen table. Seated at the rear of the table in the poor light was a large silhouette of a man. My hand grasped the butt of my pistol, carried loose in my overcoat pocket. My pulse raced. The man stood up. He was big, very big, about 6'2" tall.

'Garda Special Branch, meet RUC Special Branch,' said McMahon.

The man held out his hand. 'How are you? Séamus told me about you. And before you say anything, it was me who suggested he arrange this meeting.'

I shook his hand. 'You'll excuse me if I say I don't believe this is happening,' I said, as I sat down and shook my head in disbelief. I was still in a daze as Detective Sergeant Harry Garvin explained that McMahon had been a source for some years. When McMahon had a cash crisis and needed to sell the intelligence about the London bombs, Garvin had suggested that much more cash would be paid by the British Security Services than the Garda Síochána, who really didn't believe in paying too much for intelligence, especially about London.

'So you have known about me for some time now?' I asked the Southern detective.

'Yes, Séamus has kept me informed and he likes the way you operate, and that's good enough for me.'

'Who the fuck else knows?'

'You've asked the question early. The answer, from me, is no one.'

I looked at McMahon.

'We are a triangle,' he confirmed, 'and I swear no one else is in the picture.'

There was silence for a few seconds, then Garvin spoke. 'Look, I consider Séamus a good friend and I'll take all steps to ensure that nothing happens to him. He has been a good source for some time. I can call at his house now and then, as I do with many members of the IRA and Sinn Féin. We do it openly down here in the Republic. They know they are okay, as they just claim any offence is political. We wisecrack with them and they report our visits up the chain of IRA command. Fortunately Séamus is towards the top end of the chain of command. I have no doubt he instructs volunteers to watch me now and again. It's a great game, played well. I also think the temperature is slowly rising in Ulster. Some of the intelligence Séamus gives me, which would possibly create problems if submitted by me through Dublin—as they certainly wouldn't pass it to the RUC—could be given to you to put in through your channels. This takes any heat from Séamus, and PIRA wouldn't even think the leak was in the Republic. I think it's an awful state of affairs that there is no official co-operation between the Gardaí and the RUC. When these terrorists come to live in the Republic, after committing serious crime and murder, they are wined and dined. Some of my colleagues actually advise them. It makes me sick.'

I listened to them both for a while and then spoke slowly and deliberately. 'Is there a hidden agenda here?'

They both laughed. But I persisted.

'Am I missing something that Christmas should come so early? Is there a catch?'

I asked to see Garvin's warrant card, which he produced immediately, and I let him examine mine.

'I know all of this is a shock to you, but I really am offering you the hand of friendship,' he protested.

I cautiously nodded. 'Can I ask you a question?'

'Sure,' said Garvin.

'Did you tell Dublin HQ of the proposed bomb attacks in London?'

He looked at me hard. 'I did, but I wasn't expecting that question. I put the intelligence into the pipeline.'

He stood up and handed me an envelope. 'That's the next step,' he said. 'Read it at home. I have to leave now and if you follow me, I'll take you to Navan. You know the way from there to Dundalk?'

'Yes.' I eyeballed McMahon. 'You are some fucking man,' I said, adding, 'I'm having difficulty taking this all in.'

I followed Garvin to Navan and made my way home. It was after three in the morning when I entered the house. I set the alarm for seven to phone and cancel my golf. I didn't feel much like it now, and I planned to go to sleep again until nine. I snuggled into Eileen. She was sound asleep.

The next morning I was shaving when I remembered the envelope that Garvin had given me. I went into the bedroom, shut the door, sat on the bed and opened the envelope. I was to go to a small hotel in Naas, Co. Kildare, on the following Thursday at noon, and wait in the bar. I was instructed not to worry, that the place was totally secure. This worried me a little. Was Garvin making the place 'secure'? Would there be other eyes? I was nervous. The game I played in confidence daily was becoming blurred. Was I wise entering this new liaison?

––––

I set off on Thursday at 9 a.m., allowing myself time for a stop on the way. I drove to Dundalk, on to Drogheda and two hours later I arrived in Dublin. This gave me plenty of time for the short journey on to Naas. I stopped and bought a morning paper, reading the headline stories for fifteen minutes before setting off for Naas. At the hotel, I ordered a glass of lager in the bar. I had almost finished my drink when Garvin arrived. We shook hands and exchanged tittle tattle on the weather, houses, televisions, which were very expensive in the Republic, and each other's families. Both of us had three children and Garvin was eight years older. A punter, he liked the horses and went to many a race meeting. He had no other vices. He was a non-smoking teetotaller. He had been born in Cork and came from a mixed marriage. He hated the IRA and all they stood for. He stressed he was conservative in his ideas and viewed the Protestant people in Ulster as 'very patient', considering the abuse from the republican movement.

As Garvin talked I found myself growing to like him: to me, a sure sign of a good policeman, or a shrewd operator. I would keep an open mind on that. I found myself opening up to Garvin on various topics but always stopped short of giving all that I knew.

'Look,' said Garvin, as we finished a good lunch and he grabbed the bill. 'I will be totally honest with you. Our meetings will be a secret between the two of us. McMahon shouldn't know of them unless it is in our interest. If Dublin knew I was sharing intelligence with the RUC, I would be in big trouble.'

I nodded, but reserved the right inwardly to promise nothing.

Garvin gave me a list of about thirty names and addresses in the Republic. 'These are all IRA men who are on the run from the North for various terrorist outrages. It lists their associates in the Republic and their current addresses and modes of transport.'

He then handed me a hand-written page. 'These are the minutes of the PIRA Council meeting held near Navan on Tuesday night. It lists those present and the agenda.

'From Séamus?' I asked.

'No,' replied Garvin, with an amused look.

I didn't know whether to believe him or not.

Garvin again stressed the importance of our meetings being a secret. 'I would suggest you start a fictitious source and get him registered with an official Special Branch source number. In fact, I'll give you the name of a Sinn Féin member in Meath. You can put all the intelligence I give you, or most of it anyway, down to him, and when you give me lists of loyalist Ulster Volunteer Force players, I'll do something similar.'

Smiling, I said, 'Now we've come to the punch-line.'

I looked at him fair in the eye, and we both laughed. Finally we discussed the way the Provisional campaign was going. He told me that he had many sources in the Official IRA who would now be 'redundant', as they were turning their backs on violence. We agreed on methods of contact, urgent and otherwise.

As I drove home I thought of how we had been introduced by a senior Provo. I still couldn't take it all in. It was unbelievable, really unbelievable. Like something from a novel.

Chapter 4
Myself

I joined the RUC when I was eighteen and spent my first three years in the police, 1955–57, in Tyrone and Fermanagh. These were supposed to be my formative years in the force, but really not much can be learned riding a bicycle on country lanes, looking at the hedgerows. One thing I did learn was that police and politics don't mix, or do mix, depending on how you look at it.

I was station orderly one summer evening when an old farmer called at the door. He explained that he had been knocked off his bicycle by a motor car. The driver had driven on, but returned to the scene a few minutes later. He gave the farmer a £20 note, a sizeable sum in those days.

'That will get your bike repaired,' he said, before driving off.

The farmer set the £20 note on the table. 'I want to report this accident,' he said, handing me a piece of paper with the registration number of the offending vehicle written on it, and the £20 note.

I investigated the matter, and in due course submitted a file recommending the driver be prosecuted for a number of offences. Within a few weeks I was transferred, and never heard of the file again. Was that because the offending driver was a high sheriff?

I had been on duty at many royal visits during my service, but I consider my first one in 1956 the most amusing, if that is the correct word.

The Duke of Edinburgh was paying a visit to the Grosvenor family in their stately pile in Fermanagh. Part of the visit included a car journey along a main country road outside Enniskillen. Early on the morning of the royal journey, about a hundred police were gathered from all over, dressed in their best uniform, white gloves and all. We were taken out in open tenders, and a constable was dropped off at every minor road or laneway which touched on the royal route. The lead police car in the procession was to warn us, with headlights on, when the royal car was due and we had to stand to attention and salute as the duke passed by. We would then be collected again by a tender and our duty was finished.

We had paraded for duty at 8 a.m., and had been dropped at our points at 9 a.m. Two hours later, at 11 a.m., the lead car in the procession passed, lights blinking. I stood to attention waiting to salute the royal vehicle, but no one appeared. Five minutes passed. Ten minutes passed. It was a full twenty minutes before the royal vehicle came into view. I straightened myself up and saluted, but horror of horrors, as the car passed, the duke, who was nearest to me, had his head turned towards his fellow rear seat passenger in animated conversation. Then he was gone. Imagine, all that spit and polish, that long stand at the road junction, a stomach rumbling through lack of food, and he hadn't even looked at me! It was one of those occasions during my early service when I thought of life in Australia or Canada, or even London!

Another event that stands out in my mind was my move to Derrylin in Fermanagh on an emergency transfer. I arrived the day after the station had been badly damaged in an IRA attack, which signalled the start of the '56 campaign. The staircase had been half demolished and for a couple of days we used a ladder to reach the bedrooms. This was my first taste of real violence, when I realised that I had joined a paramilitary force. When I joined the RUC we were told it was a paramilitary force, and was recognised as such throughout the world. I suppose it was because we carried pistols and had access to, and trained in, the rifle and SMG (sub-machine-gun). The manpower at Derrylin, a sub-division of Lisnaskea district, consisted of a sergeant, four constables and two full-time 'B' Specials. One of the constables was married and lived in the village with his family. For a few weeks it was hectic. I was either in bed or standing in the sand-bags guarding the station. Again I thought of Australia—at the time I could have travelled there for £10! But, as luck would have it, within a year I would be working in Belfast, though not before the Derrylin station was 'attacked' again. The next morning we were all lined up to have our hands shaken by the prime minister—Lord Brookeborough. He thanked us for repelling the enemy. Little did he know there was no attack! One of the sentries thought he saw someone crawling through the barbed wire surrounding the station at midnight. He was trigger-happy and shot what was later found to be a stray dog. Before he could warn the personnel inside that it was a false alarm, all hell broke loose. Everyone opened fire, rockets were fired which lit up the whole countryside. After five minutes the firing stopped. There was a deathly silence, but the only death was the poor old dog. Reinforcements arrived from everywhere, and we were congratulated. It couldn't happen now, as a search would have been carried out to find the IRA firing points and the scenes would have been examined, but back then it really was Wild West rules.

I really enjoyed my short time in Derrylin. The people in the village were mannerly and helpful. They obviously didn't want this violence. In fact, the local priest invited us to his Sunday night poker school and we brought him to the station for a game on many occasions. One game I attended in the parochial house, which was close to the police station, also consisted of the priest, a Catholic constable, and a Protestant farmer. On many occasions we rode our bikes down to the border, where the unapproved roads linking to the Republic had been cratered. We were able to get around the hole in the road on foot to a shop for cigarettes. The shop-lady was always very nice, and always said, 'I hope you young men take care.'

But I was soon to forget all about the 'bogs', as country stations were called. I was going to Belfast, I was really starting a new life, but I was also going back to my home town.

———

Cullingtree Road and Hastings Street police barracks covered the whole of the Lower Falls area, from the Grosvenor Road over to the Shankill. It stretched from Fisherwick Place in the centre of Belfast up to the Royal Victoria Hospital. At the heart of the sub-division were hundreds upon hundreds of little houses in a warren of streets. The front doors opened up onto the pavement. They were old houses, small and damp, two up, two down, as the estate agents would say, with an outside toilet. On every corner there was a small shop, or a pub. In fact there were fifty-two pubs on my three beats, and in the centre of it all stood St Peter's Cathedral, towering over the Lower Falls area.

The people who lived in the long rows of tiny houses were lower working class or unemployable. In the Twenties it was very much a no-go area for police as a result of sectarian trouble in the years following the First World War. It was a full thirty years before a policeman could perform beat duty on his own in safety. The people were a fair-minded lot who drank and played to excess, but the sub-division was basically free of serious crime. Granted, there were burglaries and petty thefts, as well as many breaches of the Public Order Act, mainly through alcohol. I felt I was a shrewd young policeman and many times helped a drunk home, rather than arrest him, or lectured a minor at his or her home, instead of prosecution. I had many informants as a result and used the information wisely, I hoped.

My system of policing as a constable was different and probably a bit radical. I made policing simple by acquiring a comprehensive 'local knowledge' of my beat. If I saw someone I didn't know, it wasn't long before I knew all about them. I knew most people on my patch, the cars they drove, where they drank. My working day was spent asking questions to increase my local knowledge. Not for me the aimless plod around the beat, especially during dusk or darkness. I preferred to hide up behind some obstacles and stake out a target, be it a car with some valuables left lying in view on the rear seat by a thoughtless driver, or premises that were habitually raided by thieves. My success rate was spectacular. I rarely needed assistance in making an arrest, as I was tall, fit and strong, with the fearless temperament of the young. The commissioner of police, Belfast, a rank now abolished, and later chief constable, was on record as stating that I was probably the best practical policeman in the city, or indeed in any city. I believe I certainly became an asset to Special Branch with my knowledge of when to keep my eyes open and my mouth shut. I felt I had few peers in this respect.

The late Fifties/early Sixties was the time of the hated smog in downtown Belfast. It was fossil-burning time. Every building—whether house or factory—used coal or coke for heating and power, and on cold autumn and winter evenings this pale yellow smog descended over the city. All the major junctions were controlled by 'point duty' policemen. At rush hours they donned white gauntlets and gloves for this purpose. After such duty, when I blew my nose, two black dots would appear on my handkerchief. It certainly wasn't good for my chest. Some of the constables who did this job permanently died soon after their retirement.

The only crime in the area was petty theft or disorderly behaviour and other summary offences to do with drunkenness.

There were quite a few characters on my beats. James Young, the well-loved comedian of the time, owned a rag store in Devonshire Street. My bedroom in the station overlooked his store. The large garage type doors were always open and old ladies stood separating the old clothes into piles of wool, cotton, and other materials. James called most mornings and we used to shout down at him from the bedroom windows. He would have tried his latest jokes on us, and the craic was good. Another comedian, Frank Carson, had a TV programme in the late Fifties called 'With a Fiddle and a Flute'. He bought a pub called the Gaelic Bar on Cullingtree Road. A lovely man, his place was always full, but I think he gave away more drink than he sold at the bar.

Cullingtree Road, affectionately known as the 'Loney', was at the centre of the Lower Falls. It ran from Divis Street to the Grosvenor Road. Many small streets of houses ran off the Loney. At the heart were Irwin, Baker, Scotch, Bow and English Streets, to name a few; small streets but heavily populated. The people were hard-working, mostly employed in the local mills and foundries. They played hard too, spending all their spare cash in the pubs and bookies. Many a half-crown I loaned (maybe that's the wrong term) on a Monday morning to households near the police station. After a couple of years parading the beat, the people got to know you. If you were fair, and kept your notebook and pencil in your pocket except when really necessary to use it, then the people would co-operate, and help you when serious crime occurred. Women would call at the barracks often to request that one of us visit their home, to sort out one of their teenage family.

At that time it was all beat duty. There was one district patrol car which answered 999 calls in the area, but everyone else was on foot patrol. I got more than my share of duty in the car as none of the older members were keen to do car duty, except drive. Too much to do, and too much paperwork. I didn't mind. I enjoyed it.

I well remember being on duty on New Year's Eve 1960. I was observer in charge of the district motor patrol car, being driven by a senior constable, one who liked to get through his turn of duty without any hassle. We were cruising along Durham Street towards the Grosvenor Road, when I noticed dense smoke emitting from a house chimney. I asked the driver to stop, intending to notify the householder that their chimney might be on fire. The driver cruised on past the house.

'Never worry. This is how they clean their chimneys around here. They set them on fire purposely.'

We drove around into Fisherwick Place, and I again told the driver to return to the Durham Street house. He grudgingly turned into College Square North and headed back towards the house. When we arrived, I could see the smoke was denser and showers of sparks were rising into the night sky. When we stopped at the house, I jumped out and approached the door. I was about to knock when I realised the door was warm. I looked in the window and although the curtains were pulled shut I could see the glow of a fire. At this moment a neighbour approached. She could see the fire also and shouted, 'There are two young children in there. I saw their mother leave a while ago.'

After a few heavy kicks I managed to break open the door. The place was an inferno, but I could see the seat of the fire was a downstairs room. I shouted to the children, but there was no reply. I could see a staircase at the end of the hall and almost reached it before being beaten back by the flames. I managed to get back out. The house was part of a row of kitchen houses, as they were called, and the upstairs window sill would only have been about nine foot from the ground. I shouted to the driver to move the police car over to a spot under the window. I then stood back, took aim and hurled my baton through the bedroom window. About ten seconds later two little faces appeared, sticking their heads out of the hole in the glass. They were screaming and in dire distress. I climbed on top of the car and tried to reach them. I shouted at them to jump and I would catch them. I broke off some jagged ends of glass and one of them leaned out and I grabbed her, a little girl. I handed her down to a passer-by who had stopped to help. The other face, a little boy, disappeared back into the bedroom. Dense smoke billowed out of the hole in the glass. I shouted and shouted. The face appeared again, screaming.

'Jump, jump', I shouted.

The passer-by had climbed onto the police car, and luckily for me was there to help me when I grabbed hold of the boy's hand and pulled him out of the broken window. A few minutes later the fire brigade arrived. The house was an inferno, but thankfully the children were unharmed except for smoke inhalation, and small cuts. I was fine except I lost some hair to the flames as I tried to reach the staircase, and my uniform was burned. I never saw my baton or my cap again.

I became well known in the Lower Falls area after this incident. Maybe it was my imagination, but people appeared friendlier and more helpful.

I enjoyed going to court. There were about thirty of us in the station to cover the day turns and night duty. Half of this number had over twenty years' service, and were very set in their ways. Some had never left Ulster in their lives. The late Fifties marked the start of the package holidays, and when four of us planned over lunch in the station kitchen (all single men had to eat in the station—a lunch meal made by a cook who came each day), to go to Spain on a ten-day, 29-guinea holiday, the senior constable, one John Brennan who had over forty years' service and had marched from Cork on transfer to the new RUC in 1922, puffed on his pipe and said, 'You boys will look well walking up Spain.'

There were about a dozen of us living in the barracks and friendships developed which would last a lifetime. Some ended in later years with death at the hands of the IRA.

Communication was a big problem in the police in the Fifties and Sixties. In Tyrone and Fermanagh some stations still had the phone on the wall with separate ear and mouth pieces. The phone numbers were three digit, and were usually 222, 212 or 202. If you made a call outside your telephone area you had to go through the operator—not a very secure method. All towns had their telephone stations or exchange, staffed by locals. They knew everything about everybody! In Belfast things were slightly more advanced, but not by much. When I look back on my early days in Belfast and think how much different things would have been on the beat with a mobile phone. Good grief,

I could have covered the beats by myself. The cars were fitted with radios, which more often than not were not working, or the reception was poor. If a constable on the beat required assistance, he had to pray that the arrest was made close to a call-box, or that some member of the public would make a 999 call on his behalf. I have even used my whistle for help, a method we see in old London films, where police run about blowing their whistles. On a calm night, without wind or traffic, it was possible for neighbouring beat-men to hear a whistle. I can say it worked for me on two occasions. Once when another beat-man was nearby and heard me, and the second when a night watchman at a factory door heard me and dialled 999 for assistance. Not everyone had a phone at home, especially on my beats. The locals of the Falls used the pub phone, and on many occasions called at the police barracks. If it was any sort of half urgent call I always obliged. Private calls were to be entered in a register but this was rarely done.

The Lower Falls area was like a small town. Everyone knew their neighbours, and the local police were very much involved in daily life. In the summertime, especially on warm evenings and nights, the people would congregate outside their houses, on the footpath, having a chat. If I walked past I would be greeted with good-natured banter.

'Lend us half-a-crown, constable, we would love a wee drink.'

'Who polished your shoes for you?'

There were occasions when I would flick a half-crown at the nearest man. It was never dropped, always caught. There were a lot of street games played by adult and child alike. They had nowhere else to play. There was always a football match on one of the streets on summer evenings; I used to stand and watch. There were some very talented young players. Of course there were other games played, gambling games, the most popular being 'Pitch and Toss'. A coin was pitched from a set position towards a wall, and the nearest coin to the wall won the 'pot' of coins lying on the ground. I usually turned a blind eye to these games and walked away, but now and again the occupier of the house whose gable wall was being used would complain to the police about the noise, and we would have to act. A warning usually sufficed and they would move on somewhere else. It was against the law to play the game, but at least when they were involved in the games they weren't committing other crimes elsewhere! I well remember one game at the upper end of Leeson Street. I rounded a corner and walked straight into the game. There were about twenty men playing. Usually they had scouts or lookouts, but not that day. Some of the players scattered, others stood their ground. I was standing right beside the pot of coins lying on the ground, probably over £5, a sizeable sum in those days. What the hell am I going to do, I thought? I was quickly surrounded by about a dozen men, and one of them started to gather up the pot. Suddenly there was a shout from across the street.

'Leave him alone, let him pass.'

Two men, strangers to me, were standing on the opposite footpath, looking over at us. The crowd stood back, and I headed back down Leeson Street. A couple of stones were thrown after me. I had only recognised one of the players, a lad from Lady Street, opposite the police barracks, and when I met him a couple of days later I asked him who the men were who saved my bacon.

'One was an ex-boxer called Barney something and the other was Joe something. I think he was in jail. I think he's in the IRA,' he replied.

———

The Twelfth of July always caused problems for the police on the Lower Falls, not because there were any loyalist parades there, but because Orangemen who went and took part in the main parade to Finaghy had to return home on foot. Few had cars in those days. They naturally took the shortest route, which was across Sandy Row, along Durham Street, and left up Albert Street. They then crossed the main Falls Road to reach the Shankill. Cullingtree Road police barracks was slap bang in the middle of this migration route, and on the Twelfth of July night, extra police were on duty to marshal these Orangemen through the Catholic area. If they had all come at one time, things would have been easy, but they came in groups ranging from two up to twenty. Some were sober, some drunk, some wore their sashes, some did not, some sang sectarian songs, some were quiet. All in all it was a long night's work. The biggest problem arose from groups, who, when they reached Sandy Row, tanked up on liquor, took the long walk up Albert Street and past the Loney. The police used to pray for rain to start in the afternoon, and continue to bedtime. This drove the Orangemen home early and we never had any bother on rainy Twelfths.

One Twelfth of July stands out in my memory. It was either 1959 or 1960. It was good weather and in the evening we were paying attention to groups of Orangemen walking up Albert Street. A group of four or five stopped at the junction of Albert Street with Cullingtree Road and started to sing 'The Sash'. A nationalist group quickly gathered, and a couple of bottles were thrown. Police moved quickly and ushered the Orangemen on up Albert Street, but the damage was done, as each group after that had to run the gauntlet of bottles and bricks. The situation had now become one of nationalists versus the police. The crowd swelled to a couple of hundred. The reserve force, the forerunner to today's MSU—Mobile Support Unit—were called to the scene, and a stand-off developed. Cullingtree Road barracks was only fifty yards from the scene, and at 11 p.m. the night men left the barracks to go to their beats. One of the constables who lived in the station with me, and who had partaken of a few drinks before his turn of duty, suddenly saw fifty reserve force standing in rows awaiting orders from the commissioner of police. At that moment a bottle landed at his feet. He drew his baton and ran towards the crowd shouting 'Charge!'

The reserve force, not knowing who this man was, drew their batons and charged after him. The nationalist crowd withdrew into the Loney, and in two minutes the street was empty. The police did not pursue them into the Loney and returned to their position, and eventually away from the scene. It was a good result. I was standing beside my district inspector, Jamie Flanagan, when the commissioner asked, 'Who was that officer who gave the order to charge, Flanagan?'

The inspector, who had seen the constable lead the charge, looked at me and winked.

'I think it was someone from the reserve force, sir.'

'Oh right, well it turned out okay anyway.'

Flanagan smiled at me, and winked again.

There were many colourful characters in the Lower Falls area in the Fifties and Sixties. There was the cat lady who took her twenty plus cats out walking during the early hours like a flock of sheep. There was the rat catcher who brought his catch home in a bag and in his pockets. He then washed them in the bath with disinfectant. Then they had the run of the house. After a few days training them to eat out of his hand, he took them to the pet shop at Smithfield Market and sold them on as pet rats. Then there was the unforgettable Mickey Marley, who had a horse-drawn merry-go-round or carousel. There were about six wooden horses on the ride and he cranked it by hand. He went to the housing estates all over the city daily. In the heart of winter he only wore a vest. I spoke with him on many occasions, a rare character with a weakness for Guinness. I well remember the day I was called to Divis Street, by a member of the public, who reported a merry-go-round being pulled by a horse with no driver. I stopped the horse and found Mickey lying drunk on the ride.

'The horse knows the way to the stable, constable, just let him carry on,' shouted a passer-by.

Sure enough, the horse was heading in the right direction. I thought if I arrest him for being drunk-in-charge of a horse-drawn vehicle, I'll have the trouble of looking after the horse. I quickly jumped onto the ride and drove the horse up Divis Street. I knew where the house and stable was; it was only a few hundred yards away. The journey only took five minutes, but passers-by stood laughing, bus and car drivers sounded their horns, and I was glad to reach Marley's house. He was still fast asleep. Later his neighbour must have told him who brought him home, and a few days later he called at the station, wanting to know where I lived. He said he would bring the ride to my house and give my kids free rides. I explained I was single.

––––

It was in the summer of 1958 or 59. I was on duty in the district patrol car. We had dealt with a number of emergency calls during the night but nothing serious. It was now about two o'clock in the morning and we were considering having our tea-break when the radio 'crackled'.

'Control to M3, what is your location?'

'Just passing the RV Hospital heading citywards,' I replied.

'Can you take a 999 call to Hamill Street?'

'Roger on that,' I replied.

Control continued, 'Apparently there's fighting in the street there outside one of the houses.'

'Roger on that.'

Hamill Street was a long street of kitchen houses, two up, two down. It ran from College Square North over to Divis Street and wasn't far from the city centre, and we arrived at the scene in a couple of minutes.

There was indeed fighting in the street. Men fought men, women fought women, and there were mixed fights, all outside this particular house with the front door open. After a few minutes my partner and I separated the people fighting and then turned our attention to screams and mayhem emanating from the house. On entering, the first thing I noticed was a coffin lying on its side. Where was the body? Again we tried to separate the protagonists, both men and women. A woman lay motionless with blood pouring from her nose. An ashen-faced man lay beside her. Was this the corpse? Both bodies were being trampled on in the fight. Everyone was drunk. They could hardly stand, let alone fight.

After what seemed like an age we had the situation under control, but the women continued to scream as we got the coffin back onto the table and the corpse back into the coffin. I got hold of one woman who seemed less drunk than the others, and took her outside.

'What is this all about?' I asked.

'He came, I knew he would come, and they were waiting for him. Why did he come, oh why, oh why!'

She went on in a rather garbled fashion, but I eventually understood what the fighting was about. Apparently the family had a 'prodigal' son who had left home many years ago after causing much trouble to the house and the deceased. He hadn't been seen since. His name had cropped up during the wake, and promises were made that if this person appeared he would be 'dealt with'. There were also those on the other side of the family who thought it was good that he came, that the past should be forgotten. When he eventually arrived, drunk, in the early hours, all hell broke loose.

Everyone was by now back in the house. There was hardly room to breathe, about thirty people in a small room with a coffin. Some were squeezed into the little back kitchen.

After promises that they would be quiet and keep the peace, we left the scene. On arrival at the station a few minutes later I scrubbed my hands twice. There were no disposable gloves then! Somehow, I didn't feel like eating after handling the corpse. We were about ten minutes into our break when Control phoned.

'Are you on your break?'

'Affirmative.'

'We've had another 999 call to Hamill Street.'

'Oh no, can you get some other car to go to it?'

'Negative, M1 and M2 are both dealing with accidents.'

'Shit, okay, we'll go.'

It wasn't far to the scene and we arrived in a few minutes.

There was a group of about five men and women manhandling each other at the door of the house. We pulled them apart and entered the house. It was mayhem, and yes—you've guessed it—the pooor old corpse was lying on the floor beside the up-ended coffin.

This was beyond a joke. My partner and I started grabbing people and trailing them out the door onto the street. I found the woman I had spoken to earlier.

'How many live in this house?'

She started to count: 'Five.'

'Show them to me.'

She pointed them out and I got them back into the house and closed the door.

'This wake is now over, go to your own homes now,' I said. They milled about for a while as I stood at the door. There were a few curses and damns, and then heaven intervened: it started to rain! A good heavy shower—the policeman's friend. After a while they started to head off and peace returned. I knocked on the door. When it was opened I saw the corpse was back in the coffin, looking serene again, but the coffin was on the floor.

'Where's the table?' I enquired.

'It's broken, Constable.'

I told them not to let anyone into the house until morning.

'Okay, Constable, I'll have to clean up this mess.'

It was indeed a mess; there were broken cups and bottles and sandwiches scattered everywhere, and a couple of shoes. Nowadays when I hear of fighting at Traveller funerals, I think of Hamill Street and the wonderful fifties.

———

The only thing worse than being murdered is to have your liberty taken away. Police have to make decisions daily on whether to arrest someone for a crime. They don't take (or shouldn't take) this power lightly. They have to make an on-the-spot decision. If there is a doubt in their mind, they must ask themselves should they walk away, or should they leave the decision to a court of law? Many millions of pounds are wasted on trials in court that end with no conviction, simply because there was insufficient evidence. It all comes down in the end to the arresting officer, the man or woman who sowed the first seed of prosecution. Were they inexperienced? Or had they bad supervisory officers?

There are, of course, times when it is blindingly obvious a crime has been committed by a defendant when you apprehend him at the scene with the proceeds of the crime on his person, or when you open a car door and the driver falls out blind drunk. It is obvious he is drunk-in-charge of a motor vehicle. Having said that, the decision rests with the constable at the scene. Policing in Ireland, whether North or South, is different than that in England. In my experience I found Irish police to be less robot-like, more humane, and certainly more compassionate than the English forces, who try to achieve arrest targets, and on any occasion I had dealings with them over the years I found this obviously apparent.

A police constable on beat patrol had it in his power, in summary offences at least, to prosecute or caution. Many a time I succumbed to a tearful, apologetic woman and took the caution route. Many a time, for the greater good I thought, I cautioned the butcher, the baker, and the candlestick maker. I suppose it could be called giving a second chance. I was probably too compassionate at times. In the late Fifties, 1958 or 1959 probably, I remember coming across a young curate priest asleep at the wheel of his car in the shadow of St Peter's Cathedral. When I couldn't waken him I realised he was stupid drunk. I phoned Clonard Monastery, having found his name and address on an envelope in the car. Someone came and collected him immediately. He contacted me a few days later and thanked me for my leniency. He promised to pray for me every day. Maybe he still is!

I remember well another two instances of 'second chances'. The first was concerning a 999 call at one o'clock in the morning, to a car park at the rear of the Law Courts in May Street, concerning a man drunk and asleep at the wheel of a car. I arrived and spoke to the gentleman and, to be brief, I locked the car up and drove him home. He was a young barrister who had been working at the court all day. As chance would have it, I was a witness in a court case the very next day. I saw him, and handed him his driver's licence.

'I found this lying beside your car when I returned to it after taking you home.'

'Was it you took me home?' he enquired.

I nodded.

'I can't thank you enough, you have saved my career, saved my future,' he said.

'Well, I decided you were not drunk-in-charge of a motor vehicle, but you looked very tired, so I drove you home.'

'Is this what the record says?' he asked.

'There is no record,' I replied.

I watched his career closely over the years and, some time after he was appointed a judge, I met him in a golf club.

'How are you, Judge, do you remember me?'

He shook his head slowly.

'Many, many years ago I drove you home from the Law Courts.'

'Ah, a taxi man?' he enquired.

'No', I replied. 'You were young, you dropped your driver's licence, and I returned it to you next day in court.'

I could see the recognition crossing his face. He shook my hand, and I thought he looked as if he was going to cry.

'I've often thought of you over the years. You were my guardian angel. Only for you I wouldn't be here. I took my second chance, and I believe that experience made me a better judge.'

We spoke for ages of the old days in Belfast, until he was called to a duty he was performing in the club.

The second instance concerned a junior police officer. I suppose the rank would be inspector or chief inspector nowadays. He was caught up in an incident one night. His career was on the line. After an enquiry he was exonerated by his peers in the service, and faced no prosecution either. I didn't tell any lies for him; I just lost my notes on the matter. He kept in touch with me over the years, as he rose towards the top. If he visited a station to which I was attached he would always call at the office to say hello. This was embarrassing at times, especially when he would ask my opinion on matters in front of other officers. When he received an award in the honours list, I was invited to a celebratory function. I had to decline as I was out of the country on the date. I met him a couple of years after he retired and he was able to tell me I hadn't attended the function. I believe he also took his second chance, although I also believe he always sailed close to the wind. A real gentleman, a policeman's policeman, as we used to say in the old days!

Some years later, I was on a detective course in England, and in class I was asked what I would do in certain circumstances if I realised that, soon after arresting a suspect for a crime, he was innocent.

'I would release him,' I replied.

'No, no, no, if you can't get him on this, you may be able to get him on that, or that, or that. He's a criminal, isn't he?' replied the lecturer. He then laughed to the rest of the class. 'Paddy wouldn't be good for the crime figures, would he?'

I strongly believe that the so-called modernisation of the prosecution systems was a backward step. People now sit at desks making decisions on whether to prosecute or not, for offences of a minor nature. The system becomes bogged down with delay. It's the bad system that causes cases to be heard years after the offence date. There are those who believe that the police shouldn't have the power to decide on whether to prosecute or not. This may be acceptable with regard to serious crime, but not for summary offences. In the Fifties and Sixties when I served in Belfast, if I arrested someone during the night for larceny (now theft) from a parked motor vehicle, or loitering with intent, or disorderly behaviour, or assault, and many other offences, I took them to the police office at the Law Courts and had them charged and detained. I went back to the police barracks and typed a statement of evidence outlining the offence. I then went to the Custody Court the next morning, when the case was heard and dealt with or remanded to another court. I simply handed my statement to the prosecuting officer and proved my case from the witness box. All over and done with within twelve hours of arrest, and no expense to the taxpayer! If the defendant wished to be represented by a solicitor, the magistrate would suggest one of those present. They were always looking for work. Many countries throughout the world still operate this system, including the USA. If a police officer is given the power of arrest for a particular offence, and he finds someone committing that offence and arrests him, it seems a duplication to me that the decision to prosecute is then put in the hands of other people in a prosecution service.

In these days of political correctness, a policeman's lot is not a happy one. There are so many rules and regulations concerning the arrest, the interview, and the taking of statements properly that the constable, if not highly trained, is at a sore disadvantage, and the best training he can get is not in a training classroom, but out on the beat with experienced colleagues. The whole system of policing in Britain and Ireland needs a root and branch overhaul. Long years of young officers attending Officers Training Colleges like Bramshill, and trying to make a name for themselves inventing new forms, and policing methods, have destroyed the police service. Career officers who have never detected a crime in their lives are making day-to-day decisions, which could be handled better by a senior constable, and in England too much money, and manpower, has been thrown at traffic offences like speeding, instead of crime. There has to be a balance.

I have always believed that taking the parking problems out of the hands of the police, and appointing traffic wardens to issue tickets and prosecute was a big detrimental decision. The police have lost what was a main way of keeping in touch with the public. The constable on the beat knew the shopkeepers and businesses on his patrol area. He was able to show flexibility in his attitude to issuing parking tickets. He was able to think about public relations. He knew he couldn't call on a shopkeeper for help in solving a crime if he had booked him for being over his parking time the previous week. He had to keep a happy balance. I always showed latitude when on parking duty, except where an obstruction had been caused, stopping the free flow of traffic. The present systems in Britain have alienated the public and police. The best policeman is one who knows all the businesses and shops and characters on the area he patrols, and, more importantly, has a fair and friendly relationship with them all. Relations with the public are crucial to good police work.

In the thirty odd years since the first Troubles, in the Twenties, police in the Catholic Falls area had been slowly but surely building up trust with the Catholic population. It had taken two generations to achieve this, until suddenly in the summer of 1964 irreversible damage was done by one idiot policeman who smashed a shop window and removed a small tricolour on display. Tricolours are everywhere in Ulster now, but then in the early Sixties it was a step too far. Some politicians had heard of the flag in the window, and the matter was pushed into the public domain. The story was carried in the newspapers and sectarian strife loomed. The matter should have been resolved by dialogue, but that option was lost when the window was smashed and the flag removed. That night crowds gathered and the rioting began. I had never seen the likes of it before. For a while the police were heavily outnumbered, and were being injured by rains of bottles and bricks. My base was Hastings Street Barracks, which was only a couple of hundred yards from the shop. We initially withdrew, but as reinforcements arrived and police numbers grew, decisions were made to deal with the rioters, and regain the peace for the streets. Divis Street was a main road. It was a main traffic artery from the city centre to the Falls area. The police had a duty to protect the citizens and keep this road open. The rioting and looting continued until daylight before things quietened down. The big question was, would that be the end of it? The answer came at dusk the following night. Larger crowds gathered, and things got even worse. Buses were set on fire at the junction of Divis Street, Falls Road and Albert Street. Again decisions were taken by the police authorities. This time they wanted arrests. With my local knowledge I was chosen to drive a tender full of officers. A senior officer, D.A. Corbett, climbed into the passenger seat. We drove up the Grosvenor Road, and down the Falls Road towards the rioters. I would estimate there were over three hundred. Other tenders full of men approached from other directions. It was planned as a pincer movement. There was no other traffic on the road. It was pitch dark, as street lighting had been damaged by the rioters. The idea was that the men in the tender would jump out and try to make arrests. As I turned onto the Falls Road the officer beside me spoke.

'I want you to drive at the crowd as fast as this bloody thing will travel. I want into the middle of the crowd, do you understand?

The only lights were any headlights and as I reached the crowd I instinctively lifted my foot off the accelerator towards the brake.

The officer struck me on the left leg with his baton, and screamed, 'Don't slow, don't slow, they'll get out of your way.'

The crowd did jump, but I still can't believe how I managed to avoid mowing them down. After a couple more nights of rioting, things more or less got back to normal. Not, in my opinion, because the police were successful in their tactics, but because the crowd tired of rioting, and the people of the Falls needed the roads open to travel to their work. The aftermath was that thirty years of patient community relations work by the police in the Catholic Falls area was wasted. The two communities in the North started to move apart again, and I firmly believe that the Divis Street riots lit the fuse for the civil rights movement a couple of years later. That in turn led to the involvement of the IRA, and out of this rose the Provos and thirty years of death and misery.

———

I look back on my days working in the Lower Falls area as happy ones. I met many famous people. I met the Beatles on their 1963 visit to Belfast. They signed my notebook. John Lennon wrote under his signature, 'I've been nicked.'

I spoke to Jackie Onassis/Kennedy on her visit with Aristotle to dedicate the new giant cranes at Belfast shipyard, although the extent of our meeting was a smile and a 'Hello'.

At that time I considered myself a policeman upholding the law. I never thought that I was a Protestant foot-soldier upholding a Protestant state. I learned a lot about life, and putting trust in people. I experienced life in the raw over a few years, which would take others a lifetime to do. In 1966 my wife's health necessitated a move out of the Belfast smog and we moved to North Antrim. After a quiet, uneventful time in the north of the Province, we returned to Belfast in 1970, just as the new Provisional IRA were starting to cause havoc across the Province.

On a visit to Headquarters around this time I met Jamie Flanagan, who was now deputy chief constable. He literally dragged me into his office, where I recognised another senior officer sitting in a chair. He got up and shook hands. All three of us had served together in the Falls area. The other man was now head of Special Branch.

'George, we are sitting here discussing the enlargement of Special Branch. This must be done quickly, and we must choose the right people.'

He then looked back at the success I had had on the beat under him in the past.

'You were the best practical policeman in Belfast.'

'Well, you told me so on paper once,' I laughed.

'Did I really? I don't remember, anyway, how would you like to switch to Special Branch?'

I thought for a moment. 'Well, I'll think about it, and maybe apply to the next selection board,' I replied.

Flanagan stood up. 'George, you've just done your board.'

He looked at the other officer. 'Agreed?'

'Agreed,' was the reply.

Flanagan continued, 'Someone will be in touch with you in the next few days, and you'll be given a choice of areas you might like to work in.'

He held out his hand, and I shook it. Tea was then ordered and we sat and talked of old times, and future times. The head of Special Branch painted a grim picture.

'The Provos are enlarging daily, almost like a cell multiplying. There are so many new faces. We need to infiltrate. It'll be dangerous work, but if we can't glean good intelligence, and hold the line, law and order will be a thing of the past.'

A few days later I was given a choice of South Down, Armagh, Londonderry or Belfast. I chose South Down, and after a few weeks in the job I realised that things were much worse than I had thought whilst in uniform. Of course I had access to intelligence that I wouldn't have had on the beat. I certainly didn't foresee that the future British prime minister, James Callaghan, would be standing on the main street in Newry a few months later. At that time, he was the shadow home secretary, having held that cabinet portfolio in the former Labour government. He had played a political role in the early days of the Troubles.

————

When you get older you tend to look back more and more, to the distant past, and things pop out of your memory bank that you thought you had lost the key to; things actually become clearer. I have no real grievance about my police service. I had no real ambitions for rises in rank. I couldn't find time to study. I lived life to the full. I had a lovely wife and family. I suppose my main regret was how insensitive the government and the police authorities were to the problems of police families. No one will ever know, in any real detail, of the trauma suffered by the police and their families over the first ten years of the terrorist campaign. Police families were forced to change to an entirely new way of life. Many police had to move house to safer areas. Catholic police couldn't go to mass, and their children had to move school. Cars had to be checked for booby traps each morning before the school run.

Routes to and from the police station had to be varied almost daily. Socialising for police became a no-no. All police work became mobile, no beat duty could be performed. Emergency calls had to be checked first by the military, who then accompanied the police to the scene. Bulletproof doors and windows were installed in many police houses. As more and more police lost their lives, welfare chaos took over police households. Children became traumatised. I know that my own children lost the best years of their lives locked up in the house after school. No going out to play for them. When the phone rang or a knock came to the door, all eyes would look at me, awaiting instructions. Two of my children still suffer the effects of living in a nationalist area in the Seventies. The Provos say the war is over and everything can return to normal, but what of loved ones lost and children damaged mentally? Will they just send their nerves a message to shut down? I believe it was massive neglect that no counselling service was in place for police and their families. I certainly received none during or after my service.

The IRA campaign destroyed my life. The Second World War, 1939–45, destroyed millions of lives, but at least it was over in five years. The RUC and their families had to endure a thirty-year war against them. What was it for? Northern Ireland is still part of Britain and, according to the British and Irish governments, it will remain so until the people themselves decide otherwise. So what has changed since 1970? We have a Power-Sharing Executive at Stormont, but to the man in the street it makes no difference really. He still pays the same taxes for the same bad government.

———

I had an IRA source in the Seventies who was interned. I could have had him released quickly but he chose to accept his detention rather than risk someone putting two and two together. He studied Ancient Irish History whilst in prison. On his release after a couple of years he contacted me.

'Look, I'll continue to work for you, but I'm not going out of my way. If anything comes to my ears I'll give it to you, but don't ask me to do anything. I've a new outlook on life. I've told my OC I want out, that I don't want involved with the IRA anymore. So far they've accepted that.'

About a month later he contacted me again. We met in Belfast for a beer. He gave me a couple of names to watch for and we had a good chat.

'Did you ever study old Irish history?' he asked me.

I replied that I hadn't really, not before the eighteenth century anyway. He laughed at that.

'Did you know Brian Boru was a Scotsman?'

'No, I didn't know that,' I replied.

He went on for the next half hour telling me about the works of P.W. Joyce, a noted historian a century ago.

'The Brian Boru question was a trick,' he laughed, and went on. 'Up until the twelfth century Ireland was called Scotland, so therefore the inhabitants were Scots. The name then changed to Hibernia, and a hundred years or so later to Eire-Land and then Ireland, and the language of the country was a mixture of Saxon, Scandinavian, Danish Latin, and a Gaelic language brought over from Alban, now Scotland.'

I listened to him intently. He was a changed person, certainly not the one I had known a couple of years earlier.

'I have learned a lot from looking back. If you read things for yourself, you get a sort of achievement feeling. I am going to continue my studies and try to be a school teacher.'

'If only the people of Ireland could look forward, and not back,' I replied.

I have often thought about him, and the last conversation we had, for I never saw him again. I learned later he had gone to live in England, where he was working as a teacher.

Chapter 5
Pre-Internment Source

When a member of Special Branch receives intelligence which increases his pulse rate at the thought of capturing terrorists in the act, and then comes back to earth with a bump when told by the source that he is part of the bombing team, it's a sure thing that his brain will go into overdrive, because a solution to the problem must be found. Lives are at stake. It's a rare occasion when one is given a source in PIRA without having had to work to get him, so I was pleasantly pleased when a member of my department, who was moving on transfer, gave me a fairly new source whom he had groomed in the previous few months.

'Watch him, and hold the reins hard; he's a likeable rogue, he likes women, drink, and much more. I don't think he'll last long, he's too rough a diamond. Use code names only with him. Good luck, he may produce the goods some day.'

At our first meet, I could see he was a rough diamond. He was tall, fit, and a real risk-taker. In other times of war, I could see him making a good Para, or member of the SAS. He obviously lived a sort of day-to-day existence. On that first meet he told me that he had got drunk the previous night and had fallen asleep in bushes in the grounds of the Ballymascanlon Hotel, Dundalk. I believed him because he did smell a bit.

For a while the source would keep in touch twice weekly, but he was finding it increasingly difficult. He was on Special Branch's IRA suspect lists, and like most at that time in the same situation, he slept away from home four or five nights weekly, in fear of internment. As he got further involved in IRA training in the Republic, he went on the run together with four or five others from the South Down/South Armagh area. Not all the people in Dundalk welcomed the Provos with open arms, so at times they did sleep rough, dependent on hand-outs. The Garda Síochána knew most of them, and were aware that they were probable terrorists, but so long as they did no wrong in County Louth, they preferred a watching brief.

During this period the source proved invaluable in providing names of new volunteers to the movement and intelligence surrounding his training in the handling of weapons and explosives. I had a gut feeling that he enjoyed the buzz of being in the IRA. I soon realised that at heart he was a softie, and feared what would happen to him in the deadly game he was playing. He hadn't as yet been handed a gun and told to shoot somebody, but the day of reckoning wasn't far distant. One important task he did perform was to provide me with IRA contact telephone numbers in the Republic. These were passed through to the intelligence services who I suspect put the information to good use.

The source really came into his own one evening at a public protest rally against internment in Newry. I was moving around with the MIO at the periphery of the gathering, which was turning quite nasty. We were trying at all times to keep some uniform police and military between ourselves and the crowd in case we were spotted. The MIO became quite daring, when unable to hear properly the speeches made by the Provisionals, and suggested we approach the meeting from another direction. I wasn't happy but went along with the suggestion. We hadn't gone a hundred yards towards a large car park at the canal when the source ran past.

'Get the fuck out of here, there's two car bombs in the park, get out now, now.'

He ran on. I looked at the car park. It wasn't hard to find the vehicles, there were only four cars there. We hadn't gone fifty yards when there were two massive explosions in quick succession. We dived to the ground, as debris rained around us. It wasn't the explosions that sent fear through my body, it was the blood-curdling roar and applause that went up from the crowd. This was obviously a stage-managed bombing for dramatic effect on the crowds of IRA supporters, and it certainly succeeded. The bomb had been carefully parked, near enough to have an impact on the crowd, but not near enough to harm them. They were sheltered by the buildings of a couple of streets. There was an eerie silence for about five seconds after the explosion, and then a blood-curdling roar went up from the crowd. It was a noise I hadn't heard before. I felt the hair on my back rise, and felt fear. The crowd surged in my direction with another warlike roar. I saw uniform police run for their lives, and I ran like hell and didn't stop until I was safely in Newry police station. I thought of a shark feeding frenzy, and shivered. Neither of us were injured, but there was no doubting the fact that, only for the intervention by the source, who saw us heading for danger, we would have been walking past the car bombs when they went off. I didn't feel well for days after this, although my friend the MIO was rather excited by the danger of the whole affair. The source later explained that he had been involved in bringing the car bombs from the Republic, and hadn't had any time to phone me. He was near the scene because he had been detailed to hang around in case the bombs failed to detonate, in which case he had to keep the crowd away and dial 999 with a warning. It was pure luck that he had seen me walk towards danger, and I was to think later of the ifs and buts equation. What if the source hadn't seen us? What, indeed, if I hadn't known the source? What if the source hadn't been involved in the operation? I felt a cold shiver run down my spine. My outlook on life was changing again.

————

Some weeks passed, when one morning I received a telephone call from the source at Dundalk. By this time he was permanently on the run, and heavily involved in IRA activity. I found myself more and more travelling to meet him in the Republic. He wouldn't chance driving a vehicle, as this left him open to be detected at vehicle checkpoints in the North and the Republic. He was living from hand to mouth and each Saturday car loads of on-the-run IRA volunteers would drive to Kevin Street, Dublin, for weekly cash and clothes or food. I thought he looked too rough and had given him trousers, a jumper and some socks. This particular morning he sounded agitated and wanted to see me urgently. He said he was phoning from a call-box in Dundalk and would walk out the road towards Ballymascanlon if I would come immediately. I set off for Dundalk. I crossed the border without incident and headed into Dundalk. As I passed the Customs Clearance Depot a few hundred yards from the town, I saw a Garda police car stopped opposite a petrol garage. Both uniform members were out of the car and were talking to a tall youth. As I passed, I saw to my horror that it was the source. I slowed and our eyes made contact. The source had seen me. I drove on a hundred yards and stopped. A few minutes later the police car passed me with the source in the back seat. He looked back at me as they passed. Shit, I thought, and followed the car to Dundalk police station. I waited for a while and headed back across the border, wondering what had gone wrong. What had he done? Why had the guards detained him? Two hours later I had a phone call. It was a friend in Special Branch, Dundalk.

'How ya doin'?' he asked.

'Not too bad,' I replied, wondering what was coming next.

'I have a parcel belonging to you which I need to deliver urgently, can we meet?'

I agreed to meet in an hour, inwardly hoping my friend didn't check the daily vcp lists of traffic entering the town from Ulster. I was already on it earlier. We met in the car park of the Ballymascanlon Hotel, at Ravensdale.

My friend laughed. 'I fuckin' knew there was something about that boyo. We knew he was involved, but he was a likeable lad.'

I laughed. I had heard the description before.

'When the uniform lads called me in at his request, and he asked me to phone Newry, I fuckin' knew it was you, even before he said.'

'Did he use my name?' I enquired.

'No, he just gave me a telephone number and told me to ask for Seán, so I guessed it was you.'

'What's he in for?' I asked.

'Petty stuff, theft I think. These guys on the run live from hand to mouth, they would pinch the eye out of your head for a few quid,' replied the guard.

'I need him out quick,' I said. 'He wants me urgently.'

'Oh, I see, do you want him now?'

'Only if the uniform lads have completed their business, I don't want to advertise him.'

'Well, I think they sort of suspect something, but maybe they think he only wanted to talk to me.'

I followed my friend's car into Dundalk, and waited in sight of the Garda station. Ten minutes later the source came out and walked towards the main street. I waited until he was out of sight of the guards, and then pulled up beside him. He jumped into the car. By this time it was after 2 p.m.

'Fuck, fuck, fuck,' he said, 'the bastards had nothing on me, they just wanted info on the Provos.'

'Did you steal something?' I enquired.

'Just an old trailer, and it was worthless, rotten, I got a tenner for it.'

'Well, are you being charged?'

'No way, I admitted fuck all, and they can prove nothing, the trailer's in Forkhill now.'

'Right, what did you want me for?' I enquired.

'Right, right, stop here,' he said.

We had reached the edge of town and traffic was heavy. The source lowered the backrest of the seat and settled himself. I lowered the window. It was again obvious he was sleeping rough.

'Right, get your pen out,' he said. 'There's a bombing team set up for targets in the Newry area. They are the Newry police station, the UDR Centre, the Prod side of Sugar Island, or the town hall, Bessbrook police station, and a government building on the outskirts of Newry town, on the Dublin Road. The first hit will take place tonight at about eight o'clock, when a 30 lb bomb will be placed at the government building. One car will be used by a team of five Provo volunteers. The two bombs will be placed at the front of the building. Four of the party will carry them to the building, the fifth will cover them and act as driver.'

I felt excited. 'Good, good, that's good stuff.'

'Hold on a minute, don't get too excited, that's only the good news.'

Before he could say another word I knew. 'You're on the mission?' I said, half hoping he would reply in the negative. But no, I had no such luck.

'You're dead right,' he said. 'What the fuck can we do?'

I had two emotions running at once. One at the thought of capturing the bombers, and the other at the thought of losing the source. My mind raced. Could things be worked out some way?

'There's no way you can cry off?' I asked, more in hope than anything else.

'No fucking way, I did that once, never again, I'd stink like hell.'

We discussed the situation for some ten minutes, and ruled out various options.

'If I organise it that you and one other escape, and we capture three, would you agree?' I asked.

'If you could organise it that I escape, I would go with your plan,' replied the source.

I went to the boot of the car and retrieved a red jumper, with matching red ski cap. I got back into the car.

'Wear these tonight, and no matter what, you will not be shot. You will be allowed to escape.'

'Fuck, the shit will be crossways in me. You're going to use the military, aren't you?'

'Yes, I'll have them hidden at the building, you'll have nothing to worry about,' I replied.

'It's okay for you, what about things going wrong?'

'Nothing will go wrong,' I said, trying to appear confident, although my thoughts raced.

'Right, I'll have to go now, I have a rendezvous to keep, hope I don't see you later.'

With that he opened the car door and jumped out.

I shouted, 'Wear your red jumper and hat.'

'Too right I will,' replied the source, as he set off back into Dundalk at a brisk pace.

I headed straight back to base and discussed the situation with my chief and the MIO. The police were not trained or equipped to set up an ambush for the bombers, so it was left to the local military to perform the task. I did not talk to the troop who were detailed, but I was assured by the MIO that the bomber wearing the red sweater and hat would be allowed to escape, and, indeed, if another managed to get away, there would be no harm done. The military troop were to hide in a field adjacent to the building behind a hedge. They decided against stationing men inside the building, in case the bombs went off prematurely. I was happy with the arrangements and went home for my evening meal. I felt good. My adrenalin flowed, but was this due to worry? A couple of hours later I returned to the office to await developments. I had timed it well, as a few minutes later I received a call from the Ops room to the effect that a military patrol had contact with terrorists planting a bomb at a government building on the

Dublin Road and that they had captured one terrorist, and that the ATO (Army Technical Officer) was dismantling bombs found at the scene. I tried to sound surprised.

'Did you say they detained one terrorist?' I enquired.

'Yes, one, I have had no further details yet from the military.'

The office door opened and the MIO entered. 'You've heard the news, George?'

'Yes, I have, do you know any details?'

'I'm told by the IO that the bombing team arrived as you forecast, but that they scattered when challenged, and only one was detained.'

'I wonder how they managed to mess it up?' I said.

'I'll have the full details very soon,' replied the MIO.

I lifted the phone and rang the Ops room.

'Any name yet on the person arrested?'

'Apparently he won't give his name or address,' replied the Ops officer.

'Right, let me know when the military bring him in.'

I sat and talked with the MIO. 'How in hell can an armed military ambush allow four terrorists to escape?'

The MIO was silent.

'I mean, they could have used force, the men were carrying bombs!'

'If it is a PFU (Proper Fuck Up), then we'll soon know,' replied the MIO.

'No, we'll not know, because they'll try to hide their mistakes, and God knows what version of events we'll hear,' I replied.

The phone rang. 'Ops room here, the military have arrived with the prisoner, he's in the cell.'

'Oh, good, thank you.' I put the phone down. 'He's in the cell, I'm going down for a look at him,' I said to the MIO.

'I'll have a look too,' he replied, getting up from his chair.

We went down the stairs towards the cells. The hallway was full of soldiers and police. We walked along the cell corridor. A uniform constable was on prisoner duty. He nodded towards a cell without speaking. I slid the peep-hole cover across and looked into the cell. I felt my lower jaw drop, and couldn't believe my eyes.

'Jesus Christ,' I said under my breath.

The man in the cell was the source, resplendent in a red jumper and hat. I tried to show no emotion but was finding it difficult. My pulse raced. I turned to the uniform constable as the MIO had a look.

'Has he given any name yet?'

'No, but some of the lads know him, we think he's on the suspect lists.'

Too bloody right he is, I thought. How in hell had all this happened? What had gone wrong? I returned to the office with the MIO and sat down heavily.

'It's the source, isn't it?' enquired the MIO. 'Maybe we can work something out.'

I didn't answer. How could this happen? How could I get over this problem? I lifted the phone and rang the chief, briefing him as to what had happened. We arranged to meet first thing in the morning.

At 1 a.m., when activity in the police station had died down, I returned to the cell that housed the source. I gave the jailer a knowing look and he opened the cell door without conversation. He closed the cell door behind him. I looked at the source, who was sitting on a chair with his head in his hands.

'There's no fuckin' way I was going to get shot,' he said.

'What do you mean?' I replied.

'Well, we did a dummy run past the target, and decided all was well, so we stopped the car the second time, at the front. We lifted the bombs out of the boot, and carried them towards the front of the building. We were a few yards from the door when a radio crackled behind the hedge, and we could hear radio call signs. It was very loud. One of the boys shouted, "It's the fuckin' army." We put the bombs down and run like fuck. Then we hears, "Halt immediately or I'll fire", and the sound of soldiers shouting. The others run like hell up the Dublin Road. It was alright for them. They didn't know the fire power behind the hedge. I fuckin' did, and when a voice behind the hedge beside me again shouted "Halt or I'll fire", I halted.'

I interrupted, 'But they wouldn't have fired on you. Apart from the fact that they had to take no action against the man in the red sweater, they have rules of fire. They can't fire unless fired on.'

'Listen, if you had been in my shoes, you would have stopped too, I was shit scared.'

'What happened then?' I asked.

'I was grabbed by a soldier who said, "We have to take no action against you, you were to get away." I said, "Right then, I'll go now." He said, "You bloody won't, it's too late, too many have seen you arrested." They threw me into the back of a Land Rover, and eventually I was brought here.'

I sighed and stared at the source. I suddenly felt very sorry for him. I blamed myself, but I felt a little better when the source said, 'The arsehole of a soldier who had an open radio on, when in an ambush, should be bloody shot. He should be drummed out of the army, together with the officer who detailed him for the job. The bloody IRA wouldn't even be so stupid.'

I myself suddenly felt anger too. The military had once again ruined things. They had lost a whole bombing team, and the source was now in a dangerous situation. What was to be done?

'Get a good night's sleep, and I'll see you around 9 a.m.,' I told the source.

'I want out of here soon, bloody soon,' he replied.

At half past eight the next morning, I had a long conversation with my chief. We discussed the events of the previous night in detail.

'What does he want to do?' enquired the chief inspector.

'He wants out,' I said.

'He's mad, he'd be better doing his time, how the hell could he explain his release to the Provos?' said the chief inspector.

'I don't know, but he wants out.'

'We'll have to go to Headquarters right now,' said the chief.

We immediately set off for Belfast. We were given an immediate meeting with the ACC, Head of Department, and went over the whole business.

'It sounds to me like a piece of rotten luck, and he was shaping into a first-class source. Ah well, I think we'll have to play it as the source wants,' he said.

'He wants out, sir,' I said.

'Well, I'll leave the outcome to yourselves. You have my backing for whatever action you take.'

We returned to base and I went to see the source in the cell.

'If I let you out, how will you play it?' I asked him.

'I'll say that I told the police that I was walking past the building when I saw men running and I was grabbed by the army. Can you get a story like this published in the papers?'

'Where will you go when you're released?' I enquired.

'Straight back to the lion's den in Dundalk,' he laughed.

'Are you sure you're doing the right thing? We can probably arrange a lesser sentence,' I said.

'No, I'll take my chances, and if I think things are getting difficult, I'll blow town.'

We talked for a while and I made new arrangements for meeting him, that is if he was alive, in a couple of weeks. We would meet in Dublin, not Dundalk ever again. I told him he would be released within the hour, and headed up the stairs to the divisional commander. He had already been briefed by the chief inspector.

'I think this is an innocent man we have in the cells, sir,' I said. 'He says he was only walking past the building when he was grabbed by the soldiers, and I'm inclined to believe him. I'm releasing him.'

'Oh, right, George, just do whatever you think best. It's a pity the way things turned out.'

'You do know, sir, that this man has saved many lives for us many times.'

'I do, George, I do, and we all thank you for your input this past few months.'

I laughed. 'I bet any rewards will go to the chiefs.'

The commander laughed, and I left the office. The source was released a short time later. I went back to the office, where the MIO apologised for the military cock-up.

'Apparently the radio operator had a head cold, and his nose and ears were congested. He couldn't hear with the head phone and stupidly switched over to the speaker, when he received a call.'

'He shouldn't have received a call, the radio should have been for transmission only, it's bloody terrible work by the army,' I answered.

The MIO agreed wholeheartedly. 'I'll take it as far as I can,' he said.

I nodded. I felt tired. Had I lost a source? Was the source in serious danger? Could he convince his Provo masters that his release from custody had been genuine?

Three days later the source phoned. My first thought was to tell him he was stupid going near a phone so soon, but he seemed to believe his call from a supermarket call-box was safe.

'So far, so good, I think my story was accepted. I was drinking with them last night. One of them is packing the Provos in. He's going to live in Dublin. They got a real scare. I think they believed me when they saw my burns and my black eye.'

'What black eye?' I enquired.

'I burned two cigarettes burns on my chest, and crashed my forehead into the corner of a door, and told them it was the soldiers in the Land Rover who burned me and hit me with a rifle butt.'

I couldn't believe my ears. I was still learning about this man's personality.

_____

The source operated for another six months. He provided intelligence on the movement of PIRA members, and indeed, his information led to the capture of explosives. He also gave me good information of help to Garda Special Branch. This was passed on and led to arrests in the Republic. Over the period since his release from custody, he had been slowly squeezed out of things, as the Provo make-up in Dundalk was ever-changing. He felt he was under scrutiny. He moved to Dublin, where I went to see him on occasions. He still felt they were closing in on him. He had never been asked to partake in any outrage again, and when a good schoolfriend, also in the PIRA, told him he had been asked to keep an eye on him, he was really worried.

About two weeks later I had an urgent phone call from the source. It was late afternoon and I had just returned from a visit to the Special Branch HQ in Belfast.

'There's someone on the phone shouting for you, he says he is Seán.'

I took the call.

'For Christ's sake, come and see me quick, they got me, but I escaped, I need help.'

'Where are you?'

'I'm standing on the main street in Dundalk, near the Imperial Hotel and I'm not fucking moving. I want plenty of people around me, I'm not walking anywhere. Please, please, hurry.'

'Right,' I replied. 'Stay there.'

I headed for Dundalk and had completed half the journey when it started to rain. By the time I reached the town it was coming down quite heavily. He spotted me before I saw him, and waved at me. I stopped the car and he got in. I immediately smelt a horrible smell of human excretion.

'Jesus man, have you shit yourself?'

'Indeed I have, it saved my life!' he replied.

As I drove through the traffic I had a look at him. I was astonished to see his hands covered in blood. I could see blood running down his cheek from his head, which was matted in blood. His trousers were covered in blood and human excretion.

'Jesus, man, what happened?'

Before he could reply I spotted a Garda VCP ahead stopping and checking all traffic heading south. As we approached, heading north, they waved us through. So far, so good.

'I escaped, I escaped,' he shouted. 'I was too fuckin' smart for them. They're fuckin' animals.'

A few minutes later I was in the Ballymascanlon Hotel car park. There were quite a few cars parked, which suited fine. I parked in a space and opened all the windows.

'Jesus, man, you're rotten. Right, tell me what happened.'

I could see tears running down his cheeks. 'I'm only crying with pain,' he assured me. 'Look, they pulled out my two thumbnails with pliers.'

I looked at his hands again, and could see they were in a terrible mess. 'Just tell me exactly what occurred.'

'Well, I went into Mulligan's Pub this morning about half past eleven. I've told you before that's where most of the northerners congregate. I was talking to a couple of the lads, for about half an hour, when the local quartermaster arrived and said, "Right you guys, I need some muscle to shift some gear."

'I must admit I suspected fuck all, you had to do what this guy ordered. He drove us out of the town towards Blackrock. I thought it was a bit odd that nobody spoke on the journey. I was soon to know why! The car stopped at a house on the main Dundalk–Blackrock Road. "Right, you guys, the stuff's waiting for you in there. I'll turn the car around."

'The other guys got out and went to the door and I followed them. When we got to the door it was open and we went in. I had only walked a couple of paces when the lights went out. I had received a tremendous blow to the back of the head. I vaguely remember being trailed up the stairs by a lot of men who were shouting, "You fuckin' traitor."

'I was tied to a kitchen chair in the middle of an upstairs room, and as my head got clearer, I saw at least four hooded men. My hands were tied behind my back, and my legs to the chair. The men went into an adjoining room and I could hear them whispering, then one came forward and put what seemed to be a pillowcase over my head. I could smell perfume from it. A voice spoke: "You are being interrogated by an IRA investigation unit. Everything you say will be written down, and I'll tell you now, you can save yourself a lot of grief by admitting that you are a Special Branch or Military Intelligence tout." "Honest to Jesus", I said, "I am not talking to them."

'This was as far as I got. I received a severe blow to the head, from something padded like a boxing glove. The chair fell over. I was lifted up and received another blow to the ear. I can tell you it's worse when you can't see the punches coming. The voice kept repeating, "You are a Branch Agent, aren't you?" Each time I said "No I'm not" I got punched.'

He went on to relate that this went on for about half an hour, and then there was silence. He could smell cigarette smoke. A few minutes passed and then a cigarette was stubbed out on his neck.

'I screamed, but arms held me and again I was burned with a cigarette. The pain was unbearable. Then they removed my hood and used the pillowcase as a gag, and another one was put over my head. They kept saying "Admit it, admit it. If you admit it we'll knee-cap you and that'll be the end of it." The speaker had a Belfast accent.'

I looked at his neck—it was in an awful state. There were at least a dozen blisters. I knew he must have been in great pain. He went on to tell me that eventually the questioning ceased. He heard them going down the stairs. He heard the water cistern filling now and again, and assumed they were making a meal. He went on.

'They came back upstairs and I asked, "Can I go to the toilet?" "Piss your pants," was the reply. "You'll be pissing them shortly anyway."

'I knew I was minutes away from departing this earth unless I did something, but what? They removed my hood. There were four men, all hooded. When I saw the pliers in one of their hands my heart sunk. Then one of them jumped astride me on the chair and held me. My right hand, which was tied behind me, was firmly held. I could feel the instrument gripping my right thumbnail, and then the pulling and twisting began. After what seemed ages they showed me my thumbnail. I must have half-fainted, as their voices seemed far away in the distance. "Are you going to admit your guilt?" I could hear him saying. I don't think I answered, or if I did they didn't like it. "Take his other nail off."

'I can't remember much about this part, but I remember being shown my left thumbnail. "Are you going to cooperate?" said the voice. "Can I go to the toilet?" I asked. "Didn't I tell you to piss your pants." "It's a shit I need," I answered. "No, you can't, tell the truth and you can go to the toilet."

'Earlier I had noticed the bedroom window opposite me was about five feet wide and three feet deep. It would be a means of escape but I needed my legs untied. Then I did the only thing I could think of to force him to let me go to the bathroom. I shit my trousers. "Jesus, he's shit," said one of the captors. A voice behind, obviously the leader, said, "Carry on questioning." I have to admit myself the smell was unbearable. "Take him to the toilet, and take off his trousers," said the voice.

'My legs were untied and I was frog-marched to the toilet, which was just outside the bedroom door. My belt was undone. I was made lie down and my trousers were pulled off. I think a towel was wet and rubbed over my backside. I was pulled back to the bedroom and towards the chair. As I was about to sit down I took my chance. Two steps, and I went out the window head first. I landed in a garden and I thought I was dead. I got to my feet and staggered to the gate. A woman pushing a pram screamed at me. I was half-naked. I stumbled onto the road and stood in front of an approaching car, forcing it to stop. It was a Dundalk taxi, as it turned out. "I've been kidnapped," I shouted at him.

'I asked him to take me to the Garda station in Dundalk. He didn't speak but drove towards Dundalk. "I've changed my mind," I said, "take me to a clothes shop to get a pair of trousers." When he took me to a shop I told him I was borrowing his blanket in the back of the taxi. "Keep it," he replied.

'You want to have seen the faces of the guys in the shop. They couldn't get me out quick enough. I was in an awful state, blood and shit and vomit. They were happy to take the only fiver I had for the pants.'

'You might have picked a better colour,' I laughed.

'You're a shit, purple was all I could see in my size. What the fuck am I going to do now, I'm going to have to get off-side, fast.'

'Where do you want to go?' I asked him.

'Far, far away,' he said.

'What do you want to do, right this minute?'

'I want you to take me to Newry, I've a relative there I can stay the night with and get cleaned up and then I'll go to Belfast and get the boat to Heysham or Liverpool.'

'You'll need medical attention now.'

'Fuck the medical attention, just get me to Newry and give me some money.'

I had a total of £45 in my wallet and I gave it to him.

'Contact me when you get to England,' I said.

I drove to Newry and en route he gave me some names of voices he recognised that must have been involved in his abduction, more as a help to me in future times than anything else. I dropped him at the edge of town. That was the last I ever heard of him. I wondered if he had been killed in an accident or if the Provos had finally caught up with him and made him 'vanish' without trace. Looking back I always admired his braveness. I knew there must be others like him in the Province. They were the silent heroes who knew the risks and penalties. He knew he was a tout and nothing else. He had been coaxed to wear a green jumper and a black beret at a Fianna na hÉireann Easter parade, and had only been in the Cumann a few months when he was sworn in to the IRA at Liam Fegan's (one of the older generation of IRA, who swore in all new PIRA recruits in the border area), at Ravensdale, Co. Louth. His active service was less than a year, the ruination of a life. I felt bad about it all, but he was already in the IRA before he was recruited by Special Branch. I would have felt a lot worse if I had encouraged him to join the movement.

Chapter 6
Special Branch Intelligence-Gathering

Those in Special Branch officership in the Seventies were mainly those older Special Branch members who formed an elite force within a force. None had third-level education, indeed, few had second-level. Some of them were just not up to the job, especially as the Troubles intensified. Their knowledge of the IRA was exposed in the disastrous lists they compiled for Internment Day. I had never been ambitious, and retired a detective sergeant, but I considered myself highly intelligent, more so than many of those above me who believed a rise in rank meant a rise in intelligence. In my young days of happy marriage, a promotion would have meant a move from Belfast to the country, so I preferred to stay put. I regretted this somewhat in later years, when, at intelligence conferences, and in dealings with senior officers, I realised that I had a grasp of the particular situation, and they hadn't a clue. The reason being, they were designer officers, who spent six hours a day studying, and rose through the ranks quietly, with no practical experience whatsoever. They were then expected to show experienced sergeants how things should be done. This caused mayhem, and the belief that the higher the rank, the better the police officer, proved false to all, except that is, the senior officers.

It was a good friend, later chief constable, Sir Jamie Flanagan, who persuaded me to study, after fifteen years' service. I didn't really, but passed the exam through experience, and a photographic memory. I had been asked to join the Special Branch team by Flanagan, and the head of the department, with whom I had served in earlier years, and when the chips were down, and the Province slid towards anarchy, after internment, I worked my guts out, and risked my life to halt the slide. Others were cocooned in their own safe little worlds within the service, studying to pass law exams, few of which would be of any further use to them in their future service.

The thing which used to annoy me was that the public still thought that a good policeman who solved serious crime regularly would be promoted. Success as a policeman in that context meant nothing. Changes to the promotion regulations recommended by these designer officers meant that experience counted for nothing. Unfortunately for everyone, a lot of these useless policemen usually ended up in Special Branch. Those who pulled out all the stops to enter Special Branch were usually not the sort the department needed. The best were those recruited because of their intelligence and common sense, not because they had a strong urge, or because they were in the Masonic, or because they were Gaelic-speaking Roman Catholics. Most of them had only first-level education.

The situation was bearable until the upsurge in violence forced an enlargement of the department on an almost monthly basis. The problem was the older members of the department benefited in the promotion stakes, before the promotion regulations changed. They were in the main, with few exceptions, unfit for the task.

Also, there were some unsavoury characters recruited to the department, who were to cast a shadow over Special Branch. They just couldn't handle the life. In reality there were less than a dozen good source handlers in the department, and they had gone out and obtained the sources themselves. Some, as later courts would hear, became involved with other grey military agencies, and thought they were above the law. Some thought the end always justified the means. Most of the problems were caused by lack of supervision, or supervision by officers of the type I have already mentioned. Good supervision is the key to good police services.

Jack Hermon is a point prover in this respect. From the early days, holding supervisory rank, he was ruthless. Many a member rued the day they heard the name Hermon. In being ruthless, he made a name for himself. This name swept through the force. Everyone feared him. It wasn't that he was the best available officer for chief constable. There were many more intelligent and able officers than he, but in the end they didn't want the job as much as Hermon. He was able to make a case for himself. Others didn't even try, or feared the limelight. Jack Hermon knew there was driftwood in the detective departments, but acknowledged it was hard to detect from the outside. He did try to make them more accountable, but found it difficult because his Achilles heel was that he had not served as detective. He didn't know, in a practical way, what went on in the departments. On this ruthless rise in rank, he hadn't spared the time for a couple of years as a detective. Indeed, if he had known what went on in some Special Branch offices, he would have gone crazy. Senior officers would tend to gather around them, officers who would remain loyal to them firstly and the service second. They would promote those who would fit their bill. The American General, George Patton, once stated, 'Arsehole officers tend to promote their own kind.'

I had no doubt that MI5, MI6, and Military Intelligence operators must have had a good laugh at the situation that existed in the RUC Special Branch, when they arrived in the Province. The MIO who worked with me was astounded at the lack of records in the office, and indeed at the whole records system. Later, I knew that Special Branch had to thank the MIOs for helping to set up new index systems for the proper collation of intelligence. Some officers in charge of Special Branch offices refused to give the MIO a key of the office door, even when ordered from Headquarters. Years of doing their own thing unsupervised had made them unanswerable to anyone!

Those same Special Branch officers were to fail in their duty towards their men in the recommendation of awards. Many of these Special Branch officers received decorations and awards on the strength of the good work of their men, but the rank and file should have received far, far more recognition and awards than they did. This was proved by the fact that senior uniform officers would obtain decorations for sergeants and constables, for clearing an area where a bomb had been planted, but those members in the intelligence-gathering sections, and indeed other seriously important jobs, received nothing for risking their lives daily in Crossmaglen, or indeed Dundalk or Dublin, obtaining intelligence which was saving lives. It proves the lethargy that existed in Special Branch.

———

Being part of the United Kingdom, Northern Ireland has always had a presence of sorts, of MI5 and MI6. They would also have had a presence in the British Embassy in Dublin, just as the Russian Embassy in the Republic would have been well staffed for much of the Cold War, and I would imagine that they would have turned some of their efforts towards the republican movement to a greater degree from 1969 onwards. The responsibility for intelligence-gathering in Northern Ireland lay with Special Branch.

But, over the years from 1971 onwards others put their hand into the intelligence-gathering trough; some were helpful, most were not, and these included the military and the UDR and CID. Agents provocateurs and collusion grew out of the contaminated pipes. Inexperienced handlers of agents, which should have been passed to Special Branch, were to cause grief and misery.

Much has been talked and written about collusion in Northern Ireland, between the security forces and the loyalist paramilitaries, and I would like to make it clear I have no truck with collusion, and never did, but I can guess how it occurred. Take the UDR for instance. Its personnel were drawn mainly from Protestant areas. They knew the local police, and the police knew them. They were in and out of police stations whilst on duty and obviously they were given confidential lists of wanted terrorists. This in itself wouldn't have been wrong in principle, but they probably received nods and winks from uniform police, who would like to show they were in the know, about others suspected of involvement. Many of the UDR could be classed as loyalist, and this tittle-tattle, together with copies of the wanted lists, no doubt made their way to the UVF and UFF paramilitaries with resulting death and destruction.

With regard to specific cases of deliberate, assisted collusion by the security forces, I believe they were few, and point to inexperienced agent handlers, both military and CID. In one television exposé I watched, it was clear that the agent ended up running the CID handler. This can, and did, add up to big, big trouble. Having said that, I cannot for the life of me picture a Special Branch officer passing information to terrorists deliberately to enable them to commit murder. There have been allegations of deliberate collusion made in a number of cases, especially the murder of Pat Finucane. Were any of his killers Special Branch or Military Intelligence touts? If the answer is in the affirmative, then did the Special Branch have prior knowledge of the event? If they did not, and only knew after the murder had taken place, then they can hardly be guilty of colluding in the murder. If they were given intelligence on the murder after the crime, then they can only be guilty of withholding information. Such information should have been passed on immediately in pursuit of a criminal conviction.

As I've said before, the trouble and strife in intelligence-gathering began in 1971, when military patrols began to do their own census on inhabitants in all their specific patrol areas. When they found someone they believed to be suspect, or indeed someone who might assist them, they were given the power to detain them for a four-hour period. The local military unit intelligence officer then became more involved and they tried to recruit sources among republicans. A PIRA source of mine living in the South Down area reported as follows:

'They (the army) took me to Bessbrook and told me I was a suspect Provo. They made me stand hands against the wall, legs spread-eagled. I refused to speak. They knew I wasn't working and was signing on the dole and they offered me £50 to work for them. They put the money on the table. They said they paid big money for information. After four hours exactly, they let me out.'

By doing this the military lost me a potential good grade PIRA source, as, when he reported to his commanding officer in Dundalk that he had been held for four hours at Bessbrook, they told him to lie low for a while. They didn't contact him again for over a year. This was the start of the army running sources, and creating their own intelligence pipelines. It wasn't long before the UDR were trying the same. The pipelines became clogged with useless intelligence, wrongly graded. Then the CID decided to be actively involved in source handling. They wanted a piece of the action! And they were in a good situation to take it. They were interviewing criminals daily, and the lines between terrorism and criminality were becoming blurred as the Provos upped their campaign in the early Seventies. If during interviews CID discovered a potential informant, they should have called in Special Branch when they had finished their interviewing, but they started to recruit their own sources, with the blessing of their CID bosses at Headquarters in Knock. This situation should never have been allowed, and has led to big problems in later years. I myself used to receive extracts from intelligence submitted elsewhere to report my opinion on it. Imagine my feelings when I discovered that the report originated from CID or military in my own area. I was not to know this in the normal course of events, but having a friend on the Republican Desk at Headquarters made it possible. Everybody wanted a piece of the action!

In the Seventies, of course, when the Provo campaign was relentless, any intelligence was readily accepted, from whatever source. This was a time when the British intelligence services upped the ante, and became more and more involved. They were the only ones allowed to use mechanical intelligence-gathering, namely eavesdropping by telephone tap, or other bugging devices. Unfortunately, this included the phones of Special Branch, both in the office and at home. With regard to the office phone, all Special Branch offices in early 1971 had to go through the station switchboard, for incoming and outgoing calls. Then, without warning, a private line was installed in each office. This, we were told, was to make source handling easier. About a month after being installed, at 9 a.m. one morning the phone emitted one ring and stopped. I picked it up and said 'Hello.'

A voice on the other end which I recognised said, 'You're in early today, what can I do for you?'

'You called me,' I replied.

'No, my phone tinkled.'

The penny quickly dropped. Both phones were on one line, although twenty miles separated the offices. I was annoyed at this. I was being treated as a 'friendly Indian'. I was even more annoyed later when I discovered they had bugged my house phone as well. Although I was assured by a friend in Post Office Telephones who tested my line that my line was bugged, I decided to prove it. I didn't pay my telephone account on time and eventually ignored the final notice of disconnection. My phone was not disconnected. For years after that I talked a lot of balderdash and gibberish on the phones. I devised codes for agents, regarding times and places, to make it really hard for them. This, of course, was a useless practice when an urgent call came, requiring urgent action. In such instances I had to forget about the eavesdroppers. One can see, then, that it was extremely hard to safeguard the identity of a terrorist source, when I had to constantly look over my own shoulder at people supposedly on my side.

To obtain finance for a source requires registration. His details are written down, put in a sealed envelope and delivered by hand to a secure safe at Special Branch Headquarters. I say sealed, meaning a wax seal is used. The source is then allocated a number which is entered on all intelligence reports from him, especially when he wants compensation financially. There were times, however, when the source would say, 'For God's sake, that didn't come from me, stick it down from someone else.'

I would accede to his request and report the intelligence as coming from a casual contact and lower the grade figure. When the intelligence turned out to be good I would receive quizzical looks at Headquarters, but it was all part of the game, or to quote Rudyard Kipling 'The Great Game'.

As the intelligence-gathering agencies in Northern Ireland grew in number, so did the rivalry between them. Sometimes CID were unhappy at the way Special Branch operated in regard to the recruitment of sources. Now and again it was difficult to hide such recruitment from CID, depending on the CID official involved.

On one occasion I had a phone call to the office from a businessman I knew of, but hadn't met before. He was Catholic and ran his company throughout the Troubles without coming to the notice of Special Branch. He wanted to talk to me. I called him back at the company number to make sure he was genuine, and then arranged a meet. At the meeting he explained that a distant relative of his had a son who had become associated with some Provos. He was involved peripherally in a terrorist incident some years ago, in which a man was injured in an explosion. He had apparently been asked to drive the getaway car, but wasn't required eventually. He had knowledge of the planning of the incident and had gone on the run to the Republic immediately. He had never actually joined the IRA. His parents were distraught. They believed he had learned his lesson and wanted to know what would happen if he returned home. The mother was breaking her heart.

I arranged to meet him with the go-between the following week. A few days later I travelled to Special Branch Headquarters and spoke to the head of Special Branch. He agreed that I would try and recruit him as an agent. He agreed that if things went according to plan he would contact head of CID and request they leave him alone if and when he returned. I met the go-between again and he promised to go to Dublin personally to talk to the youth. He was to give him two choices, one to return and face the charges regarding the explosion, or to contact me. A few weeks later he made contact. I went to the house as arranged to 'arrest' him so that the locals wouldn't be questioning his sudden reappearance without being charged. He would return home after forty-eight hours, his story being that the police had no evidence to charge him, and that he had denied any involvement in the crime. This in fact was true. There was no evidence to connect him with any crime.

During this period he told me how he had become associated with the IRA, and the names of all involved with him in the outrage. He gave me a lot of further intelligence on who he had met on the run, and all they had been involved in. He gave me the name of a quartermaster who was currently involved. Provos on the run in the Republic treated him as one of their own and talked openly to him. The following week he phoned with further intelligence, and it looked good that I had recruited a useful source. But then disaster struck. A local CID officer came to me.

'You guys are not doing your job. We've just got information that so and so has returned home.'

'Is that right?' I replied. 'Don't do anything until I look into it.'

I immediately phoned the assistant chief constable (ACC SB) at Headquarters.

'This was always going to be one that would be hard to keep under wraps, but it was well worth the try. I'll contact my CID counterpart and tell them hands off. I still think it'll be worth it.'

To my horror I learned the local CID officer, who had on many occasions openly criticised Special Branch, had gone out the next morning and arrested the youth. I had to then declare my interest, and a few hours later the CID were ordered from CID Headquarters to release the youth. In the meantime I had to withstand a telephone call from the go-between, who had learned of the arrest. I was called a deceiver and a liar. The first meet I had with the youth after this CID arrest was strained to say the least.

'I just sat there and after I gave my name and date of birth I said nothing.'

I think I was able to assure him that no one in the CID knew of our contact. He worked for about a year after that and then told me one night that he thought he had repaid his 'debt'. I never saw him again, I think he returned to Dublin.

This illustrates the problems I had, but I must stress that at other times and in other areas I had no such problem with CID. On occasions they came to me and explained they had a criminal under arrest who came from a republican background, for stealing a bicycle, or a burglary, or some other non-violent crime.

'Do you want to talk to him? If he's any good to you I'll hold the file.'

I recruited two very good sources this way. Lives were saved.

Chapter 7
Criminal Injury Claims

In 1972, both factions of the IRA were soon to realise the enormous sums of money which could be earned through malicious injury claims. According to law, if any premises, business or residential, were damaged through an act of terrorism, carried out for, or on behalf of, an illegal organisation, namely the IRA, then the owner could claim compensation, not only for the bricks and mortar, but for loss of stock and profits. It was soon seen by shrewd tacticians in the movement how they could reap a two-fold benefit from this situation. Firstly, the explosion was hurting the British government financially, and secondly, by charging a fee to the property owner for services rendered, the IRA gained financially.

It worked like this, and it's anyone's guess which came first, the chicken or the egg in hatching the plans, but word soon spread. A businessman in a nationalist area is in financial difficulties. The business he runs is good, but needs modernisation. The building is old and unattractive to patrons. A deal is struck with the right contact in Provisional Sinn Féin, and a fee is paid, sometimes upwards of £20,000, but usually in the £5,000 region. The IRA come and bomb the premises. An enlarged claim is submitted for non-existent stock etc., the owner ends up with a lovely new building, and if he or she is lucky, a handsome sum of compensation for loss of earnings.

This important matter put Special Branch in a difficult situation, as each individual claim had to go through their office and be certified as having been carried out by the IRA, or other illegal organisation. In 1972, IRA sources working for the security forces, including my own, were reporting 'homers', as they were called. It would have been nice to turn down a large claim, knowing the claimant had colluded with the IRA for financial gain, but the problem would have been proving the case. There was no way in this world a source, who may even have been involved himself, could be sacrificed to prove one of these cases. It is a recognised fact that the British government lost tens of millions in false claims by this method, and the IRA made millions. The Special Branch office had to certify the bombing was carried out by the IRA, if they knew this to be the case from intelligence sources. Whether or not it was an arranged bombing was really beside the point. This was secret intelligence and couldn't be made available to anyone. Can you imagine a claim going through government departments with a note attached from Special Branch stating the claimant had paid the IRA to do the job? It wouldn't travel far before the IRA and every Tom, Dick and Harry knew of this information. Then it would be curtains for the source.

Although on most occasions the Special Branch were powerless to act, nevertheless, they didn't stop trying to obtain evidence from other areas to block false claims, and if the matter wasn't serious, then some of the results were funny in the extreme. Some of these entrepreneur claimants really went the whole hog to collect as much in compensation as they possibly could, and forgot that when you play with the devil and he then eats you, the blame is your own. The directors of a large business were well aware that the authorities were becoming wise and were no fools when it came to estimating amounts due for stock and loss of profits. The premises were purchased for the sting, and the plan drawn up to cover two years' trading. During this time large quantities of stock were 'diddled' through the books, and private cash from the directors was put through as turnover. To all intents, the place was really flourishing, and lack of cash flow was put down to fictitious alterations and improvements. The IRA were eventually tasked to do the bombing, and were promised 10 per cent of what would be a huge claim, for the building, contents, and loss of profits. According to the source, when the cheque finally arrived at the directors' solicitor's office, the IRA had a mole in the office. They arrived soon after and took the gentleman to a bank in Dundalk by 'arrangement', and relieved the firm of the total sum. There was a lot of tears and gnashing of teeth. The losers couldn't call in the police and tell them that money they had stolen from the government had now been stolen from them.

In another instance a businessman paid £5,000, and half of his stock, to have his premises bombed. A year later his newly repaired building was doing a roaring trade, and things were looking up. Unfortunately, those who carried out the bombing were arrested or interned on other charges and the new members of the unit decided on a bombing campaign. His premises were flattened again, beyond recognition. His claim was not to his satisfaction, and he ended up living in England.

Then, of course, there were the claims for personal injuries and shock. Shock was later removed from the statutes. When a bomb exploded in Derry, Newry or Armagh at this time, in 1972/1973, the population of the particular town descended on the area en masse, within minutes of the blast. They then reported injuries, mainly shock. Each of these claims was probably small, under £1,000, but when added up over a period of years they became a very large sum indeed. Add to this the fact that in the early years of claiming most claims were inflated, and one can realise the huge amount paid out by the government. Has anyone ever sat down and totalled all claims paid out since 1970?

Intelligence would also suggest that those who paid the IRA up-front to carry out a 'homer' were lucky to get away with a one-off payment. In many cases the terrorists would return for another bite of the cherry, and claimants would find themselves out of pocket in the long run.

There were many instances indeed where Special Branch were well aware who had carried out various crimes, but because of the intelligence system and source protection, CID could not be informed, even with a nod and a wink. Especially with a nod and a wink. Although the local divisional commander was usually briefed on a need-to-know basis, there were many instances where even he had to be kept in the dark. The vast well of intelligence remained hidden from CID until the Regional Crime Squads were formed on 1 June 1976. Each squad contained a Special Branch sergeant and two or three Special Branch detective constables. They were to perform a liaison role with new tasking co-ordination groups, and evaluate how much of this intelligence could be put to use in maximising arrests for terrorism, without endangering the original source. This eventually led to the use of supergrasses, and the acceptance by the courts of their evidence. This may have made the IRA sit up and worry, and helped the situation for some time, but in the end it proved disastrous.

To return to 'arranged' terrorist outrages in return for cash, I received a telephone call from a source the day following a bank robbery, which netted official IRA terrorists a large sum of money. His intelligence ran thus. The manager of the bank was an astute card player and played in games at a number of towns south of the border, on a Sunday evening. Sometimes these games had commenced on a Saturday evening and lasted for upwards of thirty hours. The manager went down a couple of thousand, and issued a cheque. The source heard him say, 'don't lodge this for a week,' in a jocular but serious manner. The game eventually ended, and even continued the following weekend. The manager had brought cash and taken back his cheque. Again he had a bad streak and the source saw him in serious conversation with a known Official IRA man. A few days later, the same manager was relieved of the contents of the bank safe, before any staff had arrived. The source knew he had an 'arranged' robbery, and when he again went to the poker school a couple of weeks later the bank manager was conspicuous by his absence. One of the Official IRA told my source the bank manager wanted £15,000 of the cash returned to him for personal debt, as promised when the robbery was arranged, but he was eventually told the cash was required for the widows and dependants of the IRA. He took sick retirement.

At that time, in the early Seventies, the Official IRA and their clingers-on were carrying out far more fundraising robberies than the Provisionals, especially in the South Down/South Armagh areas. Many of these were arranged, none more so than the post office van robberies. The drivers of these vehicles, even at that time, carried upwards of £10,000 on their weekly pension day runs. They lived in nationalist areas and weren't hard to persuade, by threat or otherwise, to hand over the cash bags on a remote country road. Special Branch were aware of these robberies from good sources within the movement but were powerless to act, because of source protection. Eventually, the number of robberies was cut drastically by new methods of delivery of the money, and police/military protection.

Chapter 8

Proposed Bombing of Newry RUC Station

I was in the divisional commander's office when the telephone rang. 'It's for you, George,' said the commander, passing the phone.

'Hello,' I said.

'Hello,' said the voice on the other line.

I recognised the caller. 'It's difficult to talk now,' I said.

'Right,' said the caller, 'I will phone you at home tonight, just make sure you are at home.'

I set the phone down, finished my business with the commander and left the office.

That night I received no telephone call as arranged, so I went to bed about 11.30 p.m. I had just fallen asleep when the phone rang.

'Can you come and see me now?' said the caller.

'I sat in all evening,' I replied. 'Jesus, it's a quarter to midnight.'

There was silence for a few seconds and I then asked the source the rendezvous point.

'Do you remember where we met when you admired my car?'

I replied in the affirmative.

'Right, wait behind the wall at the rear of the car park.'

'I'll be one hour,' I said, setting down the phone.

It was a warm night in June 1971. As I approached the border, I slowly increased my speed and turned the radio off. I wound down the driver's window halfway. The road was straight at this point and my headlights cut out a path ahead in the darkness. About a hundred yards from the actual border, I passed the burnt-out British customs post, which had stood in the middle of the road at this point. The road quickly narrowed again and I was in the Irish Republic, and although the Irish customs post was only a quarter of a mile ahead, I kept up this speed. Only a fool crawled through 'hijack alley', as this section of the main Belfast/Dublin Road was known. This particular area, Killeen, was famous for hijackings, bombings and many murders. The area had witnessed exchanges between the IRA and the British Army. About 100 yards short of the Irish customs post, I slowed to 20 mph, and in the absence of any customs officer I increased speed again. It was after 12.30 a.m., and the post would show no sign of activity again until 7.30 a.m. I travelled a further half mile into County Louth until suddenly the road was brightly lit by a hotel on the left. I braked and pulled in to the car park, which was full of cars. Loud music was coming from the building, probably a dance, and people were entering and leaving the main door. I selected a parking space near the rear wall and switched off the engine. I had a good look at the vehicles in the car park to ascertain if any were occupied, and started to walk away from the car. The pebble-dashed wall ran the length of the car park to the hotel wall. I crouched and tried to control my breathing, glad to be out of the glare of the lights. The line of trees ran almost parallel with the wall, and was set back about four yards. I looked along this avenue and saw a figure sitting with his back to the wall. The figure lifted an arm in recognition, and I moved in a crouched position towards him. I sat down.

'Jesus, it's bloody suicide me coming here at this time!'

The source chuckled. 'Part of the game,' he said.

Before I could say any more, he spoke earnestly. 'Look, a claymore mine has been planted on the concession road near Crossmaglen, you'd better keep the army patrols away for a while.'

He went on to explain that about 30 lb of commercial explosive with 2 cwt mix had been laid, and that a team of PIRA would watch each evening from a distance to shoot any survivors.

'The operation will start this Friday night, and the mine will be detonated by a command wire from the Republic.'

He handed me a crumpled piece of paper. 'That's a good map showing the bomb location,' he said.

I took the map. 'Who is in on the job?' I asked.

'The Crossmaglen boys and a couple of the Dundalk ASU.'

The source stated he had been visiting a safe house at Hackballscross to collect something, when he had stumbled on the intelligence by chance. The owner of the safe house had an unsafe tongue.

'Look, I'll phone you if I learn anything else, but I don't think I will.'

I nodded. 'The only thing we can do is keep the military out of the area,' I said. 'If we start looking for the damned thing during the daylight hours, they'll know their operation has been compromised.'

'Put the SAS in after dark to take on the ASU,' laughed the source.

'Into the Republic?' I said.

'Aye,' he laughed.

It was my turn to laugh now. The source looked at his watch. 'Creeps, got to go. See you soon, God bless.'

And with that he was off.

I waited for ten minutes, then returned to my vehicle and set off to re-cross the border at Killeen. It was a really pitch-black night. Mine was the only vehicle on the road and as I passed the closed customs posts I felt very alone, but wasn't I always alone, keeping secrets secret.

There are many hotels and roadhouses between Dundalk and Drogheda. Most of them are usually very busy, being on the main arterial road from Belfast to Dublin. These premises were ideal for a meet between myself and my Garda Special Branch friends, who were usually very astute in selecting the venue on any particular day. We would spend an hour over lunch and be able to do our 'business' without much chance of being observed.

The day after my midnight meeting in the hotel car park I received a call from a source at 9.30 a.m. requesting a meet, the only problem being he had no wheels. He made it clear to me that it was in my interests to come and see him. He named a hostelry south of Dundalk, and I agreed. There would be no obvious contact between us in the place, so I warned him I would be in company having lunch. When the source rang off I lifted the phone and rang my new Garda friend. I suggested a meet and a bite to eat. The offer was accepted and we agreed to meet at noon, in the roadhouse named by the source. I had a real reason for combining the two meets—I had to pass on intelligence of the previous night regarding the bomb at the border near Crossmaglen. With bombs going off all over the place in Northern Ireland at that time, and the increase in IRA activity from both PIRA and OIRA along the border, I felt more secure when visiting the Republic if I was accompanied by a member of the Garda, although I knew damn fine I would probably be back in a couple of days, on my own, as usual.

We were halfway through lunch when I saw the source arrive with an unknown, rough-looking companion. They went to the bar and ordered a drink. I knew that the mirror behind the bar gave a good scope for seeing around the place, and I knew I would be spotted shortly. Five minutes passed and I excused myself to go to the gents. I was only in the cloakroom a few seconds when the source entered. He stood beside me at the urinals and when another customer left, he quickly handed me a note.

'Give me a tenner quick, and remember for fuck sake I am involved in this as a driver, I'll get more off you when I see you again.'

I gave him the tenner and quickly returned to my table. A few minutes later I saw the source return to the company of his friend at the bar. We finished our meal, and we discussed the current threat on the border area.

'We down here think Brian Faulkner will be a tough nut, but he seems a fair person,' he said.

We had a long, open and frank discussion and both aired our views on many subjects ranging from the Charlie Haughey arms trial, to Cathal Goulding, Joe Cahill, and Seán Mac Stíofáin. The Provisionals were in their infancy and they were having a hard time getting off the ground in the Dundalk/Newry areas, which seemed to be retaining their members in the Officials. My Garda friend told me his fears about our meetings and exchanges of intelligence.

'This time last year there is no way I would have met you,' he said. 'But we can now see that the RUC are acting impartially, and only trying to save lives, we know these scum would just as quick shoot a guard.'

We agreed that any intelligence given one to the other would be submitted and attributed to someone else. Not the thing to do, but I for the moment was happy enough with the situation.

When I saw the source and his unknown companion eventually leave the premises I stood up and said I would have to go. We had been there over an hour and a half. My friend followed me to the border at Killeen, and it was only then that I opened the note given to me in the toilet. I held it in my left hand as I drove.

'Oh shit,' I said out loud.

I drove straight to Newry police station and knocked on the divisional commander's door.

'Come in,' I heard.

I opened the door and saw the uniform chief inspector and another gentleman I didn't know.

'I need to see you, sir,' I stated.

The commander looked at the chief.

'Can you excuse us, gentlemen.'

They both left the office.

The commander's office was on the ground floor and a wide footpath ran the length of the building outside the window. A line of cars was as usual parked along the footpath but there was still plenty of room for people to walk. I looked out the window.

'Around 1 p.m. tomorrow, give or take an hour, a car bomb will be parked on the footpath outside this office. It will contain a 100 lb bomb.'

The commander sat back in his chair. He looked pale.

'Tell me about it,' he said.

I told him the source may be involved, probably as the driver, and named the other three. One to accompany the source and the other two in a lead vehicle. I described the vehicles.

'We'll have to park a military pig (troop carrier) at the spot. This will deter them and they'll clear off,' I said.

'You mean bring the army in on it?'

'No way,' I said. 'They will only be told to do a VCP. I don't want a dead source.'

'Surely they'll have a secondary target?' said the commander.

'If they had he would have told me.'

We discussed various other ways we could play the situation the next day and I left.

Next morning, a warm sunny one at that, I arranged to have an army armoured vehicle parked outside the commander's office at 11.45 a.m. At about ten minutes to one the two cars cruised past, as stated in the note. The source was driving the second car containing the bomb. A close watch was kept for the next hour and a half but they didn't return. I hadn't returned to my office very long when the phone rang. It was the source.

'I knew you would put a pig there, they were fucking mad. Seán wanted to leave it at the police station rear gate, but that would have meant going round again and drawing suspicion.'

'Where is it now?' I said.

'On the way to Forkhill to await further instructions.'

'Will you know the new target?'

'I would say no to that.'

'Thanks anyway.'

'You owe me.'

'You're a cool bastard,' I replied.

'I love you too,' replied the source and hung up the phone.

Chapter 9
Bridge Vehicle Checkpoint Incident

In 1971, especially after internment, Dundalk really became a frontier town, where members of both factions of the IRA sought safe haven after their terrorist exertions in the North. It was without doubt not the best place for a member of the RUC Special Branch to be. I felt better when I could time my visits to the area during the first hours of darkness or early in the morning between 9 a.m. and noon. If the reason for my trip was to visit a dead letter-box, then I would sometimes take another member of the department with me. But on visits to a source, I normally went unaccompanied. On other occasions I would be accompanied to meet a pair of Garda Special Branch and the four of us would lunch together and compare notes. I got to know the town of Dundalk well, although with its traffic system it was nigh impossible to choose more than a couple of ways through the town travelling north or south. One had to cross a bridge entering the town on the northern side and another one leaving on the southern side. When I had been on a particularly dangerous meeting I would always feel better once I'd crossed the bridge on the northern side. If I was stopped by uniform Gardaí at a vehicle check, I would show my driver's licence and give my reason for the visit to the Republic as shopping or pleasure. As often as not, from the summer of 1971 onwards, with the increasing loyalist activity, and the early nucleus of the UDA being formed, a Garda/Irish Army road check was always in force at the northern bridge in Dundalk.

In early 1972, I had occasion to visit a source in Dublin. The intelligence obtained wasn't spectacular and referred to some Official IRA on the run. I returned in the late afternoon and was stopped on the bridge mentioned on my way back. I returned to the office, and eventually went home for my dinner. At about 10 p.m. the phone rang. It was a Provo source.

'I have some vegetables for you, three or four different types, are you hungry?'

Within half an hour, I was heading south again, accompanied by a colleague. As we approached Dundalk, I saw the VCP had been removed from the bridge. I felt a bit more comfortable. We journeyed on south through Dundalk, to Drogheda, where we met the source, a Provisional, standing on the chapel steps. He climbed into the car and directed us northwards again, into the countryside, where he eventually disembarked at a country lane. I had no idea where we were, and was by no means happy with the situation. Ten minutes later the source climbed into the rear seat with a bag. As he left it on the floor in the rear, the sound of metal on metal could be heard.

'There's some shooters for you,' he said.

I set off for home as the source explained he was happy the finger would not point his way when the loss was discovered from the dump.

'They have just arrived in from America. The guy who stashed them was drunk. There's plenty of stuff there. They won't be missed,' he said.

As we neared Dundalk, where the source now resided, he made a request I wasn't happy with.

'Can you take me back up with you and drop me on the southern side of Newry?'

'Are you mad?' I replied. 'What about a road stop, Garda or British Army?'

'I really need up tonight, I must be in Newry in the morning, I'll lie on the floor in the back and put this coat over me.'

Before I could answer, he lay on the floor and covered himself with my coat. Against my better instincts, and not wanting to argue with a source who had just given me weapons, I drove on. We passed along the main street, and finally reached the bridge. My heart missed a beat.

'Shit,' said my colleague. 'A bloody VCP!'

'Fuck, fuck,' shouted the source.

'Turn, turn, they'll not shoot.'

I was in two minds what to do. My mind worked overtime. A few yards and I was on the VCP. There were two Irish Army soldiers on the pavement, one on either side of the bridge. Their vehicle was parked 25 yards ahead. A lone Garda stood in the centre of the road. As it was 1 a.m., and traffic was fairly light, all vehicles were being checked. I stopped.

'Hello,' said the guard, leaning in to the window. 'Can I see your driver's licence please?'

As I held my licence up for inspection, the guard stood back from the car, and was looking at and speaking to one of the soldiers. I said, 'thank you,' put the car in gear and moved off, not in a fast way but steadily increasing speed. The guard was taken aback and, looking in the mirror, I saw him gesticulate to one of the soldiers, who ran across to the other soldier. By this time I was about 30 yards away and increasing speed.

My partner said, 'Drive, drive.' He had been quiet most of the trip, but he started to talk now: 'They'll shoot, they'll shoot.'

I now realised we were safe from this action. I knew the Irish Army wouldn't shoot. I realised later that when I stopped at the vehicle checkpoint, and the guard had leaned down to speak to me, and stood up again, the soldiers probably thought he had told me to proceed. In the next vital five seconds, what with the noise of my car, and another car coming from the other direction stopping as I moved off, the indecision was created in the mind of the guard. I drove fast towards the border, and mindful of the Garda station at Drumad, turned left half a mile short of the border and crossed at the unapproved road at Jonesboro Church. As we reached the outskirts of Newry the source jumped out of the vehicle.

'You're a fuckin' good un,' he said to me. 'You should be in the IRA.'

I drove towards the office. I felt elated at the recovery of the weapons of the IRA but very worried at what may have happened if the Garda had discovered the weapons, and worse still, the identity of the source. There would no doubt have been many repercussions, as I was armed, and had an SMG under my seat. In any event my car number plates would need to be changed in the morning. A question of changing false plates for further false plates!

Chapter 10
Proposed Bomb to Kevin Street

Sources within a terrorist movement are very hard to come by, and the very nature of such organisations, always wary of a member talking, makes it hard indeed to pass on to Special Branch all that is happening within that organisation. Intelligence is mostly disjointed, and arrives in dribs and drabs, with the odd gush to hard stuff. This is why it is imperative for the Special Branch handler to exercise extreme caution when acting on such intelligence, as source protection is paramount. It does not do to eat the goose as well as the eggs. There is no doubt that some handlers would sacrifice the source if the intelligence would lead to a spectacular security forces coup. Thus far, I had always found a way out if the source himself was involved in an outrage, of which he was giving prior intelligence. If acting on such intelligence meant the capture of the source, then, obviously, much thought went into the possible actions of the security forces.

I had one source, pre-internment period, in the summer of 1971, who had worked his way into the organisation fairly quickly. He had no full-time job, and was quite useful to Sinn Féin carrying messages from Dundalk to Newry and vice versa. He would steal the odd vehicle for use by PIRA and very soon knew all the active members of the organisation in the border areas. He knew, and was known well by, Seán Mac Stíofáin, the PIRA chief of staff, who resided in the Navan area. I liked the young lad, and the way he operated. At a prearranged meeting place he would arrive from the most unexpected places—out of a car boot, out from a hedge, from the back of a lorry, and once down from a tree! I felt glad that he had already been in PIRA before I had commenced my association with him. I was submitting good intelligence from him on a weekly basis, for what was really drink money.

The source only had use of a car on an intermittent basis, but I worried about the many military road checks on the main Newry/Dundalk Road. Both of us were well aware that any arrest or detention, even for an identity check, a ruse used ever-increasingly by the military to question a suspect, would lead to an automatic six-month suspension from the PIRA. This was to ensure that volunteers in the movement hadn't been got at and 'turned'. When the source reported that he had actually driven the chief of staff, Seán Mac Stíofáin, to Kevin Street in Dublin on a couple of occasions, I knew he was going to be a useful source indeed; in fact, he was already saving lives in the South Down/Armagh/Newry areas with good intelligence leading to the capture of weapons and explosives. He would go to Kevin Street in Dublin on most Saturday mornings when a small sum of money was paid to all those members in the Republic who were on the run from Northern Ireland. He would often drive a carload down to Dublin from Dundalk, when he was able to gain good intelligence, just by keeping his ears open, although few volunteers would talk of their actions. Joe Cahill seemed to be there most Saturday mornings.

In July of 1971, just prior to internment, I was invited to a drinks get-together at RUC Headquarters at Knock. Guests were from Special Branch, Military Intelligence, and the Security Services in the form of MI5 and others. It was really a matter of mingling with a glass in hand. After a few introductions a gentleman introduced himself from the Director of Intelligence staff. He led me quietly to a corner and made no secret of the fact he had seen some of my reports on a source's visits to Kevin Street, the Provisional Sinn Féin Headquarters in Dublin. He had read that on many occasions Kevin Street was visited by Joe Cahill, David O'Connell, Seán Mac Stíofáin, Séamus Twomey, Rory Brady and many other senior Provisionals. He explained he might have a job for me and questioned me on the character of the source.

'Would the source take a duffle bag to Kevin Street some Saturday morning soon?' he asked. 'And more importantly, would you say he could forget he had done so afterwards?'

I looked at him. We moved over to the side of the room.

'You know what you're asking, don't you?'

'Of course, George, but you could assure him he would be in no danger, as the device would be set up already on a twelve-hour clock, all he has to do is put it in a downstairs room, or preferably under a staircase, oh, and he would be well rewarded, that goes without saying.'

I said nothing.

'Look,' he said, 'I'll be in touch with you next week.'

With that he left my company, as the MIO had just joined us. The gentleman winked as he left me, and I knew to say nothing of the conversation. But inwardly I was really surprised at the request. It was fraught with danger and would, if it happened, give the source a powerful hold over me, and indeed, the Security Services in London. This wasn't only agent provocateur, it was conspiracy to murder. I wasn't happy to say the least. When I returned to the office that very evening the phone rang and it was the source in question. He sounded agitated and was requesting a meeting urgently.

'I need to see you anyway,' I told him.

An hour later we met as dusk fell on the Rostrevor/Hilltown Road. We left the vehicle and walked across open ground until out of sight of the road. The source was in an agitated state.

'Fuck this,' he said. 'I think they're on to me.'

'Why do you think this?' I asked.

'Oh, I just have this feeling, I can't bloody sit, I think my nerve is going.'

'Would a tenner help your nerves?' I enquired.

'It sure would,' replied the source, laughing.

I asked the source what he had for me and he told me that a leading 'Stickie' (Official IRA) wasn't playing by the rules in the South Down area, and that funds or proceeds from various robberies were not being handed to IRA Headquarters. (At Easter of 1971 when the Official IRA and the Provisional IRA sold their Easter badges outside the Post Office in O'Connell Street, the OIRA badge stuck to the lapel whilst the PIRA badges required a pin, thus: Stickies and Pinheads.) The intelligence was that an internal feud was imminent. I knew that the Official IRA, were dominant in the Warrenpoint/ Rostrevor area. The source intimated that he had eavesdropped the intelligence at a poker school of the OTR (on the run) men in the Imperial Hotel in

Dundalk the previous night. I thanked him and said nothing for a moment. I was considering whether to ask the source about taking the package to Kevin Street. Finally I decided to ask him.

'If I asked you to carry a duffle bag, or another receptacle of your choice and take it with you on your next visit to Kevin Street, what would you say?'

'I would say this proves you lot are up to anything, probably running around bumping people off all over the place.'

I smiled and waited.

'If I did, it would fuckin' cost you, you know that.'

I nodded. 'All I want to know is, would you do it, and could you handle it?'

'You mean the device?'

'No,' I replied. 'I know you could do that, but could you handle the whole situation?'

'How much would I get?'

'I don't know,' I replied.

'Would they pay £500?'

'I'm sure they would,' I replied.

'Jesus, I could have done a good job last week, I drove Seán Mac Stíofáin and another man down from Navan. There were four or five of the top brass there.'

As he spoke, I worried about the whole situation. Was I going crazy? Here I was asking a member of the IRA to place a bomb, on behalf of the British Security Services, at the Headquarters of Provisional Sinn Féin in Dublin, in another country! There may be mayhem and murder in Belfast, but did this justify what I was doing? I felt very uneasy.

I dropped the source off in Hilltown, having told him I would be in touch if any new developments took place. On the way there in the car the source enquired if this was my idea, or was I being briefed by others. I laughed. 'You ask too much,' I replied.

'It must be orders from above, or where would you get £500?' the source replied.

About a week later I visited the Special Branch Registry at Knock, and met the ACC of the Special Branch in the corridor.

'I want to see you, George,' he said, waving me into his office.

As I entered the room I saw the gentleman from the DOI's office get up from a chair. Before the ACC could speak he said, 'Ah, George, how are you?' He then said quietly, 'I was going to contact you today, you can forget that little job I asked of you, we have decided against it.'

'Ah, you two know each other,' said the ACC.

'Oh yes, yes,' replied the gentleman from MI5, heading for the door. 'Goodbye, George, we'll meet again soon.'

He left the office and myself and the ACC chatted about one of his recent intelligence reports for a few minutes before saying our farewells. As I entered the Registry a few minutes later I felt easier. A weight had been taken from my shoulders.

———

Some months after the intelligence services gentleman cancelled the proposed mission to place a bomb in Kevin Street, home of the Provisional movement, I was to meet him again, whilst on a visit to the chief superintendent, Special Branch, at Headquarters. The previous day I had received a contact from an IRA source to the effect that he, the source, was in possession of a new type of car booby trap. He phoned from Dundalk and I attempted to arrange a meeting. The source was none too happy about transporting the device by road anywhere, even in the Republic, for fear of being caught at a VCP, and as he later explained it wasn't really a fear of being caught by police, but fear of having to explain to his Provo masters why he had removed the device from the cache in the first place.

I agreed to travel to County Louth to pick up the box device, which measured 8" x 5" x 2" approximately. I met the source in the car park of the Fairways Hotel on the Dublin Road south of Dundalk, and agreed to return the box without fail at 8 p.m. the following evening. He told me the device contained a pound of plastic explosive, but required arming. I returned to the office and telephoned the deputy head of the Special Branch, explained the situation, and that I would bring it up to Headquarters the next morning for examination by technical explosives experts. It would be dismantled, photographed and all component parts would be examined for tracing purposes. It might even be doctored in an expert fashion, to ensure that when eventually used, it would not explode. In later years it would probably have been bugged.

The next morning I travelled to Belfast. My chief was on leave, and I had to get back to the office as quickly as I could. I had no worries about the drive. I had worried the previous day driving through Dundalk. As usual I had been stopped going into County Louth by a Garda vehicle checkpoint, but the production of a driver's licence facilitated my entry through the stop. Never had I been requested to open my boot, or had the car been searched. The vehicle checkpoints were really only a deterrent, and were otherwise useless, unless a vehicle was properly searched. This would require half an hour by experienced personnel, so the chances of detections were small. I personally thought it better to do one car per half hour than to look at twenty driving licences without even recording any details for future reference.

As I walked up the rear stairs at Headquarters, passing the canteen, I met the gentleman from the director of intelligence's office coming down.

'Hello, George, how are you, how are things on the border?'

'I'm fine thank you,' I replied.

'Look, I need to talk to you for a few minutes, can I see you after your visit? I know why you're here.'

'Okay,' I replied.

I continued to the Special Branch corridor, where I eventually handed the booby trap device to the deputy head of department. There were others present, so after some small talk I excused myself.

'I'll go for a coffee, sir, until you've finished,' I said, standing up and leaving for the canteen.

I hadn't walked ten yards until I felt a hand on my shoulder. It was him.

'I'm just heading for coffee,' I said.

'That's fine, I'll join you,' he said.

I picked a corner of the canteen and sat down. The man got straight to the point, like a rapier. In a hushed voice he said, 'George, it's obvious that you have at least a couple of sources who have access to weapons dumps, can you do something for me?'

I slowly nodded, not knowing what was coming next. 'If I gave you some assorted ammunition, would the source be willing to leave them in the dump?'

Looking back on the matter later, I realised how naive I was. I actually wondered what on earth was going on. It was only when the conversation continued and it was explained that the ammunition was doctored, that the penny slowly dropped.

'What do you mean doctored?' I asked enquiringly.

'Well, er, some have had most of the powder removed and the round will only travel a few yards, others have had twice the powder required inserted, others have been doctored to explode in the breech, and so on.'

I finished my coffee thoughtfully.

'Do I make the source aware of the reasons I am giving him ammunition for the IRA?' I asked.

'Definitely not, they must be completely in the dark.'

'He'll smell a rat, I've no doubt about that, he's no fool,' I said.

'I'll let you think about it, and I'll be in touch.'

He stood up, shook hands, and left the canteen. I had another coffee. I thought of these people in the Security Services. Did they sit about all day devising new games, I wondered? I never saw the gentleman again after that meeting. I was later aware in Special Branch circles of doctored ammo being used, with devastating results in some cases. I felt happy I wasn't involved. It was at this time I realised the Security Services were using every trick in the book against the Provos. The war was getting dirty.

Chapter 11

Robert Nairac and the SAS

Internment wasn't working. At least that's what the press stated, but those on the inside knew that no one would ever really know if things would have been better if the event hadn't taken place at all. A lot of dangerous people had been locked up, and although 'innocent' people had also been arrested initially, they were mainly released. Those that were left and those terrorists subsequently detained, on better intelligence, soon formed themselves into IRA units within the jails. A lot of good intelligence was gleaned from the interrogations of those arrested, concerning the main players, location of weapons, the future threat. Although sources were obtained within the organisation from this dialogue, things were constantly changing. PIRA kept changing their rules, and also kept producing new faces. It made the game hard, but I revelled in it. I was working round the clock, always available.

In Belfast, PIRA had started a ruthless sniper campaign. Their aim was to kill a British soldier, or policeman, on an almost daily basis. There is no answer to a sniper. The military became over-zealous in their response, and, in the propaganda war that followed, came second best. The balance had to be moved, and after high-level discussion the SAS were officially brought into the Province. Their three main bases were Belfast, Londonderry and Bessbrook, outside Newry.

The first contact I had was when my chief introduced me to two men who arrived at the office one evening. One of them was an SAS captain, Tony Ball, and the other was a young Guards Lt, seconded to the regiment, called Robert Nairac. I liked the lieutenant and was to strike up a good friendship with him for a couple of years. He was in his late twenties, wore torn jeans, and a loose shirt. He always had a two-day growth. He was a university graduate, and spoke Gaelic fairly well. He was a product of Ampleforth, the top Catholic college in England, and had studied Irish History at university. I took a liking to him, but I could see the MIO kept a wary eye. He didn't much like any direct contact between Special Branch and the SAS. This was not how things were to be done. The SAS needed to be supplied with hard intelligence to enable them to perform their covert operations. It didn't matter to them who supplied it. They weren't much concerned about rules anyway. They had access to the pipelines, and the SAS hierarchy had no doubt been given a nod and a wink as to who in the Special Branch office was supplying the goods.

Nairac started arriving at the office late at night and suggesting going for a beer to the officers' mess, or going for a Chinese meal. It wasn't very long before I realised that the SAS had tunnel vision, tunnelled towards a kill or kills. There would be no prisoners. I arrived at the office one evening about 8 p.m. and the MIO was sitting at his desk speaking to Robert Nairac. We greeted each other, and a few minutes later the MIO excused himself and left the office.

'Anything new in South Armagh, any new faces?' said Nairac. 'Come on, we must have more trust, let's start sharing.'

'For Christ's sake Robert, you know I can't.'

'Look,' replied Nairac, 'come on up to the canteen and I'll buy you a coffee.'

After some small talk Robert got to the point. 'You like to know all that goes on in your area, don't you? What would you say if I told you that the explosion at the cross-border repeater telephone station last week wasn't the IRA!'

I looked at him. 'I'm not with you,' I said.

Robert got up from his seat and went to the counter to get two more coffees. When he returned to his seat he continued. 'Right,' he said. 'It looks like I'll have to give first.' He took a deep breath. 'The explosion was carried out by SAS under instructions from the intelligence services. This was to enable them during repair to tap into the cables carrying the North-South links.'

I was somewhat taken aback; it was my first direct association with the department of 'Dirty Tricks'.

'Why?' I asked.

Nairac went on. 'We will shortly be able to listen in to calls taking place in the Republic, and we intend to target certain telephone numbers of known players. You yourself have submitted telephone numbers in the Republic of known PIRA activists.'

I didn't speak for a minute. He laughed.

'Look, George, I'm just letting you know that although you work your ass off, and think from the good intelligence you submit from your sources that you go to bed at night knowing all, well you don't, you never know the half of it, nothing is ever as it seems, what I'm telling you is probably the tip of the iceberg. Other ops are taking place that I know nothing about. I don't think I'm taking any risk in telling you anything you want to know. There'll be situations I won't willingly wish to share, but if you were to ask I would tell you.'

I must admit I was surprised at all this.

'What other police of any department or rank know of this?'

'I don't honestly know,' replied Nairac. 'But if the situation arose, I'll declare I had to tell you.'

I finished my coffee and got up to go.

'Before you go,' said Nairac, 'I'll finish the story.'

He then explained how the repairs to the link were not carried out by post office telephone personnel, but by Security Services experts, under the guise of post office personnel.

'I have no doubt you will hear of this from your own people. It couldn't work properly without Special Branch involvement. I have told you this to show my trust in you; I hope you will reciprocate and be open with me.'

I was to become acutely aware that the SAS were mounting operations in the border area, and in the Irish Republic. A few weeks after our conversation Nairac admitted that they had an ongoing operation across the border, and one day as I was driving past the courthouse in Newry I saw him emerge from the gates. The court was in session, and I wondered what on earth he was doing inside the building. I stopped fifty yards away, and as Nairac walked past I wound down the window.

'Where are you going?' I said, smiling.

'Hello there,' replied Nairac. 'I'm just out for a walk.'

'You were in the courthouse,' I said.

'I was, I was, George,' he replied, in his best Dublin accent.

I said nothing and just looked at him.

'You want to know what I was doing in there, don't you?' smiled Nairac.

'I'm curious,' I said.

'Well, I was looking at somebody, the court days are good for that, you know,' laughed Nairac.

'What identification did you show to get in?' I asked.

'My very own Belfast driver's licence,' said Nairac.

He didn't offer to show this to me but jumped into the passenger seat.

'You're going home for lunch, aren't you?' he said.

'I am,' I said.

'Would there be enough in the pot for me?'

I laughed.

'I'm having a bowl of soup and a sandwich, the wife's at her mother's for a couple of days, so you may as well join me.'

I drove home and when we had finished our meal, we sat in the lounge for a chat.

'I hear you are becoming quite adept at dirty tricks,' laughed Nairac suddenly.

I was taken aback. 'What do you mean?' I asked.

'Well, I heard that when a list of subscribers to a weekly pools system in aid of prisoners' dependants was found lying in the road, and reached your hands, before it was handed back to the Pools Collection Office, you copied about ten names from the list. Then the following few weeks you telephoned a couple at a time and told them they had won the jackpot draw. The office was inundated with complaints and allegations, and the poor unfortunate collector, who just happened to be in Provisional Sinn Féin, got into extreme difficulties, ending a promising career.' Nairac roared with laughter. 'You wouldn't call that dirty tricks?'

'That's only a practical joke,' I said, smiling.

'Sure, sure,' laughed Nairac. 'I hear there were quite a few practical jokes,' he said, still laughing.

'Who has been telling you this?' I enquired.

'Your boss,' he replied, laughing again.

I knew it had to be someone in the office, but I wasn't really annoyed.

'You still haven't told me what you were doing in the courthouse,' I said, trying to make Nairac embarrassed.

Nairac answered with a question. 'Can I use your phone?'

'You can, but watch out, I've no doubt it's tapped,' I replied.

Nairac didn't question this statement, but said, 'It's okay.'

He dialled a number and said, 'Hello there, change my ETA to 4 p.m., thank you,' and set down the phone.

I got up to go back to work, but Nairac asked me to wait a moment. 'I want you to take me into Dundalk within the next few days. I'll call you later tonight.'

'If you guys want to chance going to Dundalk, go, I'm sure you don't need me,' I replied.

'I do need you, honestly, I'll explain later, I need you to drive, and be able to negotiate Garda VCPs without any suspicion, if such a situation arose.'

'What on earth do you need to go to Dundalk for?' I enquired.

'I need to, honestly, and I need you to help.'

'Is this official?' I asked.

'Everything I do is official,' smiled Nairac, standing up.

I dropped him where requested and returned to work. Later that evening Nairac phoned. 'Can we do that tomorrow?' he asked. 'Oh, and keep it between ourselves.'

I reluctantly agreed, and arranged to meet Nairac the following morning. I wasn't terribly happy about the situation. I felt I was crossing the border too regularly, especially to the Dundalk area. I had been doing so, without backup, at all times of the day and night. My colleagues knew locally, and were doing the same themselves, and my ACC Special Branch was aware at Headquarters. On occasions, I had to telephone Special Branch Headquarters when leaving for the Republic and again on my return. As long as the intelligence kept flowing, no one voiced any real concern. I realised that I should ease up, but I couldn't, I had been on a high since internment. Each piece of intelligence I gained fed me like a drug until the next, but was it all going to be worth it in the long term? I always tried to keep out of politics. The motto 'Without fear or favour' was one I liked to serve under. A terrorist was a terrorist and that was that. I wasn't happy travelling to the Republic with the SAS. I hadn't cleared the trip with my immediate superior, as it was never necessary. Each man did his own thing, and ran his own agents, although lately the words 'teamwork', 'sharing', and 'accompanied' had started to enter Special Branch vocabulary, although each intelligence report from Special Branch members, irrespective of rank, went directly, in a sealed envelope, on a special form, to the ACC, SB. The desk officer then decided who should have access to the report, or an extract thereof. This was based on a strict need to know basis.

Nairac was at the rendezvous point outside the police station. I stopped the car and he jumped in. He was eating an apple and offered one to me. He pointed at a tinker woman walking on the footpath.

'Would you bloody believe it? I gave her some change and she then asked for more. She even wanted my bloomin' apples.'

I laughed and drove towards the border at Killeen.

'Can you tell me what you want me to do and where you want to go?' I said.

'I can,' said Nairac. 'I want you to take me to Dundalk and then drive me to Crossmaglen, via the concession road. I need to approach Crossmaglen from the south and I want to look at a place south of Culloville. I know where I'm going. I've been there approaching from the north, although only in darkness, and now I need to approach from the south.'

We had an uneventful journey to Dundalk, where I swung back north and west, heading towards Crossmaglen.

'I thought you might have taken me a wee run around Dundalk,' laughed Nairac.

'No way, and anyway I would guess you've been around Dundalk before this,' I replied.

Nairac produced an ordnance survey map and proceeded to study it. We didn't speak for a while, and then I said, 'I don't like it here. Crossmaglen is not my favourite place.'

We were about half a mile from Culloville when Nairac suddenly said, 'Stop here, George.'

He jumped out of the car and ran towards a lane where he disappeared. He returned after about five minutes, breathless. I reckoned he had run about 200 yards to be in such a state.

'Go,' he said. I had kept the engine running and headed off again towards Culloville. He mentioned nothing about his stop at the laneway.

'Do you still want to go to Crossmaglen?' I enquired.

'Not quite,' replied Nairac. 'Can you drop me at Forkhill Base instead of Crossmaglen?'

'No problem,' I replied.

I was slightly puzzled by the whole affair, and was reviewing my opinion of Nairac. I knew that the Special Forces were a law unto themselves, but just what was Nairac's role? He had told me he was a liaison between Special Branch and the SAS, and was able to rattle off the names of Special Branch personnel all over the Province. Was he now intelligence-gathering, or just setting up another operation in the Republic? Was he really experienced or just in the learning process? I crossed back into Northern Ireland and left Nairac in the main street in Forkhill. I would remember this day some time later when I overheard him being admonished by the Special Branch chief as to his risk-taking in visiting certain licensed premises in South Armagh. On another occasion, I was sitting at my desk when Nairac arrived in one afternoon and persuaded the clerk to make him a cup of tea. We talked for a while. I looked at my watch and said 'shit.' I jumped up. 'I've got to go on a message.'

Nairac stood up also. 'Want some company?' he enquired.

I laughed. 'No, thanks,' and opened the office door. 'I'll be back in two hours,' I informed Jean, the clerk.

Nairac followed me down the stairs. 'Come on, George, take me for company, I'm bored stiff today.'

I thought for a moment. I was only going to do a drop of money to a source, at a prearranged spot. The source would be somewhere nearby watching but no contact was to be made.

'Okay, okay,' I said to Nairac.

We hurried to the car and drove off, heading for the border crossing at Killeen on the Newry to Dundalk Road. About half a mile across into the Republic, we reached the Border Inn, a roadhouse with a large car park. I pulled up in the car park.

'Wait here, I'll be back in two minutes,' I said to Nairac.

I went into the pub. It was a warm day and there were about a dozen customers, probably all passing trade, customers going to or coming from Dundalk. When my eyes got used to the darkness I saw the source sitting with another man in the corner. I ordered a Coke from the barman and drank it all at once. I set the glass down.

'I enjoyed that,' I said to the barman, who laughed.

I headed for the gents toilet and quickly reached up and left a cigarette pack on top of the cistern. It contained four £5 notes. I left quickly, waving goodbye to the barman. I felt I had done everything right. I returned to the car and got into the driver's seat. Before I could start the engine Nairac spoke.

'I take it you know the cottage over there?'

I immediately knew what he was talking about, but for the moment I pleaded ignorance.

Nairac laughed. 'Come on, George, no pissing around, you bloody know what I'm talking about.'

I laughed. 'How the hell do you know about this cottage?'

'Because at this very moment in time we are in the sights of two of my men who are "dug in" in the middle of that field of whin bushes opposite the cottage.'

I couldn't believe what I was hearing. The cottage in question was about 100 yards away from where I was parked in the pub car park; this was half a mile into the Republic. Intelligence from a reliable source a few weeks previously had shown that certain 'wanted' members of the PIRA used the building some weekends. These members were on the run from the Newry/South Down area. Nairac went on to state that they had been given the information via the intelligence pipeline. It was a top secret operation.

'What do you intend?' I asked Nairac.

'To detain and return them to Northern Ireland, one in particular,' he replied.

'Do you think you are too close to that building down the road?' I asked, pointing at a Garda police station.

He laughed. 'No problems.'

'How long has the op been taking place?' I enquired.

'About ten days or so,' he replied.

I started the engine and headed towards the border and Northern Ireland. I wondered why he had told me of the op. I certainly didn't need to know of the SAS op in the Republic, and had no doubt Nairac would be looking for a reciprocate goodwill offering from me down the line sometime. Still thinking, I found myself agreeing to have a pint of beer before my evening meal.

I was to see Nairac regularly on his liaison visits to the office. I met him socially, and he even babysat on a couple of occasions for me, giving one of my boys an SAS cap badge. He loved to get talking about Irish history, and was convinced he knew more of the famous speeches made by some of the more well-known United Irishmen than any member of the IRA. He was sure that if the Special Forces were given a free hand, there would be fewer joining the Provisionals. On the other hand, he was also convinced that politicians would solve nothing, and that the people actually doing the fighting should sit down, talk, and help make Ireland a great country. He thought it inevitable that Britain would have to leave Ireland. He was all for that, but, in the meantime, people who murdered and bombed had to be dealt with in a civilised society. Everybody had their job to do. I was aware that Robert Nairac had associations with others in the office, and socialised with them also. This wasn't unusual, as each member was responsible for certain geographical areas, but he did get around, and from his conversations it was obvious he was doing the same at Special Branch offices all over the Province. He was always smiling and game for a practical joke, but I was always acutely aware that Nairac was always trying to keep on top of his game. He always gave that public school image of work hard and play harder. His SAS superior in South Armagh, Major Tony Ball, was different; he was quiet, studious and didn't believe in wasting breath in unnecessary conversation. On the few occasions that I met him, he gave the appearance of having built a wall around himself, which one climbed at one's own risk.

I was on holiday when I heard of the IRA abduction of Robert Nairac on Saturday 14 May 1977, from the Three Steps Inn, Drumintee, South Armagh. I was shocked, but not entirely surprised. I had overheard the chief admonish him for actions such as visiting public places like the Three Steps Inn. I myself knew Nairac took more risks than I would ever dare. I had heard him practise his Irish accent, and felt that he was being rather naive in carrying out overt missions in the most violent and dangerous parts of Northern Ireland, on his own. I was part of a Special Branch team who knew how to operate in South Armagh, and had been doing so successfully for some time. There were many do's and don'ts, if you wanted to stay alive, and I knew Nairac had broken one of the don't rules in visiting the Three Steps Inn. He had paid for the mistake with his life. His major, Tony Ball, would also lose his life not many years later in what has been described as a mysterious car accident in the Saudi Arabian desert, where he had gone to work as an intelligence consultant. When I spoke to his former SAS colonel, shortly after news of the accident broke, he said: 'I did everything to get him to remain in the regiment.

He would probably have achieved colonel rank, but he was hard set on leaving his SAS life, and the big money being offered for security consultants in the Middle East was too hard to resist.'

The one thing that stands clear in the whole sorry episode of the abduction and murder of Nairac is the complete and utter mess that the IRA abductors made of the whole operation. They acted like a complete bunch of amateurs, and broke all IRA rules on drinking alcohol before, or during, an operation. When the story unfolded after a few days, and the IRA hierarchy realised how senior an officer in the SAS Robert Nairac had been, and how much high-grade information on the whole security forces' covert operations in Northern Ireland he could have supplied, including the names of 90 per cent of RUC Special Branch, probably all the SAS and many in MI5/MI6, they were really sick. In a proper operation, Nairac would have been interrogated over a period of time by those who could persuade him to reveal all. The IRA could have made life very difficult for the security forces north of the border for some considerable time. They took the credit for executing Nairac, as he was such an important officer, but at heart they realised that the drunken rabble, who were later charged in connection with the abduction and murder, had acted like the proverbial 'Browns Cows'. One, Liam Townsen, was charged with and convicted of his murder. Five others were charged on offences connected to his abduction. A source in PIRA later told me that initially the IRA were going to deal severely with those involved in the premature execution, but relented as this would have been an admission that a complete mess had been made of the operation, or that there had been no one with any terrorist experience involved that night. They were in a no-win situation and tried to delay the confirmation of Nairac's death, by making sure no body was found. There have, in fact, been many theories put forward regarding the disposal of the body, the last one I heard being that the body had been put down a freshwater well shaft at Ravensdale, and by the sheer logistics was 'irretrievable'.

One thing is certain, Robert Nairac was a brave man, a gentleman, and the sort of person you wanted on your side. In fact, when I spoke to a Garda detective who interviewed his abductors, I was pleased to learn they thought he was a brave man and a true Special Forces soldier. At one stage, although badly injured, he wrestled one of them to the ground and got his pistol; unfortunately for Robert the gun misfired and they were able to overpower him again. He had a premature death at the hands of so-called Irish patriots, for being suspected of being a British spy. These are the same people who lick the Queen's head on their stamps and who draw British government Social Service allowances, pensions and unemployment benefit, yet they'll kill a soldier working for such a government, ignorant of the fact that this soldier believed a United Ireland was inevitable and should happen eventually. It's a funny world. The one thing that I was certain of in the whole story was that Robert Nairac was very deserving of his posthumous George Cross. I was proud to have known him and worked with him, and although I only knew of some of his operations in South Armagh, I believe that there is no doubt that more lives were saved than taken by the use of the SAS.

Chapter 12

Internment

Much has been written about the decision in August 1971 to intern, without trial, those suspected of being engaged in terrorism. It is now generally believed that the decision was wrong. Many of those arrested in the first wave, on 9 August, were neither republicans nor members of the IRA. The decision to intern by the prime minister, Brian Faulkner, led to an increase in violence, and encouraged IRA recruitment in nationalist areas. Faulkner was in a no-win situation. There would be problems if he did and problems if he didn't. In the end it was down to the intelligence being submitted by the Security Services that forced his decision.

I myself played a part in this, as I was submitting intelligence from one particular source close to Seán Mac Stíofáin and his Dundalk quartermaster. This source reported seeing new boxes of Kalashnikov rifles at Drogheda, and that the Provisionals appeared to have plenty of commercial explosives. He also reported an intended bombing and sniping campaign. He stated that Seán Mac Stíofáin had told him that the aim would be to kill a policeman daily. I later had no doubt that this intelligence must have played a part in the decision to intern, although I never knew the full story.

The first I officially knew of the decision to intern was at a briefing the previous day, 8 August. There had been whispers in the previous weeks, but nothing definite. The head of Special Branch, of each police division, had, in the days before, submitted a list to a secret team at RUC Headquarters, of those in the area whom he considered active in terrorism, and a direct threat to the community at large. These lists, as later proved, were based on outdated intelligence in many instances. The main perpetrators of violence were, of course, the Provisionals—an organisation that was only a year old! Many on the lists were suspects in the 1956 campaign, now living normal lives and involved in nothing. Many were arrested by mistake, and on very dubious intelligence from unreliable sources, including ungraded intelligence from any Tom, Dick or Harry.

It was only when I was detailed my duties on 9 August, and handed the files of those I had to interview, that I realised the shambles we were in. My first prisoner was under twenty years old. I and another detective had to interview him in an army Nissen hut within Ballykinler military camp. The hut was split in two by a screen, a highly unsatisfactory state of affairs. When the prisoner was seated opposite me, I opened his file. It contained a sheet of paper on which was written 'It is reported that subject is a member of the Provisional IRA.' This was not a lot to talk about, or put to the prisoner, who immediately protested his innocence. The idea was to have him confess to membership of the IRA, and he could then be recommended for detention. I was losing interest after the first interview. Most of the interviews I took part in were of a similar vein, that is, a sheet of paper in a folder, with a piece of scant intelligence written on it.

Of course there were those who made the recommendation to intern easy, by stating, my name is Seán Bloggs, I reside at such and such an address, I am a member of the Irish Republican Army and I refuse to answer any further questions. I felt sorry for some of them from lower-class working homes, with little future. Easy prey for the IRA! It didn't take much persuading for some of them to break down and bare their souls. How they went from membership of the Sinn Féin Cumann into the IRA.

The interviews were helpful for various reasons: to obtain an admission to membership of the IRA; to obtain good intelligence leading to further arrests for internment; and most importantly, from my point of view, to turn IRA volunteers around to work for the intelligence services, and release them back into society, hopefully to continue to provide good intelligence.

A large number of Special Branch, assisted by some CID, had been called in to interview those arrested. Many of these detectives were woefully inexperienced, and completely useless as interviewers. I was sure that some of them gave more intelligence listed on the files to the subject than they actually received! As the day wore on, those having no success with their interviews were changed over, and other detectives tried to obtain a confession to membership. Some detectives became frustrated and began to copy the military tactic of standing the prisoner with his legs apart and fingertips on the wall. After a while the arms gave up. They were then abused verbally. I am no angel, but I didn't like what I saw. I saw no reason for it. I didn't feel good. I thought a persuasive tongue was a much better sword of battle. I believed their attitude to be wrong and counter-productive, but I knew these detectives realised it was internment day. They were the modern Galahads about to save Ulster. They had witnessed the military man-handle the detainees on arrest, and an interrogation frenzy had built up. This violence soon stopped, and it must be realised that very violent and dangerous men were locked up.

I became aware that certain senior PIRA members were being taken to Ballykelly military camp, later Ballykelly Holding Centre, for interrogation of an intense nature. It was felt that these so-called godfathers had to be 'broken'. I later learned that the techniques used were severe, and included hoods, loud noise, and deprivation of sleep. I was also aware the military were involved in this matter. The mode of transport was helicopter. I knew a Special Branch detective who was involved in these interrogations, and he told me a few days later all that had happened at Ballykelly. He also told me the prisoners were not physically assaulted. This time of internment was a time to make a name for oneself, and, more importantly for some detectives, it was a time to acquire a source within the IRA. From intelligence gathered at internment many lives were saved and weapons and explosives dumps located. But, in reality, the whole interviewing system was haphazard and without any real supervision.

Some members of CID had been drafted into each detention centre, and if they achieved a confession of membership of the IRA and the source agreed to tout to secure his release, the CID member kept the source, using the excuse that the source would work for no one but him. This was, of course, nonsense, and this system would later prove disastrous in many cases, as intelligence gained, instead of being sent through CID channels and eventually to Special Branch, was being withheld. This caused friction between the departments, and these

CID personnel, and indeed many inexperienced Special Branch detectives, would quickly lose their sources through stupidity. They should have had protection of such sources as paramount in their minds.

The internment arrest interviews on 9 August lasted a couple of days. Those found to be members of the IRA and a danger to the public at large were interned, and those found otherwise, or arrested in mistake, were released. I know of no innocent man being interned. Internment became a continuous process after that, but in each instance Special Branch had to convince the appropriate authorities in the Northern Ireland Office at Stormont that there was no other option. The intelligence flow swelled, and others were arrested, but the big question in each case was this: if a suspect admitted involvement in terrorist activity and membership of the IRA, but now wanted to go home to his family with a promise to be a good citizen and to renounce violence, while flatly refusing to be a Special Branch agent, was it better to chance his release or intern him?

While I did obtain good sources from internment arrests to add to my existing ones, I felt at times like the proverbial mother hen, running around protecting them from their own organisation, and indeed from the military. The military arrived for a four-month tour, and to be quite honest, all they thought about was the chance to engage the enemy with fire-power, to detect IRA men, and to capture weapons and explosives. The protection of sources meant absolutely nothing to them, and although some regiments had good intelligence officers, most came down on the side of their colonel and his aims.

I tried to interview some who didn't speak from arrest to detention, over forty-eight hours. I will never forget the hate in their eyes. At this time I was to interview a Provisional who talked non-stop about any subject but the IRA, or the trouble in Ulster. There was no real hard intelligence on this man but he was named by others in the movement as being involved. He kept stating he was in Sinn Féin, not the IRA. He was released but subsequently arrested again on receipt of further intelligence. As I entered the interview room I looked at the prisoner, who said, 'I'm glad it's you, we'll have another talk on Irish history.'

We did indeed talk on many subjects all day, but when things got to the nitty gritty and the IRA, he changed the topic of conversation.

'Look, I'm in Provisional Sinn Féin, if I'm asked to help the IRA, I don't know what I'll do.'

'You'll be handed a gun and told to shoot a policeman,' I said.

'I'll be killing nobody,' he replied.

He was eventually released. A month later, a Sinn Féin rally in Newry got out of hand, and a pitched battle ensued between the rioters and the police/military. Shots were fired. I was with another detective observing the proceedings. We were suddenly separated from the main crowd of police. A crowd rushed past us and a pair of eyes met mine. It was him. He surged past us in the crowd and winked at me. If the man had chosen to stop and point me out, I would have been lynched, shot or badly injured. Had the man eventually helped me after all his refusals? I liked to think he had and felt good about it later.

It's easy to be right in hindsight, but I believe the decision to intern without trial was wrong. It gave a legitimacy to the Provisional IRA campaign, and it actually increased the violence on the streets. It gave the IRA their biggest ever recruitment tool.

The police service then was not trained, or indeed equipped, to deal with this increase in violence. They were heavily dependent on their Special Branch officers to provide intelligence, which was the key with which to defeat the terrorist, and since the only way to obtain a good source is through dialogue, I found myself involved in a long series of arrests and detentions, in an effort to defeat the IRA. One arrest would lead to intelligence which would lead to another arrest and so on. Out of these arrests I, and indeed others in the department, would obtain sources of information. These informants, touts, call them what you will, were only obtained after long hours and indeed days of continuous persuasion, never of a violent sort. I didn't have to resort to violence. You couldn't very well work with him later, after having assaulted him. There would be no trust. I really enjoyed talking to these terrorists, and felt a real buzz when I turned one to my way of thinking. I liked to find out how they ticked. How they came to join the movement. What they expected from this New Ireland they felt they were shaping. Some had come forward to the IRA and offered themselves for recruitment. Some were brought into the movement by friends, but most had started by joining the local PSF Cumann. These Cumanns or clubs were more likely than not organised by older men, probably old IRA, or a member of an old republican family. I was intrigued when I saw that each Cumann had an education officer.

'What does he teach you?' I enquired of volunteers who talked to me. I was told that the EO taught them socialist doctrines, and how a socialist Republic was the main aim of the movement, apart from the removal of the British. These were Provisional volunteers, and when I eventually got to talk to a friendly education officer, I learned a good deal about the future aims of PIRA. I was astonished to hear that he really believed the one man one vote nonsense; he really believed that Catholics had no vote in elections. He seemed surprised when I explained that Catholics had a vote just like their Protestant neighbours. I was intrigued to learn that their proposed system of policing their New Ireland would be to draw members from the housing estates to the police service. Each area would police themselves, and hold their own area courts. They should also join other organisations to push for improvement of social issues in their community, but never admit to membership of the IRA. They should encourage the public to complain about the RUC. The RUC would have to be disbanded and a new police service started. Cumanns should have organisers willing to work many hours, but should always be under the covert command of the local IRA unit.

It was, however, in my opinion, a rather childish system and it was to be many years later, in the late Seventies and Eighties, before Sinn Féin/IRA woke up and started to streamline their political operation. In relation to the Garda Síochána, they proposed that they would eventually have to be disbanded too, as phase two of their take-over of the island continued. The RUC would be stood down in phase one. All members of the Cumanns would eventually have to speak the Gaelic language as their everyday tongue. The Irish language would have to play an important part in future. I found that when I told them that I myself had no wish for English soldiers on the streets, and that Irishmen should solve their own problems, they looked at me strangely, in a disbelieving fashion. Although there were one or two from middle-class households, most of these volunteers were from the lower classes. I felt sorry for some, and felt a strange admiration for some who really believed that the Provisionals would one day rule Ireland, and be in government. Have they been partially right?

I believed, as previously stated, that the decision to intern was wrong. Even more so when a source much later told me that he had given me false intelligence on weaponry just before internment. I often wondered how the conflict would have turned out if no decision on internment had been made. One would never know, but the four months from September to December 1971 would set the rules for the years that followed. Mechanical intelligence-gathering was in its infancy in the Province, and was strictly controlled by MI5. Special Branch surveillance units had not yet been born, so, as already stated, Special Branch had to pull out all the stops in the battle for intelligence. When three or four persons were arrested as suspect terrorists, and realised that they were staring at an unknown period of internment, at least one in the group would prefer to chance working for Special Branch, and be at home each night with his family, married or otherwise. There were rare occasions, of course, when a volunteer would agree to 'work', but when he was released he would leg it across the border, never to be seen again, or he might join an active service unit. Some would appear to have terrific potential as informants, only to prove a damp squib. Others would get cold feet, and when they were re-arrested would plead to be let out of the unwritten 'contract'. I was usually happy with this, especially if they had come clean about all their involvement and associates up to that date.

The IRA were no fools and treated very warily any volunteer who had been arrested and released, but they couldn't suspend them all, and as Special Branch kept up a relentless arrest policy on suspects, things became difficult for the Provos. There were, of course, innocent men arrested. I would get rid of them quietly, apologising, and more or less explain, within reason, how they came to be arrested. Special Branch also had to watch out in their informant recruiting policies. If say, six men were arrested as suspects and found to be involved with PIRA, and one agreed to be an informant if released, it would be madness to intern the other five. The one released would have a short life-span. Two would be interned, and the potential source and three others, including the highest-ranking terrorist, would be released. This made it very hard indeed for the movement to detect any touts. On other occasions, a couple of others, usually hard men, would be released first, with smiles and cheerios, and the potential source kept until the next day. It was a game, which if played hard and well, could reap huge rewards.

During this period, September to December 1971, in which the PIRA re-grouped again and again, I was to obtain three or four good sources within the Provisional movement. Some were to last only a year, others a couple of years, and one until 1977, but in those vital months of mayhem in late 1971 and early 1972, they were gold dust. The beautiful thing was that they were all in the South Down/South Armagh PIRA. None knew that the others in their unit were also working for Special Branch. PIRA personnel wastage was high. Some were killed in action. Some were arrested and charged with specific offences. Some were interned. Some went on the run to the Republic. The end result was an ever-changing make-up in the units. I was able to hear two or three versions of intelligence and grade it properly. A proper grading of intelligence is essential for future actions by the security forces. Some Special Branch were tempted to grade information B2, when it was more than likely C3 or even F6. To put it simply, the source is graded A–F, and the information 1–6. A1 is usually applied only to documentary fact, or other means of proving the information is true, therefore B2 is one of the best gradings possible from a source. A B2 would be better than a B3; 2 relates to probable, 3 to possible. The only thing that we in the department worried about was our continued success. The Provos were bound to realise that our success rate was down to infiltration of their movement.

My association with the Garda Síochána was in its infancy in these months, but was very crucial in the terrorist war. From this wealth of intelligence coming in from my IRA sources, who spent as much of their time in the Republic at Dundalk, as in Ulster, information on PIRA movements and safe houses in County Louth could be passed to my new friends in Garda Special Branch. There were houses or pubs where volunteers would congregate in apparent safety. These premises were used to swear-in new recruits, and leave and collect messages. Some were between Dundalk and the border, which made it extremely handy for PIRA. One important house, that of Liam Fegan, one of the older generation of IRA, was increasingly mentioned by sources, and Garda Special Branch were informed accordingly, with the result that they swooped in the first week of December 1971. Ammunition was found, and Fegan was arrested. All new recruits to the PIRA in the border area had been sworn in by Fegan.

This was a heady time for me, and one source in particular wouldn't return to South Down for fear of arrest. He knew his photo was plastered all over military lists. The result of this and other necessities meant that between September and December 1971, I made forty-seven trips to the Republic, to Dublin, Dundalk, Drogheda,

Navan, Blackrock, Bailieborough, Port Laoise, and many more. I was made very aware from Headquarters that I was their only contact with the Garda Síochána. I was encouraged to continue my covert liaison. I had to keep a step ahead. The South Down and Newry PIRA were in Special Branch control. I myself had three volunteers of the Provo units working for me. As previously stated, arrests and detentions caused an ever-changing officer-ship in the IRA! There came a day when an informant returned from a trip to Dundalk and a visit to his area OC. The source had been asked by this man who should be the new OC, as the previous OC had been arrested. I put certain ideas in his head to assist the area OC with the result that another source of mine was appointed OC. I felt really good, my hard work was paying off, and I was saving lives daily. During this period mentioned, my intelligence efforts averted what would have been death and destruction ambushes at Crossmaglen, Killeen, Newry and Mayobridge. If the sources themselves were involved in an outrage, and couldn't avoid taking part without smelling, I looked after them, by setting up an 'accidental' army VCP or other ruse to make PIRA abort the attempt.

During this period, the help and assistance from our Garda counterparts was immeasurable and was essential. On-the-run IRA volunteers moved about together freely, without constraint, in Dundalk, and the guards were able to see associations of members far more easily than RUC Special Branch. They were often able to fit a piece into a jigsaw. It should be remembered that my Garda Special Branch friends at this time were cooperating without the knowledge of their government. They were always at pains to make this situation clear, and worried about their authorities discovering their association with the Northern Special Branch.

The success I was enjoying was soon to be covered over by a dark cloud looming on the horizon. PIRA knew that the success rate of the security forces in South Down/South Armagh wasn't by accident, and the day wasn't too far off when they would suspend the whole of the Newry, South Down, unit and force them to operate as part of the cross-border active service units based at Dundalk. Our problem in Special Branch was that we had been too successful. During this period from September to December 1971, and indeed early 1972, our southern area of South Down/South Armagh had a dozen bombings, numerous shootings and armed robberies. What would the figures have been without Special Branch input? It should also be remembered that most of these bombings happened during a three-month campaign by PIRA to destroy all the British customs posts at Fathom, Tullydonnell and Killeen, as well as the customs clearance stations nearer Newry. These were easy targets and the bombers could be back safely in Louth before the bombs exploded. During this period of late 1971, the Official republican movement, whilst strong in the Newry/Warrenpoint/Rostrevor areas, confined themselves to the acquisition of funds from banks and post offices, with the odd half-hearted shooting. The officers in the Official movement in South Down were in the main from good nationalist families who had no heart for shooting policemen, or bombing Catholic businesses. I had an Official IRA source with whom I had a good association. He actually hated the Provisionals and their methods.

'They are putting us back fifty years,' he would say.

He was also to accuse some of his own within the Official movement of turning into gangsters, and he alleged that a lot of the money from robberies never reached Official IRA Headquarters. This member was so disgusted, he went to live in the Republic and I introduced him to one of my counterparts in the Garda Special Branch. I believe he assisted Garda Special Branch for a long period of time.

Special Branch, at this critical period in the months after internment, had another fight on their hands. This was the battle to keep one step ahead of, and protect their sources from, the British Army. This may sound strange, as they were both fighting the war against the IRA, but it was perfectly true. There were no clear lines drawn in the sand as to the exact nature of the intelligence-gathering operations in respect of the RUC/British Army. The military were recruiting potential sources, by arrests at VCPs, and only some of the intelligence gleaned was finding its way into the pipeline. The problems with Special Branch arose when the army would arrest one of their sources, causing embarrassment at least, and suspension from the IRA at worst, rendering them useless. It was a very difficult situation. If we removed an informant's name from wanted lists, then we were advertising to all that we had an interest in him. If we requested the military to leave him alone, again we were advertising our interest. Sources had to take their chances, and did so, often with disastrous results. Although we had the services of a good MIO in the office, he too was powerless against gossip in the officers' mess of the local military unit. Special Branch had a good success one day, leading to the capture of three IRA bombers and their bombs. The very next morning a national newspaper in London carried the headline: 'Intelligence tip-off leads to capture'. When the news editor received a visit from Scotland Yard Special Branch officers, he revealed his source as a military officer friend in Ulster. In fact, the officer serving in Ulster had only been given a nod and a wink in the mess when news of the arrests broke. These were everyday problems encountered in Special Branch. At the end of this turbulent four months at the end of 1971, the IRA would change. A cell system would develop, making the gathering of intelligence that much harder, and I would come to value my extending influence with Garda Special Branch more and more. What I would lose one way, I was going to gain by another.

Chapter 13

Further Meet with McMahon

I continued my association with Garvin and indeed with McMahon, against the express wishes of Special Branch London, and also, I suspect, the Intelligence Services. Some of the intelligence was so sensitive that I did not put pen to paper, but went to Special Branch Headquarters in Belfast and gave it verbally to the Republican Desk Officer, who I was acquainted with and whom I had served with in earlier years. In fact, when I eventually moved from the border areas I handed over McMahon to him. Unfortunately he was killed years later, when a helicopter carrying intelligence staff to a conference in Scotland crashed on the Mull of Kintyre. I received a continuous flow of good intelligence from both McMahon and Garvin that I have no doubt saved countless lives in Ulster, and led to the arrest and detention of many evil men.

From my conversations with Garvin I learned that lines of contact were now being set up between the Special Branches in Belfast and Dublin, but I was also assured by him that Dublin were only giving what suited their political masters. He mentioned the rise of a senior officer whom he didn't like, and told anyone else he knew.

'If I can't trust him, how can RUC Headquarters? If he feckin' knew what I was giving you, he'd destroy me,' he said.

One morning in early May 1974, I received a request for a meet from Garvin. He asked me to drive on down from Dundalk to Slane, where he would meet me and buy lunch. I drove down without incident, and we were soon installed in a hotel dining room having lunch.

'Have you seen Pal lately?' I enquired.

This was our pet name for McMahon.

'By heavens I have, did you see on the news the seizure of a large amount of commercial explosive? Well, that was Pal.'

'Yes, I thought that was your patch,' I replied. 'I'll bet it cost you.'

'Not a penny, not a penny, he told me to take it. Dublin were happy.'

'I'll bet they were, but it's us who should be thankful, it was destined for Ulster,' I replied.

Garvin nodded. 'I'll tell you why I asked you down,' he said. 'Dublin is crying out for intelligence on any possible loyalist paramilitary action here in the Republic. The dissent to any power-sharing is gathering in pace and they are worried about previous loyalist threats to bomb the Republic.'

I agreed that things in the North looked bad. 'I'm sure Headquarters are now giving Dublin intelligence which I am sure includes anything regarding loyalist paramilitaries operating in the Republic,' I replied.

'I know, I know, but I thought you might have heard something,' said Garvin.

'Unfortunately, or maybe fortunately, as I've told you many times, we have no Protestant paramilitary problems in my area, it is 99 per cent Catholic so I have no sources who could help,' I replied. I went on. 'From what we read and hear on the news, a Council of Ireland, as in the Sunningdale Agreement, is not on for the unionists and therefore for the paramilitaries, things don't look good.'

'Well, I think we are increasing our vehicle checkpoints on northern traffic, and can only hope for the best, I suppose,' said Garvin. He then raised another topic with me. 'George, you remember how we planned to keep our contact secret and submit the intelligence from a bogus third party,' said Garvin.

'I do,' I replied. 'Why, is anything wrong?'

'Not really, but I was asked a funny question at Headquarters the other day by one of our Special Branch liaison officers, who are now, believe it or not, travelling to Belfast Special Branch Headquarters. Isn't this great?'

'It sure is. What was said at the meeting?' I replied.

'Well, it's hard to put a finger on it but I think that he gave RUC

Headquarters, Knock, some intelligence which originally came from me, then discovered they already had it. He smells something fishy. I denied any knowledge of any leak, but he's pro, he knows something isn't right.'

'It's maybe my fault, in requesting no DD (downward dissemination),' I replied.

'Well, we'll feckin' have to watch ourselves from now on,' replied Garvin.

We had almost finished the meal when a man who obviously knew Garvin well approached our table. He proffered his hand to Garvin and thanked him for arranging to have some tinkers removed by the Gardaí from a piece of his land.

'I know it's early in the day, but will you and your friend have a drink?' he enquired.

Garvin introduced me as a friend, 'Seán' from Belfast, and politely refused, but nothing would do the man and I found myself accepting a beer. The man turned away, saying his goodbyes, and suddenly turned back again. 'Hand me your pen,' he asked Garvin.

Garvin handed him a biro and he wrote something on the menu, set the pen down and walked away smiling. I leaned over and read it with Garvin. It was the name of a horse running at a meeting the following week. Before the lunch was over, Garvin gave me his usual lists of new arrivals from the North.

'Can you do the usual on these half dozen, there's no hurry, and I have a present for you from Pal. It's in the boot of the car.'

After a further ten-minute chat we made our way to the car park. Garvin opened the boot of his car, and opened a sack. I could see the butt of a rifle.

'I'll not bring it out,' he said, wrapping it up again. 'You'll see it's an Armalite. Pal has been given a couple for rifle training. He says you're to examine this one, and you should be able to trace it in the States, it's US Army issue. He wants it back in a week. You're to leave it behind the pillar. Do you understand?'

'Right, okay, I know where he wants it left,' I replied.

'Do you want me to travel up to the border with you in case you are searched at a Garda VCP?' asked Garvin.

'No, it's okay, when I get out of the car park here I'll transfer it to under my seat. I should be okay. They'll be looking for danger from the other direction,' I laughed.

Inwardly I knew I would worry like hell until I crossed the border, and even after that. I didn't feel like explaining to a British Army road stop what I was doing with an IRA Armalite in the car.

About a week after a visit to my home by Scotland Yard Special Branch, who were worried McMahon was refusing to contact them, I made contact with McMahon. I requested a meeting in Drogheda. I felt uneasy around Dundalk and liked a place in Drogheda McMahon had taken me to previously. McMahon didn't want this and requested me to come to him, at his home.

'Jesus, I've had enough of that, my nerves wouldn't stand it,' I replied.

'You'll not meet a soul,' replied McMahon, laughing.

It was apparent that McMahon was going to insist on me coming to his house, so I reluctantly agreed. I passed through Dundalk at about noon, skirting the main thoroughfare by going round past the dog track to the Dublin Road, and travelled on to Ardee where I stopped in the main street to buy a newspaper and a can of Coke. I saw a youth standing near the shop selling *An Phoblacht*, the Provisional Sinn Féin paper. I bought one, and let him keep the change. I journeyed on and around one o'clock I arrived at the house. There were two men sitting on the wall of a nearby cottage, who seemed to take an interest in me as I parked at McMahon's gate. I had just got out of the car when McMahon came walking towards me. We met about five yards from the door, and as McMahon turned back towards his door, he lifted his arm to these two men and shouted, 'How's the lads?'

Both men waved back. When we were safely inside, I asked about the men. McMahon laughed, 'I knew you'd worry.'

'Who are they, for fuck sake?' I asked.

McMahon laughed again. 'They're two of the boys from Crossmaglen.'

'Who are they?' I insisted.

'They're with the border ASU but it's okay, they think you're one of the boys from Belfast. They called earlier and I had to tell them something, so that when you arrived they wouldn't be alarmed.'

'Jesus Christ, I don't believe this,' I said. 'I knew I shouldn't have come here.'

'It's okay, really,' laughed McMahon.

'Who are they?' I repeated.

'One of them is Mickey McVerry, and I think the other is Murphy. McVerry is the operations officer of the South Armagh boys.'

I felt ill.

'It's okay,' repeated McMahon, 'I taught McVerry how to shoot.'

I knew of McVerry, a much wanted man. 'What are they doing here?' I asked.

'Och, they're helping to build a wall, it passes the time for them, and they get a bed now and then, when they urgently require it.'

'I left the Armalite at the drop pillar,' I interrupted.

'Yeah, I got it.'

I sat down and we spoke again of the visit from Scotland Yard Special Branch.

'I thought you had settled with them,' I said.

'Och, they're a shower, I know what they want, they'll just wait,' he replied.

'They'll be on to me again soon to see if I found you,' I said.

'Don't say you were at my house,' said McMahon.

'Are you going to get in touch soon?' I asked McMahon.

'The fuckers want to fly into Dublin airport and meet me in the city,' said McMahon. 'I flatly refused and didn't phone back.'

He went on to say that he wasn't happy with the way Scotland Yard operated, and wasn't satisfied that they placed source protection high on their list of priorities.

'You are some man to talk of protection, look at the bloody chances you take!' I said.

McMahon laughed. He went to the back room of the house and returned with a rifle. He took the magazine off and handed it to me.

'This is another Armalite. It came into Ireland from the mainland. They are being brought from America on a passenger liner, maybe even the QE2, by Irish stewards working on board.'

'What are you going to do with it?' I asked.

'Use it for training, what else,' he replied.

'How many were brought in?' I asked.

'It's an ongoing operation, they bring two or three in now and again,' replied McMahon, returning the weapon to the back room.

When he returned I asked him if he had any further intelligence which would be of use to me. McMahon outlined the current situation within the Provo hierarchy.

'It's a Joe Cahill inspired war now. He and Twoomey are planning the direction now. No one is sure where David O'Connell stands, he has policies like a Federal Ireland, with the four Provinces controlling their own politics, sending delegations to a main parliament in Dublin. This is too radical for Cahill. The young bloods, like McGuinness in Derry, are taking an iron grip on the movement.'

'Anything else?' I enquired.

McMahon went on to state that the IRA Army Council had decided that the fight must be continued on the mainland, and long-term policies were being set in motion to this end.

'It's becoming very hard indeed to get a whisper of any impending operation, because they are paranoid about informers. They are developing the cell system really well.'

I looked out the window at a van which had appeared outside.

'It's only some blocks for the wall down the road,' said McMahon.

I nodded, although I wasn't too happy at Mickey McVerry standing outside. His history to then was short, but certainly full of incident. He had achieved notoriety within the republican movement within a short space of time, and was considered to be one of their top men in South Armagh.

'What am I to tell London?' I asked, standing up.

'Tell them I'll be in touch, I know what they want, you know,' replied McMahon.

I didn't answer.

McMahon went on. 'Certain people have received letter bombs in London, and they want me to provide intelligence on it.'

'Can you?' I enquired.

'Not without difficulty, but I have an idea who is behind the operation.'

I said nothing. I didn't want to get involved in this, I had been told to break my association with McMahon, and although I would have loved to be involved, I desisted from any further questioning. I would phone Special Branch Headquarters on my return and tell them to pass on the information that McMahon would be in touch shortly. My problem now was getting back home. Had any of the Provisionals outside recognised me? Did they know my car? I left the house shortly afterwards after some small talk. McMahon came to the gate with me.

'I'll see you, Seán,' he shouted. 'Keep your head down and good luck.'

The men working at the wall heard him and waved at me as I passed. I had a long run up to the border and was sort of relieved when I reached the northern side of Dundalk.

A few days later I was summoned to Special Branch Headquarters by the deputy head of the department.

'Hello, George,' he said as he welcomed me into his office. I sat down.

'London say the source has been in touch, they're coming over tomorrow.'

I wondered at that. I wondered where they would meet, and thought I was going to be asked to take them to Dublin or some other destination in the Republic.

'They are organising a meet in Derry,' said the deputy.

I was surprised. The deputy went on to explain that only one Special Branch officer from London would be going to Derry and that, as he was advised to take company, he had asked for me.

'Well, he knows that you and the source know each other, he would be worried if anyone else might identify him.'

'Do you know why the Met Special Branch want to go to Derry?' I asked.

'No,' said the deputy. 'I can honestly say I know nothing, only that the source wanted them to come to Derry.'

I received further instructions and returned home. The next afternoon I drove to Derry, and went to a military base as instructed. I was shown to the bar in the officers' mess and there stood John Hewson of New Scotland Yard.

'Hello, George, thanks for coming.'

He asked me what I would like to drink, and we sat down with two beers.

'I appreciate you coming,' said Hewson. 'How's your good wife?'

'She's fine, thank you,' I replied.

Hewson continued, 'We have two bedrooms in the mess for tonight, and I want you to take me to the local Special Branch office.'

He explained this was a courtesy call, but that he wanted them to organise a vehicle checkpoint in Derry City that very night. I felt like asking a lot of questions, but I resisted.

I introduced Hewson to the local Special Branch, and wasn't even present in the room when the vcp was organised. We returned to the military base and had an evening meal, after a quick wash-up. The meal had hardly begun when Hewson spoke. 'Did he mention anything to you about letter bombs in London?'

I lied, 'No, he didn't say anything.'

'Well, I'll explain the score tonight,' replied Hewson. 'The source is in Donegal, and later tonight he'll cross the bridge in the city. The people we want will be a few cars behind, I'll know them from our arrangements.'

'What do you want me to do?' I asked.

'I want you to wait here in case I need you if there's a cock-up, or we need to take some action to safeguard the source.'

I nodded. We finished our meal and the last I saw of Hewson was when he headed out of the mess in military uniform with a cheery wave. Two hours later I was sitting in the mess when Hewson arrived back. It was about eleven o'clock. He was all smiles.

'How did it go?' I asked.

'Great, great, we had a good scoop. Look, George, I don't need you any further, so if you want you can go on home, or if you wish you can use your room here.'

'Where are you taking your catch?'

'You don't want to know,' replied Hewson. 'Just leave it at that.'

I made up my mind there and then to go home. I never heard anything further about any arrests, but before we parted I heard a helicopter being ordered for Hewson. I was never to know the outcome of the Derry visit. I knew not to ask McMahon when I next met him.

Chapter 14
Dublin Trip with MIO

The MIO entered the office. 'Fancy a coffee?' he asked. I nodded. We walked along the corridor to the canteen. It was empty except for two staff on duty.

'Two coffees and biscuits please,' ordered Laycock.

We sat at a table near the door. I was coming around to thinking that Laycock was a genuine sort. I had started to like him and found it easier and easier to talk shop with him in the office. Even though Headquarters had ordered each Special Branch officer to treat their newfound military colleague as if he was one of their own, difficulties were arising across the Province. Not so here at Armagh/Down. Laycock was confiding easily with me on matters which I myself would have had no knowledge of. We were also playing the game by allowing Laycock access to anything in the office, including intelligence reports just completed for transmission to Headquarters at Knock. We had spent a couple of long evenings together drinking Black Bush, the beautiful Bushmills special blend whiskey. Laycock had told me his life story to date. He was twenty-seven and probably upper middle class. He had been at university, and was Conservative in his outlook. He had been approached and offered a commission in the Intelligence Corps. He had accepted and settled down well into an officer's life. He was sharp-witted and believed in a soldier being blind to all else when he received an order to do something. He read a lot, played a fair game of chess, and looked forward to the *Times* crossword daily. He fully realised that this was the time to make a name in the service, to build up his cv for future senior rank. He was ruthless and quite prepared to cut corners if necessary. He was posted to the Special Branch office for the next two years, and had no doubt whatsoever he would be helped enormously in his task by myself and all I could offer at the office. His success really depended on Special Branch success. As we sipped our coffee, Laycock blurted out, 'Look, George, I've been wondering, would it be possible to go with you on a source contact? I'd love to see you operate and hear these guys first hand.'

I was taken aback for a moment, and then laughed. 'I don't think the 100 per cent cooperation included this.'

Laycock laughed. 'Look, I'm only here for two years, then I'm gone forever. I've been taught all there is to know about cultivation and running sources at Ashford Military College, but I've never yet been involved. If you do this for me, I promise you, then I'll return the favour two-fold.'

I sort of made up my mind immediately. I had been about to ask one of my colleagues to accompany me that very night, now I didn't have to.

'Be here at the office at six o'clock tonight,' I said.

'Where are we going?' asked Laycock.

'Dublin,' I replied, 'and we're using your car—have you Northern Ireland or English plates on her at the moment?'

'Northern Ireland plates, I changed them only this morning,' replied Laycock.

'Right, see you at six, I've got to go out.'

As I got up from the canteen table, Detective Inspector Jack Bishop entered and said, 'There's a phone call from HQ for you, George.'

'Right, just going.'

I heard the chief inspector accept the offer of a coffee from the MIO. I knew he wouldn't mention our trip. I lifted the phone.

'Is that you George? Chief Supt Jones here.'

'Yes, sir,' I replied.

'I want you to come up and see me tomorrow, I must brief you on something.'

'Right, sir, I'll see you about ten o'clock then.'

'Right, George, that's fine, see you then.'

I met the MIO at six o'clock and shortly afterwards took the main road south towards Dundalk. We were stopped twice, by the military at a VCP in South Armagh, and by the Gardaí at a VCP near Castlebellingham on the main Dundalk to Drogheda Road. On each occasion the production of a driver's licence and an examination of an empty car boot were sufficient. We talked of this and that on the journey. Laycock was teasing me about the office systems in the Special Branch office, especially the filing systems.

'I don't know how you manage,' he said.

'Well, we file a lot in our heads, you know.'

He smiled. We reached the northern outskirts of Dublin at about 7.15 p.m. and fifteen minutes later we pulled into a large supermarket car park on the south side. The place was packed with late night shoppers. We found a space, parked, and entered the store.

'We're looking for the toy department,' I said.

The MIO didn't speak, but pointed to a sign, Toys and Gifts. I watched for a minute and then walked up to a youth in his early twenties examining a child's bicycle.

'How you doing? You made it then.'

The youth looked at Laycock, apprehensively.

'One of the lads,' I said.

The youth, a tall, sandy-haired, freckly individual, nodded at Laycock.

'We've gotta go now,' he said. 'Follow me at a discreet distance. The meeting is in a hall, a community hall I think.'

We walked through the store.

The youth spoke again. 'Any vehicles parked near or at the hall should be of interest to you, as there are a lot of OTR men going. I will contact you tomorrow or sooner on the phone if anything urgent arises at the meeting.'

We followed the source for about a mile, and saw him park and enter a building, still on the south-west side of the city. We drove around calling all the registration numbers of parked vehicles into a small Dictaphone, at the same time observing a number of men entering the hall. As some of these men walked up a short flight of steps to the door they donned black berets. Laycock was totally amazed at this.

'Where are the police?' he asked.

I assured him they were breaking no rules in the Republic. 'The Special Branch are probably watching us if we only knew it,' I told him.

It had started to rain and, spotting a carry-out fish and chip shop near the hall, Laycock said, 'Fancy a fish and a Coke?'

I was apprehensive about stopping at the door of the hall, the only vacant parking spot, but I agreed.

'I'll get them,' I said. 'We don't want upper-class English heard here, especially tonight.'

I returned to the car in just over five minutes. 'Right, let's go.'

Laycock turned the ignition key. There was a dull click. He tried again, but there was no life at all in the engine. He looked at me.

'I've something to confess,' he said. 'I had to get a push start this morning, I think I've battery trouble, it's the damn military radio runs it down and it's so far to go to the bloody Transport Depot at Lisburn, I was hoping I'd be okay for a couple of days.'

I said, 'Fuck, we're facing up an incline.'

It was still raining. Laycock opened his bag of fish and chips.

'These are not bad at all, George, not bad at all.'

'You do realise our situation,' I said. 'It wouldn't surprise me if the Garda Special Branch are carrying out an observation of this place tonight.'

Laycock didn't reply. I jumped out of the car, asking Laycock to pull the bonnet catch. I lifted it up and by the light of the street lamps gave a forlorn tweek to each terminal on the battery. It was raining cats and dogs, and as I closed the bonnet and jumped back into the car, I said, 'We could always park up and go to a garage and organise a tow or a set of jump leads.'

'I can't leave the car,' said Laycock.

'Why not?' I enquired.

'I have an SMG under the driver's seat,' he replied.

'Holy shit, what about those vehicle checkpoints we came through?' I said, annoyed.

'Well, you had your police pass, which would have got us through if a search looked imminent,' Laycock laughed. 'No sweat, no sweat.'

I opened my bag of fish and chips, and sat eating quietly. We sat for over an hour, chatting about this and that, having realised our only hope was a clutch start when the other cars moved off and we could get turned. The rain had stopped when the door opened and the first of the PSF members came down the steps. They came out in two's and three's, chatting as they walked. Suddenly the source appeared alone.

We saw each other at the same time, and I got out of the car and waved him over.

'The fuckin' car won't start, we need a push.'

The source turned quickly to a group coming down the steps behind him.

'Tony,' he shouted, 'the lads need a push, come on boys.'

Within a short time, about six of them were pushing us up the hill. Laycock jumped the clutch, and, after a couple of tries, the engine fired and away we went. I rolled down the window and shouted, 'Thanks, lads.'

I felt very relieved, and after a while I turned to Laycock. 'If only they had known that this car was owned by the British Defence Ministry, and the driver and passenger were members of the intelligence services.' I breathed deeply.

Laycock imitated an Ulster accent and said, 'Sure the craic's good.'

Chapter 15

Further Meet of the Triangle re: Rogue Members of RUC/Gardaí

Until 1971, the only close contact I had ever had with the Garda Síochána in the Republic of Ireland was when I had occasion to call at a Garda station in County Clare to report some gypsies who had damaged my car. This was in the early Sixties. I was amused at their telephone system then, and the uninterested attitude of the guard on duty. I felt they were fifty years behind the times. My attitude was to change completely many years later during my association with D/Sgt Harry Garvin of their Special Branch. It wasn't long before I discovered that Garvin was astute, courageous, intelligent, shrewd, and honest to a fault. In fact, leaving the police service to one side, he was one of the nicest people I had occasion to meet. I looked forward to our meetings. I was to learn a lot from Garvin, and in this respect I remember one particular visit to the Republic in response to a call from McMahon. I hadn't heard from him for a couple of weeks, and indeed was lucky to have been in the office when he telephoned.

'Can you come to the same meeting place as we met the time before last?'

I thought for a moment, and quickly realised McMahon wanted me to come to his own house.

'No way,' I replied.

'You must,' replied McMahon. 'I've no wheels and there is another reason.'

I reluctantly agreed. I went home, garaged the car and changed my registration number plates. Then, having told the office I was going to Headquarters in Belfast, I drove south towards 'Apache' country, as I liked to call it, around Dundalk. I passed through the town without any problem and headed south-west. I hadn't noticed anyone I knew going through the town and had not made any eye contact. I would try and return in the rush hour traffic. I felt better in a crowd. I travelled on and eventually pulled up in McMahon's road just as it started to rain. I liked the rain, and liked to travel in bad weather. There were fewer people on the roads, and it was difficult to see the driver of a car clearly. I felt it made my journey easier.

McMahon's door was open, and I said, 'Anyone at home?'

'Come on in,' replied McMahon. He was putting some turf on the fire, and looked his usual dishevelled self. 'Sit down, sit down,' he said. 'I see you've brought the rain with you.'

I laughed, and turned down an offer of something to eat. McMahon talked of the merits of Flora and how he had stopped eating butter and drinking coffee. 'My stomach felt better after a week and I am saving a fortune on Rennies,' he laughed.

We talked for about five minutes about good food, then McMahon said, 'I've a few things for you.'

I waited.

'They're going to step things up in Belfast. They want to hurt London economically, so you will see a lot of businesses being targeted.'

'Only Belfast?' I enquired.

'No, it's target at will as usual, but they want it stepped up in Belfast.'

'That'll be good for jobs,' I replied sarcastically.

'Units have been instructed to give a fair warning of the placing of the bombs with a code word, to ensure the police know the caller is, in fact, the IRA. After a couple of months, they will again revert to a sniping campaign.'

I let him continue.

'They have access to a lot of nitrates, and a couple of madmen who are good at mixing the stuff, and they can get it to Belfast without much difficulty.'

McMahon went on to tell me of lectures being given in Dundalk to PIRA from Belfast on improving techniques in their booby trap devices for vehicles, and three members of the border ASU at Crossmaglen (now on the run in the Republic) were lecturing on large claymore mines. He then spoke of some new names.

'I've been putting these guys through their paces on the rifle,' he said, handing me a list of seven names.

'I'm not sure of some Christian names, and not sure of some surnames, it's like that, but the towns in the North are probably right. You can do your own detective work. Oh, and you haven't closed the door to America, the Armalites continue to come in.'

McMahon was interrupted by a knock on the door. My hand went into my pocket and gripped my Walther pistol. Before I could speak, McMahon opened the door. There stood D/Sgt Garvin, Garda Special Branch. He walked in, holding out his hand. 'Hello there, George, how are you?'

I looked at McMahon. 'You bloody knew he was coming,' I said.

McMahon laughed. 'I thought it would help if we all met up again.'

'Did you not know I was coming?' asked Garvin.

'No, I didn't, did you know I would be here?' I asked.

'Yeah, he did say.'

'Sit down, will you,' said McMahon.

We all sat around the table. Garvin accepted the offer of a cup of tea which had been stewing for five minutes. I again declined.

'Is he giving you something good?' asked Garvin.

McMahon outlined to Garvin what he had just told me and continued. 'The Army Council are not happy with the situation in Belfast. The military and Special Branch are having too much success with their new covert surveillance units. Their use of new sophisticated technology has them really worried, and they know Special Branch have a couple of well-placed sources deep in the Belfast Brigade. They are also worried about the rise of the loyalist paramilitaries, and the fact that a lot of their important IRA people have been interned or imprisoned. You can expect changes in the Belfast leadership. The last time I spoke to Joe Cahill he told me he had great faith in some young eagles in Belfast who would take the organisation to new levels. This was just before he left on his fateful arms trip on the *Claudia*. Brian Keenan is now the QMG of the Provos. He will tighten things up. He believes too many weapons are being seized by the Security Services. Keenan has overseas contacts in the Middle East and Libya. He's definitely getting the stuff in. Only last week I was shown another new RPG 7 rocket launcher. The South Armagh lads had it.'

McMahon went on to say how the Provo hierarchy had been dealt a crushing blow by the arrest of Cahill on the *Claudia*, and how David O'Connell's view on the whole military campaign was changing. O'Connell realised that a long war was proving futile and that their window of opportunity was closing fast with the rise of the UDA. He had told McMahon that he was starting to believe that a federal solution may be the best way forward, each Province having their own assembly. McMahon also told us that the anti-internment campaign was to be intensified, especially in New York and Washington, and that there were now those in the Irish Caucus in New York actively engaged in purchasing and supplying small numbers of rifles and pistols, which were getting through to Ireland in passenger and cargo vessels.

Garvin interrupted, 'Yeah, a source of one of my men told me about two rifles which had been brought into Dublin on a cargo ship from Chicago.'

'Do you know where they've gone?' asked McMahon.

'No I don't, do you?'

'To Derry,' replied McMahon.

'Oh, that's something I was to tell you, George,' continued Garvin. 'The Derryman, McGuinness, was seen outside Navan a few days ago with another guy, also from Derry. He was down for a meet but I haven't heard anything on it yet.'

I nodded. 'You seem to have a lot of PIRA activity down here recently,' I added.

'Internment has given us a hell of a lot more work,' said Garvin. 'At the start they congregated around Dundalk, but increased Special Branch activity has sent a lot of them down to west Meath, and even to Drogheda and Dublin.'

'It depends how much more they want involved,' added McMahon. 'The dedicated ones will hang around Dundalk, looking for action with the ASUs in South Down and South Armagh. The ones who are not so dedicated, or don't fancy a long spell in prison, or who have a nagging wife and children to worry about, move on down to Dublin. In fact, some are going as far as Cork and Kerry to resettle.'

Garvin handed me a list of names. 'These are the recent arrivals to my area. Could you check if the DOBs and addresses are correct?'

I looked at the list of five names. All were from Belfast.

'No problem, I'll have them checked out and will phone you ASAP.'

McMahon turned to Garvin. 'There's one of your guards passing information to one of my unit.'

Garvin didn't say anything for a moment, letting the statement sink in. 'Jesus, one of my lads in my office?' he replied.

'No, no,' said McMahon. 'It's one of your uniform guards.'

He named the guard and Garvin said, 'What's he passing to the Provos?'

'Information on Garda escorts to the bank cash transports,' said McMahon.

'Fuck me, I'll deal with him pronto,' said Garvin.

'You can't, I would be in difficulties, and you don't want that, do you?' replied McMahon.

Garvin looked visibly embarrassed. I commiserated with him and said, 'You have a problem, Harry.'

'So do you,' said McMahon. He turned to me and named two on-the-run terrorists known to be living in the Dundalk area. 'You have a policeman from the RUC who plays poker most Sunday nights with them south of the border.' He named him.

It was my turn to be shocked. 'I know the constable, I know he was once a good sportsman, but this really is a shock.'

'Has he been any use to you?' enquired McMahon.

'Come to think of it, no he hasn't,' I replied.

'We have our problems,' laughed Garvin. 'At least you have an independent police service now, we have still to look over our shoulders at the politicians. They are our masters, in all aspects. The old-timers in Fianna Fáil, themselves ex-IRA, still wield a lot of influence. I know a superintendent who joined the force with me. His father was old IRA, his father-in-law was old IRA. The whole family are republican through and through. I used to visit them a lot. When I entered Special Branch, they sort of stopped our association. They still talked to me if the occasion arose, but really that was the end of it.'

McMahon interrupted, laughing, 'Sure half the guards are republicans.'

Garvin enjoyed the joke.

McMahon added, 'I forgot to tell you, George, there are a lot of reports of sightings of RUC Special Branch and SAS in Dundalk, by volunteers. I know they are paranoid about this, and it's all nonsense, but watch yourself.'

'Thanks,' I replied, and thought of my visits with Robert Nairac.

'Right, one last thing for the two of you,' said McMahon. 'The very latest whisper is that a new weapons purchase is being organised again, following the *Claudia* disaster. They must immediately try again, if only for morale. The story is they will attempt another foray in Libya. That's all I know. I'll keep a listen. Before you go, George, the powers that be down here are worried about the loyalist paramilitaries. Anything new?'

'You have good reason, the intelligence on the loyalist paramilitaries is not good,' I replied. 'They rumble now and then about doing a spectacular in the Republic, but really they haven't the same expertise with explosives as the Provos.'

I could maybe have given Garvin more, but was very hesitant, as I felt that it wasn't really my place to be giving this intelligence, as I had no loyalist paramilitaries in my area. It wasn't that I didn't think Garvin should have it, but Headquarters should have been assuming such a role with Dublin. I had no loyalist problems in my nationalist police area of South Down/South Armagh, so any intelligence I would have been giving Garvin would have been taken from general Intelligence Summaries. I wasn't happy with that. If I had personal knowledge of loyalist paramilitary activity in my own area I would have shared it with Garvin. I again refused the offer of a cup of tea.

'If you want to leave now, George, I'll stay on here for another ten minutes,' said Garvin.

I stood up and shook hands with both men. As I walked down the path to my car I wondered what I was doing here. I had a habit of taking my pulse two or three times daily, and when I counted my heartbeats in the car they numbered 120. Too many, I thought, too many. I made a mental note not to take my pulse heading home through Dundalk. It may have frightened me. I set off for Dundalk and the road home. On the journey I was making decisions mentally, and the next day I went to see a senior Special Branch officer in charge of the Republican Desk whom I'd known well for quite some time. I realised that I had to share my secret about Garvin. I had heard that lines of communication being established between Special Branch, Dublin, and their counterparts in the RUC, would make it increasingly difficult for my submissions from Garvin to be put in the pipeline as coming from another source, and although I gave a lot of my intelligence verbally to the ACC Special Branch, I decided it was time to make a big decision. I sat down, and after some small talk, I started and told him that I had a Garda Special Branch source deep in the Republic and that by mutual agreement we were disguising our intelligence input as if from another source. Recently this was proving difficult and so I had decided to bring another member into the equation. He was already aware that I had contact with Dundalk Garda Special Branch.

'Some of the stuff is very high grade, and eyebrows are being raised at Headquarters because I'm not requesting any payment, and also I am worried about doing harm eventually to a very decent Garda member, who, I have no doubt, because his masters are politicians, could get hurt.'

'I thought you had Garda contacts around Dundalk and Drogheda?' said the chief.

'So I have, but this is another one,' I replied.

The superintendent laughed. 'How the hell do you do it?'

'Well, I didn't really go looking for him,' I said.

I was on the verge of telling him the whole story, but held back, even though I had made up my mind that on any future date if I was transferred, or for any other reason had to leave, then I would hand my sources to this man. It would be better to wait until then. In the meantime we had to talk about Garvin.

'Are you worried about the glory of the whole affair?' asked the officer.

'No, I'm not, what do you mean?' I asked.

'Would you want to give him to someone else to handle?' he asked.

'No, I can't,' I replied. 'There's more to it.'

'Well then, what you should do is put his name and details on paper and seal the details in an envelope. Put the envelope in the safe of ACC Special Branch. This will keep you right in any future difficulties.'

'You mean register him as an agent.'

'No, just to keep you right!'

I was starting to think I should have kept the whole matter to myself, but then I thought of Garvin, and indeed McMahon. McMahon was very content with the triangle situation. He thought the threesome was working well. Why should I disturb matters?

Chapter 16
The Cherry Blossom Kid

When I served in the nationalist Lower Falls area of Belfast in the Fifties, I was to found many relationships which have lasted through the years, both in local community and amongst my own comrades in the force. One of the latter was later to work with me in Special Branch, namely Seán Campbell. We had both lived in the police station, as all single men were expected to do, as the force then was really semi-military. Everyone had to parade and be accounted for morning and night. If any single men wanted to go out to a dance or other late-night venue, a late pass after 11 p.m. had to be obtained. All members were allowed two days off per month, although it wasn't really two full days, but a period of thirty-two hours. I loved the life and without doubt boys grew into men very quickly. Young policemen ate, worked and played as a family. A cook came to the station each day to cook lunch. Lasting friendships were forged. We gave each other nicknames, and Campbell was known as Cherry Blossom. No matter what time of day or night one would meet him he was shining. His boots and leather belt were spit and polished, his brass shone, and even the skin on his face glowed. He always had a knife-edged crease on his trousers, and last but not least, he had gleaming white teeth always breaking into a half smile, with eyebrows lifted in a quizzical fashion. Campbell and I had adjoining bedrooms, and shared all but our toothbrushes. We both married around the same time, and went our own ways, to different police divisions.

Irishmen are great marchers, and are famous throughout the world for this famous sport. They also use this pastime to air their grievances, and so it was from 1969 to 1971, when marching was the order of the day. There were daytime marches, or parades as the Yanks would call them, and there were night-time candlelit marches. These marchers walked under different banners, including civil rights, People's Democracy, and the Trade Unions even joined the show. Anyone who was anyone in the nationalist community had to be seen at the head of the parade, or at least in the front half dozen rows. In this respect many misguided English people of left-wing backgrounds, including the middle and upper classes, marched to show their solidarity with Irish nationalism. The Provisional IRA was in its infancy in this period, and any march or parade was blood and succour to its aims and objectives. The Provos infiltrated these marching committees and used the occasions to foment further hatred and division in the community.

Special Branch, being well aware of the situation, could use these gatherings to build up their dossiers on known militants, and more importantly to note the new recruits by association. On learning of a prospective march or protest parade, Special Branch would ensure that their members were drafted in from other divisions for observation duties. PIRA didn't keep to police divisional boundaries when detailing their units. It was indeed a great opportunity to gather intelligence, although to be able to identify any individual or make any recording one had to take part in the proceedings, which was fraught with extreme danger. This was developing into a terrorist war of a kind unheard of before in Western Europe. Special Branch was making the ground rules as the days passed by. Nothing was hard and fast, except the danger. In later years when I watched the news, and saw two army corporals who had strayed into a funeral procession being pounced on and led away to their certain deaths, I shuddered, and a chill ran down my spine at the thought of the risks I had taken.

At one of these marches, at Newry in County Down, when the Special Branch members met before the parade I was pleased to see my old friend Campbell, the Cherry Blossom Kid. I hadn't met him for some years. I knew he was in the department, but this was the first time we had performed duty together for about ten years. We both were appropriately attired to blend in with the usual casual dress of the marchers, and both had longish hair. Campbell had a small placard stating 'Civil Rights for Nationalists' and wore a Glasgow Celtic scarf. I was more conservative, but wore a tricolour pin in my lapel. I carried a walking stick and appeared to limp. In reality the walking stick was for defence, if I had to cut and run. We arrived at the departure point for the protest march, at Hill Street, Newry. It was an evening parade due to start at 7 p.m., but being early summer no candles were required. We both mingled with the ever-growing crowd, trying not to make eye contact with anyone, but the crowd pressure grew and eventually we got slightly separated. I got my back to the wall of a building. I could see Campbell now and again, probably searching for me. I refrained from shouting. At the point where I was standing I could see the usual leaders at the front, and eventually a loud hailer got the march under way. In the front couple of rows I could see a group of about a dozen well-dressed men and women. They had English accents. Some could be considered well known. They had appeared before in parades and were quite open with their support of the civil rights movement. Suddenly my mouth fell slowly open. There was the Cherry Blossom Kid marching with those women and chatting away to one of the ladies, his teeth shining in his usual grin. I pushed forward and eventually ended up marching about ten rows behind him. I wasn't to see Campbell again until the end of the proceedings. He was standing with the group of women. He waved me over.

'George, these young ladies are over from England, isn't it great?'

I smiled and nodded.

'Are you chaps going to the gathering in the Imperial?' enquired one of the ladies.

I knew of the venue she spoke of, and shook my head in the negative. She meant the Imperial Hotel in Dundalk.

'Sure we are,' interrupted Campbell.

I couldn't believe my ears, and quickly tried to change Campbell's mind.

'We have no car tonight, Seán,' I replied, thinking this would deter Campbell.

'We can give you a lift,' replied one of the ladies.

'No, thanks, I've got things to do for the next hour,' I replied, hoping this would end matters.

I was shocked to hear Campbell reply, 'Right, ladies, I'll go with you, and George, you can come on over later and meet us.'

With a knowing look he was off. 'You'll come over about eleven o'clock then?' he shouted.

I nodded. I couldn't believe this. I returned to base and debriefed. I made an excuse for Campbell, and eventually set off for Dundalk. I wasn't at all happy with the situation, but I was new to the area and should be unknown to anyone. The hotel was packed and it was quite some time before I saw Campbell, still resplendent in his Celtic scarf. He was standing with the actresses and three unknown males. He introduced them to me, knowing I would recognise the names. They were Official IRA from Newry. Campbell bought me a beer. I could see he held one of the actresses by the hand. Where the hell was this leading, I thought to myself. I made small talk with the company for a few minutes. I didn't know what Campbell had told for a cover story, so I was non-committal about anything. When Campbell looked at me, and headed for the toilet, I waited a couple of minutes and followed.

'For Christ's sake, Seán, you're fuckin' mad,' I whispered in the safety of the loo.

'It's great, look at the intelligence I'm gathering, look at the contacts I'm making,' whispered Campbell.

'I know the contact you're trying to make,' I said.

'Isn't she great?' laughed Campbell.

'Right, I don't like this, it's too dangerous, I'm leaving now,' I said.

'Just you go on home, I'm staying the night here with her.'

'Jesus man, forget it, come on home now, before it's too late.'

'I'll be fine,' laughed Campbell. 'I'll see you tomorrow.'

'Don't come to the office, phone and I'll meet you,' I said.

With that Campbell was off back to the company. I joined them for another five minutes and then drifted away. As I drove home, I chided myself for not insisting Campbell return with me. I had left him in the lion's den.

I needn't have worried. Next day at eleven o'clock Campbell phoned from a call-box and we met for a coffee. Now he wasn't so talkative.

'Had too much to drink?' I enquired.

'Not really, but I'll not be going to Dundalk again for a long time.'

'What happened?' I enquired.

Campbell was pensive. 'Promise this is between us,' he asked.

'I promise,' I replied, laughing.

'It's no bloody joke. After you left we went to a couple of pubs,' he replied.

'Who went with you?'

'A whole gang of us, and eventually I ended up back in the Imperial Hotel with you know who.'

I whistled.

'She paid in advance for the room,' he continued, and it was only when I started to undress I remembered about my pistol.'

'Jesus, you weren't carrying, were you?' I said.

'Aye, I was going to give it to you in the toilet last night, but changed my mind.'

'What did you do?' I asked.

'I managed to hide it between my clothes on a bedside chair,' he replied.

He stopped talking for a minute.

'Go on, go on, what happened?' I said.

Campbell continued. 'Well, I woke early, and found I was in bed on my own. I sat up and there she was, sitting on one of the armchairs and pointing my gun at me.'

I stared at him.

'She said, "Don't move, I want to know who you are."'

He continued. 'I knew I had absolutely nothing on me except cash and my pistol, so she couldn't have any clues, so I told her to put the gun down. "Are you a cop?" she asked. "You must be joking," I replied. "Well, only police and terrorists carry guns, so you are one or the other," she answered.'

I was speechless.

'I just jumped out of bed, grabbed the gun, and started to dress,' continued Campbell.

'What did she do?' I asked.

'She told me she thought that I was a cop, and that I hadn't the feel of a terrorist. I replied, "Why, have you felt many?" in a jocular fashion. "You bastard," she replied. "You are a cop."'

'What did you do then?' I asked.

'Well, I dressed, but she got back into bed and sat staring at me. I then left and within five minutes I was leaving the taxi rank near the hotel, bound for the border and Newry. It cost me a bloody tenner.'

I said nothing for a few minutes.

'You were bloody lucky, you acted so much out of character last night,' I eventually replied.

'I know, I know, I'm having problems at home,' he replied.

We compared notes for a while on the previous night's proceedings, and before Campbell left for home, he told me he had obtained some good high-grade intelligence on the Official IRA that he couldn't wait to get into the pipeline. We crossed paths rarely after 1971, when the marching cult waned. The Cherry Blossom Kid had a premature death. I felt a sad, sad loss. I was sick when I heard the news, and over the years since his death I have thought about him, and our young carefree days in the Lower Falls Road area of Belfast. I can still see his grin.

Chapter 17
Bomb at Forkhill

From early 1971 onwards, intelligence became the growth area of the Security Services. Each intelligence-gathering group, Special Branch, Military Intelligence, SAS, MI5 and the SIS, started to draw lines in the sand and compete against each other. This produced rivalry and unnecessary infighting to prove who was superior. As the SAS carried out more and more covert operations tasked by Special Branch, and gathered, in the process, invaluable intelligence, a lot of this didn't come back in the pipeline to Special Branch as it should have. Strange as it may seem, these different agencies were not averse to stealing sources of good intelligence from each other. This could be done in many ways, the best being the old mafia method of getting in close; that is, to establish friendship, gain confidence of the other, and be given the prize without a fight, or arousing any suspicion. The military were adept at holding get-togethers to establish friendships with those they considered could be of use to them in their quest. They would wine and dine, and then brazenly start a brain-picking exercise. It was by these methods that the intelligence network pipeline became clogged with useless over-graded intelligence; C3 became B2 overnight.

I was on one of these exercises organised by the SAS when I was to receive an important phone call from Dundalk. It had been a lovely early summer day in 1971. Some Special Branch staff in my operational area had been invited to the Ballykinler Army Camp, Co.

Down, for a day's shooting with a difference, as the weapons to be fired were those currently being used by terrorists. Some of them, like the Thompson SMG and the M1 Carbine, I had never fired. Some of the pistols were rare models, and this would probably be the only chance I would ever have of firing any of them. As usual, the outing turned into a match which was eventually won easily by Special Branch. I don't think the SAS were too happy at the outcome. With a well done lads, and congratulations chaps, all and sundry adjourned to the mess, for food and liquor refreshment. It was the late afternoon and we looked forward to an evening's entertainment. When we entered the mess, I was given a message to phone the office. Damn this, I thought, and was in two minds whether to phone or wait till later. I decided I'd better phone in case it had been my wife looking for me urgently. As it happened, she had phoned the office asking that I phone her as soon as possible.

When I rang her she was very excited. 'A male caller rang you, and gave his name as Tony, that's all he would say. He said you would know what to do.'

'It's okay, dear, I know who it is, thank you, I'll not be home until late.'

'Are you going where I think you are?' she enquired.

'What do you mean?' I replied.

'I know by his accent,' she replied.

'It's okay, dear, see you later, bye.' I set the phone down.

I made my excuses to the company, 'Got to go, lads, thanks for the craic,' and headed for the car. It was lucky I had been in my own vehicle and hadn't travelled to the shoot with someone else. I travelled through Castlewellan towards Newry, on the Hilltown Road, and just short of Hilltown came upon a military vehicle checkpoint. Damn, damn, I thought, just what I need when I'm in a hurry. There were about ten cars ahead of me in a queue and it was nearly ten minutes before I reached the checkpoint. I rolled down the window.

'Good afternoon sir, can I see your driving licence?' enquired the soldier.

I produced my licence.

'Is this a business or pleasure trip, sir?'

'Pleasure,' I replied.

'Can you open your boot, sir?'

I got out of the car and opened the boot and stood back. The next thing there was a shout.

'Over here quick,' from the soldier to another, and immediately, 'Put your hands on your head, sir, now, now.'

The penny then dropped. After the shoot, I had thrown my Walther pistol into the boot, together with the holster. At one stage the military had fired our Walthers, and we had fired various military pistols.

'I'm a police officer,' I said. 'And that's my pistol.'

I was eventually allowed to put my hands in my pockets to show my warrant card, but the patrol refused to let me proceed until they had checked me out on their radio. I knew it was useless to protest, as the military NCOs were a robot-like bunch. The do's and don'ts and musts and must nots are drilled into their brains. They took no chances. I sat and waited another ten minutes before the radio operator spoke to the corporal troop commander.

'The IO says you have to release this man immediately.'

I saw him look uncomfortable before he said, 'Carry on, sir, thank you.'

I breathed a sigh of relief and drove on towards Newry. I passed through the town without incident and headed towards Dundalk. I crossed the bridge into the town, turned sharp left along the estuary, and found a telephone box near the dog track. The code name Tony was one of my Garda friends, and was only to be used if he had very urgent intelligence which might save lives. In other words, intelligence on a proposed terrorist outrage! I phoned the guard's home number.

'Hiya,' he said. 'Where are you?'

'I'm in Dundalk, I got your message a couple of hours ago, I was a fair distance away,' I replied.

'Look, things are hectic for me at the moment, I've something big on myself and your stuff sort of cropped up too. I have to go to Drogheda urgently. Could you meet me there in an hour? I'm sorry I can't go to Dundalk. I can't miss this contact.'

'That's okay,' I replied. 'I'll head there now, where shall we meet?'

'Do you remember we met once in a place on the Dublin Road out of town?'

'Yes, I do, okay, see you there,' I said, setting down the phone.

I drove without incident to the hostelry and had eaten a chicken sandwich and drunk a beer, before my Garda friend arrived.

'Hello, George, how are you?'

He scanned the half dozen customers in the bar and sat down.

'It's like this, George. One of the lads in the office had been grooming a young lad who works in Dundalk. He was only sworn into the Provos, in Kate's Pub in Dundalk, a few weeks ago. Now, our lad is on holiday, and this young lad phoned looking for him urgently. Luckily he had made arrangements with him that in his absence anything urgent was to be given to me. He phoned this morning and I met him in Ardee. He has pinpointed some stuff here in the Republic for me, and I'm meeting him in an hour, when we will continue our operation. When I was talking to him this morning he started to talk about a bomb at Forkhill, in Armagh, but thought it would be no use to me. I immediately thought of you and the story is this. The source was present when two new recruits to the Provos, just like himself, were given a bomb of about 50 lb. This was then built into the rear seat of a Mini car, and they were to drive it to the police station in Forkhill, Co. Armagh, tonight. This was to be a sort of tester for the two of them.'

'Do you know their names and any details on the car?' I enquired.

'I haven't the reg. number, but I have the make and colour, and the two names,' replied the Garda officer. 'Oh, and regarding the time tonight, it will be fairly late, more than likely a.m. even, as one of them works part-time in the Ballymascanlon Hotel. They haven't too far to travel from the hotel across to Forkhill, of course.'

I took all the details.

'Right, thanks for everything, that's one I owe you, I'd better get back to make arrangements for a reception committee, I'm glad we had made arrangements for urgent meetings.'

My friend laughed. 'I must go now myself.'

We got up and left the premises. I drove straight to Newry and had a meeting with the commander. We then had an urgent meeting with the military IO of the local unit, ensuring that the operation was mounted with source protection paramount. It had to be a chance passing patrol that found the car and the bomb, during a routine vehicle checkpoint. I had to ensure no one in the military set-up let the two men be aware that they were looking for them specifically. This was done by ensuring the IO only briefed one man in the patrol, the troop commander, and that he kept the details to himself. There was nothing more I could do and I headed home. It was past eleven o'clock. I was tired. At eight o'clock next morning, as I hadn't had any news of the outcome of the military VCP, I phoned the MIO.

'It was a blank,' he replied.

'What do you mean a blank?' I asked.

'The two names were correct, but the car was clean, and we released them.'

'You should have phoned me,' I said.

I was fuming. When I was told the car was still parked in the village, I requested the MIO to have a further examination carried out. A short time later, after a detailed search, the bomb was discovered built into the back seat of the vehicle. What more could I have done? I felt helpless. Why oh why did the military release them? The only consolation was they hadn't had time to prime the bomb, and there was no loss of life. Years later it would seem small consolation, as one of the two IRA men went on to play a leading role in the Provos. He could have been captured on one of his first jobs, if all had gone according to plan.

Chapter 18

Meeting with Source and with Garda Special Branch

I continued to travel to the Republic for meetings with McMahon, against the wishes of London, but only because McMahon demanded it. I had built up a good relationship with him. We trusted each other, and as he continued to supply high-grade intelligence, my own authorities were more than happy. I obeyed his wishes to refrain from putting some of the intelligence into report form, and went to Special Branch Headquarters and reported direct to the ACC SB verbally. He then acted as he thought fit, paying very close heed to the protection of the source. Everyone was happy with the arrangement and McMahon trusted me to hand over any very sensitive material, verbally. We were now meeting on a weekly basis almost, and I remember him requesting a meeting on a very wet day, in the autumn of 1973. We arranged to meet at meeting place D, which was a car park area in Drogheda. We could sit there in the car and talk undisturbed for hours. He wasn't in a very good mood as his stomach was giving him trouble. He kept sipping a thick white liquid from a bottle.

'The chemist made this up for me a couple of days ago but it's nearly finished,' he said.

'Do you not use Rennies?' I enquired.

'I used to use a packet a day, but they're a waste of money.'

We chatted for a while and he talked about Charlie Haughey, who had been in the news the previous day, for some reason or other.

'I don't like him, he backed out of helping when the chips were down,' he said. 'He wanted to be a hero, but hadn't the balls.'

We chatted on and it was a good ten minutes before he got to the reason for our meet.

'You're in for the long haul,' he said.

'What do you mean?' I replied.

'This will be the last campaign, this one goes on to the end, there may be tactical ceasefires from time to time, but this war goes on to the end.'

'Where did you get this from?'

'I saw a draft document yesterday, which outlines the future strategy of the movement. They will oppose Whitelaw's proposal for this Councils of Ireland idea, and will boycott the local elections. They realise the SDLP will benefit electorally, but are counting on reversing that later. Their main worries at present concern the British infiltration of the movement. McKenna, McKevitt and Keenan seem to be the main players now, after Adams and Hughes were interned, and thankfully for me, the Belfast Brigades now believe the information given to the British about the bombs in London came from a Belfast tout.'

'I'm sure you're happy with that,' I laughed.

'I sure am,' he replied. 'It's a pity Joe Cahill was arrested on the arms boat.'

'Will this knock the Provos onto the back foot?'

'I doubt it, they have opened up other routes to bring weapons in from Europe. I remember Cahill telling me a year ago that Brian Keenan had been successful in that respect. The *Claudia* capture was a big loss but it wasn't the first shipment, nor will it be the last. They managed to import a lot of stuff. It's stashed everywhere.'

He then went on to say that the main worry the PIRA command had at the moment was leaks.

'They are really worried that they are being infiltrated at a high rate. They know, or are fairly certain, that some senior members of the organisation are working for the British. David O'Connell has told the Northern command to sort themselves out. According to him, the problem lies in the Belfast Brigade. He reckons that the dialogue between those members arrested and interned in Belfast and the Special Branch was bound to spawn informants for the British. Séamus Twoomey told O'Connell that no matter what, the fight went on. They should reply to every security force success with another IRA success and that informants don't last forever, but are part and parcel of the overall campaign.'

'Are you worried about our meets?'

'No I'm not, I trust you, and by that I mean I trust you to keep to the rules when we meet. Make sure you're not followed and keep phone calls short and coded, I try and use different call-boxes each time, your lot are more than likely tapping your phone.'

'I realise that,' I replied.

'No names, no places, and from now on we will meet one hour before the time mentioned.' He went on. 'Just think, the Officials are calling off their armed struggle. If I hadn't been with the Provos I could have peace and quiet now.' He laughed.

'Why did you go with the Provisionals?' I asked him.

'I bloody didn't. No one ever asked me. It was just assumed I was switching. They just sent new lads to me for training. I think for a while a lot of the lads didn't know what they were in. There are guys sent to me from all over. They tell me their names are Seán, Séamus, Declan or whatever, and that's it. I don't ask their address, and they don't give it. If a UVF man arrived down to me for training, and said he was James from Belfast, that would be it. He would get away with it.'

I laughed.

'In fact,' he continued, 'why don't you come on a training session? No one will ask who you are.'

I laughed again. 'Now wouldn't that be something,' I said.

He went on to speak about the Official IRA. 'I knew, or suspected, the Officials would cease their military campaign after I read a secret "Policy Objectives" document issued to members of the official Sinn Féin executive some months back. In this document they talk of their aim of a Democratic Socialist Republic in which state power will be in the hands of the working class. In other words their aim is to overthrow British imperialism and capitalism in Ireland, that they must organise the people on those issues which affect them most.'

He went on to relate that the Officials believed that whilst there had been much self-sacrifice by many people in Ireland, it had been in a disjointed, conspiratorial fashion. The mass of the people must be involved to create a revolution. In the 1920s the people were faced with the Treaty soon after the Truce. When the Civil War was fought and lost due to the lack of substantive objectives and indeed leadership, the losers, who considered themselves as the republicans, looked for a scapegoat. This was easy. Blame the politicians—they had signed and adapted it. Those who had fought the British decided the armed struggle was the only way forward. They tried to make politics a dirty word.'

I interrupted him.

'Do you want an all-Ireland socialist Republic?' I asked.

'An all-Ireland, certainly, but a communist state, definitely not!'

He continued. 'In the Thirties there were people in the republican movement capable of starting a true political revolution in Ireland. Unfortunately the presence of McBride, Barry, Twoomey and Russell, all fighting men in the leadership, stifled any attempt at radical political change in the organisation. According to the document these men were sort of middle class, and Russell was a conspirator who secretly made contact with the upper tier of Fianna Fáil, and tried to use them without success. The present leadership of the Official republican movement believe that in this day and age armed struggle is futile. It turns Irishman against Irishman, and when the British eventually go from the island of Ireland, whatever system of government takes over will be troubled over a long period of time, probably generations, with mistrust between people . . . and many scars will need to be healed.'

'I have enjoyed your history lesson, are you sure you have finished?' I interrupted.

'I can go on and on if you want,' he replied.

'How do you feel about your own involvement in all this death and destruction?' I enquired.

'To be honest, at times I'm sick of it, I know you consider me to be an armchair general, but I have principles.'

'Have you ever murdered anyone?'

'No, thank God I haven't. I know you will say that I teach others to do just that. Well, I can't deny that, but I don't order them to any particular target, that's for others.'

'What do you think of the PIRA leadership?'

'Now that's a hard one, they change so often as they are jailed or interned. Some of them are bloody madmen. Can you picture one of those guys as Taoiseach of a United Ireland? I'd bloody go to Australia.'

He laughed at himself.

'Have you heard from London recently?' I enquired.

'I have actually, I phoned them last week with an address in Manchester which may be of use to them. I got it quite by chance listening to a conversation.'

'Did Hewson mention me?'

'No, he didn't, he asked me about certain people in Belfast, but I couldn't answer his questions, and told him I wasn't going to try and find the answers. It would be dangerous. The English don't really understand how things are done in Ireland, do they?'

I agreed with him.

'Are you heading home now?' he asked.

'I am,' I replied.

He instructed me to follow him to Dundalk.

'I'm going to a housing estate where I'll show you a very, very safe house. I'll bet the Dundalk Special Branch don't know of this one. It's only known to a very select few. I won't stop at the house but as I pass it, I'll hit the brake light twice. You can then carry on home.'

I thanked him, and had a laugh when I saw what he was driving— an old battered red van that looked like it had never ever been washed. I followed him without incident and was shown the house. I then headed home. I would pass the information on to the Dundalk Garda sooner rather than later; it was of no use to me.

Chapter 19
Meeting with Garvin

A s the violence increased my job became rather hectic and I didn't get much sleep. I found it increasingly difficult to switch my brain off at night and on again in the morning. It was getting difficult to keep up with the pace. Special Branch might have a mystical aura around it, like a fog, but those within knew that it was a never-ending slog to keep abreast of a situation that was really a terrorist war on innocent people. It was at its height in the mid-1970s, and as the security forces had more and more success, it caused more and more problems for Special Branch. The IRA tightened its network and created small cells of two or three volunteers. If a volunteer was caught he couldn't give much intelligence except concerning his own cell. This made it imperative that Special Branch had to work ceaselessly to obtain and cultivate new sources. What had been a low-grade source one week may progress to high-grade the following week, or vice-versa. It was a great game but a highly dangerous one.

For a source to be of real use he needed to be involved heavily in the operational end of things. This meant he was in danger from two fronts: from the security forces for his involvement, and from the IRA for touting. These men had nerves balanced on a tightrope, and they had to be handled very carefully. 'Agent provocateur' were two words that we didn't dwell on, although I always kept them in my mind, and tried to keep to the Rule of Law; this is the reason why I always took out 'insurance' against any future problems with agents provocateurs. That is, if a good PIRA source who supplied good intelligence leading to the capture of weapons and explosives on a regular basis, told me that he was part of an IRA team carrying out a robbery on a post office or a shop the next day, and that if he cried off he would stink, I would immediately send a report or phone the situation to my Special Branch ACC in Belfast, and would be guided by his advice on the matter. I would devise a plan which would force the terrorists to change their plans; for example, having a military vehicle parked at the scene of the proposed raid or a vehicle checkpoint in the area. It was a matter then of keeping fingers crossed that the source wasn't arrested. Headquarters were happy with these arrangements and thought it was a small price to pay for high-grade intelligence, the supply of which would have ended if the source had been arrested carrying out the crime. This is how things were done in the Seventies. Rules were probably being bent, but we were saving lives. There were of course particular touts to keep a wary eye on, and in these instances we might play things differently. Never ever would a source be allowed to commit murder or even withhold information on a murder. I told them in no uncertain way that they would be charged accordingly. This is how Special Branch worked. This is how I was trained. Nothing was in, nothing was out.

I arrived at the office early. I had to go to Dundalk urgently. The source had phoned late the previous night. I had to go to Castlebellingham. I lifted the phone and rang Garvin.

'Hello there,' I said. 'I have a message to Dundalk, can we meet?'

'No problem,' replied Garvin.

'I'll see you at the chip shop.'

'Right, half past one.'

I put the phone down and wrote a note to the office clerk saying I had gone to Belfast, and left the office. It was a bright day, and, having told my wife that I would be home late, I drove towards the border. I reached Castlebellingham and parked near the castle gates. The source had been working for me for over a year. He had joined the IRA because all his mates were involved or loved to think they were involved. It would be true to say the IRA never had a definitive list of members. There were probably sometimes less than two people who knew whether or not a person was a volunteer. It was all rather haphazard to say the least. If you claimed to be a volunteer, that was okay, it was accepted. At least until someone decided to check you out. I had recruited the source from a wave of arrests following a Sinn Féin parade which turned into a riot, with several vehicles and shop premises destroyed. He was twenty-four years old and from an old family in a South Down town, with large business premises. After twenty-four hours in custody, I had no difficulty in turning him to my way of thinking. Before his arrest he had begun to realise his situation, and the devastation that would be caused to his family if they knew of his involvement. He had had a bit of bravado one night in Dundalk, when some school friends who had joined the Provos persuaded him to get involved. He agreed to help me, and proved an easily obtained source. Since that date he had made contact on a regular basis. He had been registered with Special Branch Headquarters. Initially, he had given names and details of those he knew were involved in terrorist activity. Twice he had put two and two together in Dundalk, and phoned me with details of Belfast cars leaving the 'right' place in the town heading home; both cars were followed with successful results. He was in touch almost weekly with a quick phone report of the latest situation as known to him. He was dreading being handed a rifle and ordered to join others on a shooting. He had been on one rifle training exercise at a bog near Bailieborough and didn't want to go near there again. He had been really frightened by what he had seen. Being a mild-mannered lad from a middle-class home he reported being frightened by some of the ruthless men he had met at training.

I waited in the car for a while, then the passenger door opened and the source got in.

'Hi, how's things?'

'Not bad,' I replied. 'What's new?'

'Drive towards Drogheda and I'll tell you.'

I set off, but found it hard to concentrate due to heavy traffic on the main Dublin Road. I turned off the first side road and parked beside a farm gate. I got out and lifted the bonnet. We both looked at the engine and I said, 'Right, I don't like this, what have you got for me?'

'I think there's a jail break planned for Port Laoise, here in the Republic, they have a couple in there that have to get out.'

'How did you get this?'

'Keeping my ears open and meeting a Crossmaglen man who knows I'm involved.'

'What's planned?'

'Don't know except that it's soon, and they are using a helicopter, oh, and my Crossmaglen man has a friend who supplied 100 metres of heavy duty rope bought from Belfast or Bangor.'

'Is this in connection with the break?'

'Yes, this is all I know.'

'Will you get any more on it?'

'No, it was quite by chance I got it.'

'Right, I'll drop you back at the castle.'

'No, you go on, I'll dander back from here, it's only half a mile, and by the way I need £50 to pay a bill.'

I opened my wallet, and glanced at my cash. I needed some for the rest of the day! I gave him £40. 'It's all I can give you now,' I said.

The source headed up the road, and I set out for the 'chip shop', the code name for a café in Navan, Co. Meath. The café was fairly crowded when I arrived at about 1.35 p.m. Garvin was sitting at a table for two at the rear. I sat down opposite him.

'What would you like, I've ordered a pizza and coffee.'

'That would do nicely, a ham and pineapple and an espresso.'

'Did you get your job done?' asked Garvin.

'Yeah, I suppose you've guessed I was seeing someone.'

'Successful trip?' enquired Garvin.

I screwed my face. 'This visit is to your benefit,' I replied.

I went on to tell Garvin of the proposed jail break.

'It's all rather vague, no dates, no personalities,' said Garvin.

'It is,' I agreed, 'but the source is fairly high grade, and I would think the forecast event is probable more than possible.'

'Right,' said Garvin. 'I'll get moving on this right away.'

'I brought you something,' he said, handing me a list of four names. 'These four are on the continent at the moment, Holland has been mentioned, on PIRA business, probably connected with weaponry according to the source. I haven't put it into my pipeline yet so you can act as you wish. Oh, and I nearly forgot, our mutual friend has a meeting tomorrow with a friend of the Derryman, you know who, and two from Belfast, who were in Navan yesterday, so stand by for something good re: future policy.'

'Right,' I replied.

We finished our pizzas and coffees. Garvin rose first and when he went out the door, I followed suit. I was going to be home earlier than expected, and already my brain was planning a surprise Chinese meal with my wife.

Chapter 20

Ending of Customs Checks at Border Posts

Although Reginald Maudling gave the okay to Brian Faulkner on his decision to bring in internment without trial, leading to riots and death on the streets, he was very soon to call the decision a disastrous one. The Provos stepped up their campaign, while the ordinary nationalist population joined in with rent and rate strikes, and other civil disobedience. The two traditions grew further and further apart. Internment was to last until December 1975. During that period over 1,700 were killed.

In the period August–December 1971 the IRA commenced a border campaign across the Down/Armagh border area. They had no shortage of manpower, as more and more Provos went on the run to Dundalk, and joined the border active service units. They mingled with the South Armagh Brigade units initially, but later there was mistrust. The South Armagh lads didn't like Belfast men and the initial gloss in their friendship soon wore thin.

The Officials were active militarily also just after internment began, and a couple of weeks after internment day, in early September, they targeted an army patrol on the Newry-Bessbrook Road with a landmine, killing a young soldier. When I later spoke to Official republican sources in Newry they were not happy with the killing. They would have gone to any lengths to pursue their socialist agenda for a socialist Ireland, but many baulked at the killings. I believe it was at this time that the Official IRA leadership started to re-examine its agenda. They didn't want to be carried along in a Provo slipstream with the murder of Irishmen by Irishmen. They were soon to announce a ceasefire. I remember the last week in November 1971, about three months after internment. I received a phone call from a young Provo source. He was phoning from Dundalk.

'There's something going on, I can't put my finger on it but something's fishy.'

'Do you want to meet me?' I enquired.

'No way, I'm not going up near that border today.'

'Why do you say that?' I enquired.

'I was looking for a lift into Dundalk this morning. I had walked across at Killeen and was hitching a lift. As I passed the car park of the Border Inn I saw a guy from Forkhill. I can't remember his name, it might be Michael. He was standing with three strangers beside an old Cortina. Now this lad knows I'm involved and I know he's involved. We drink in the same Dundalk pub. We have spoken on a couple of occasions. I started to cross the road towards them. "If you're going to Dundalk, any chance of a lift?" I called. For a minute no one spoke, and then one of the strangers said, "Fuck off." He was an unshaven, evil-looking bastard. The Forkhill lad dropped his head and looked at the ground, so I knew these fuckers were IRA. I knew not to get involved so I continued towards Dundalk hitching. I was so scared I didn't even think of taking the registration of the car.'

I interrupted him.

'What are you trying to tell me?'

'I'm fucking telling you something's going on up there at the border crossing.'

'Right, okay, I'll see you.'

I replaced the receiver and told a colleague about my telephone call. We decided to go down to Killeen and have a look for anything suspicious. A stupid thing to do and something I certainly wouldn't do in later years. We drove to Killeen, stopped for five minutes and turned back just before reaching the Northern customs post. We saw nothing, except an army Land Rover parked 400 yards north of the border. We headed towards Newry and had gone about half a mile when an explosion rattled the vehicle. The customs post had been blown up. We turned around, heading south again. Traffic was building up in the aftermath of the explosion, and when we reached the customs post debris lay where a building had been. The military vehicle had moved north a couple of hundred yards and was carrying out a vehicle stop check on vehicles coming from the scene. On ascertaining there were no casualties we headed back to base. Other uniform police were arriving at the scene to carry out their investigation. A couple of hours later two customs officers who were operating from the only part of the customs post left standing were shot dead by the IRA, who had returned to the scene. It was later ascertained that the IRA unit had fired on the men from County Louth, about 100 yards south of the actual border. The distance between the two customs posts on the main road was about 400 metres. This was known to the security forces on both sides of the border as no man's land. This marked the end of the customs posts on the Northern side of the border. They were never re-established, probably because they were indefensible, and it was about this time that the military set down rules to ensure no military vehicle went within 500 metres of the land boundary, obviously to avoid easy ambushes by the IRA. The source was right in thinking that an IRA operation was imminent that day. Two poor souls were executed at somebody's whim. The men were unarmed and I believe both had been customs officers for many years.

———

I remember another incident a couple of weeks after internment came into force. I had been down to Crossmaglen with the MIO. This was a time when one could drive around the area covertly checking on addresses of people who had been mentioned in various ways as being members of, or associating with the IRA. Within a few short months this type of work would be very difficult and, as for the military, only armoured vehicles would travel in and out of Crossmaglen. Within a year, even armoured vehicles would suffer death and destruction, and it became a helicopter only base. However, the MIO asked me to go with him to visit an elderly farmer who had been more than friendly towards a military patrol who had crossed a field adjacent to his house. His tractor wouldn't start, and six soldiers were able to push it up an incline to fire the engine. The house was only about half a mile from the border, and the old man told them he had seen men wearing balaclavas outside the house one night late. He asked them what they were doing. They were carrying rifles, and one of them called out his name and told him they were the IRA. They then ordered him to go to bed, and keep his mouth shut. We spoke to him for a while, but there was no way he would pass any information to us.

'I've never had a phone. I don't agree with killing. The British shouldn't be here, and these other idiots here shouldn't be shooting at people. I'm not afraid of them, but I won't inform on them.'

He offered us tea, but we declined and said our goodbyes. We made our way to Crossmaglen police station, which was now also a military base. The MIO had a general conversation with the military officer in charge and soon learned that two military semi-armoured vehicles had apparently inadvertently crossed the border a couple of hundred metres into the Republic. When they realised their mistake and tried to re-cross back into Armagh, a vehicle was parked across the road blocking their route. We listened to other military being sent to the scene. A crowd was apparently gathering and attacking the vehicles. It was no place for us, but we sat for a while listening to the radio transmissions. Military reinforcements were instructed not to cross the border under any circumstances to assist the trapped vehicles. About an hour after we had first heard of the event we heard the Gardaí and Irish Army were at the scene. I thought that would be the matter sorted, but apparently not, as according to transmissions they were doing very little. The crowd had grown. One vehicle was set on fire by this mob. The soldiers made it into the second vehicle. Then armed men arrived on the scene and opened fire. A soldier was fatally injured as the surviving vehicle made it back over the border. The next morning the soldiers involved complained that the Irish Army had stood by doing nothing when the shooting started. They reported being frightened of the hostile crowd more than the armed men.

'They were after our blood, and I know they would have killed us with their bare hands if they had got us. At least we could return fire on the IRA snipers, but you can't fire on a mob of people, can you?'

The next day I arranged a meeting with Special Branch, Co. Louth. We went over the events surrounding the incident.

The Special Branch officer said, 'I can't speak for the Irish Army, but I know of a disgusted uniform guard who was kept awaiting instructions which never came. It could have been handled much better than it was. It's a pity the soldier lost his life, I would hate to think it could have been avoided.'

Internment certainly wasn't working and when Direct Rule was imposed in early 1972, a PIRA source informed me that Cahill was quoted as ordering the Belfast Brigades to up the ante.

'The cracks are showing, we need pressure, pressure, pressure.'

This is just what happened; 1972 was probably the bloodiest of all. The Provos did indeed up the ante, although their success was tempered by some good security force actions against them, and later in 1972 when 'No Jury' trials were proposed it was a severe blow to the Provisionals. My own job became harder and harder, as new faces kept appearing in the ranks of the Provos. The government were crying out for intelligence. The violence must be kept at an acceptable level. I never really knew what this meant. It was no surprise to me when a Provo source in Dundalk told me that the British government wanted ceasefire talks. He took great delight in telling me they had won the war, that Mac Stíofáin and his Army Council were going to London.

When I phoned head of Special Branch, he said, 'Right you've told me, forget about it.'

That's when I felt small and inadequate. Nothing is ever as it seems.

Chapter 21
Enoch Powell

The first time I met Enoch Powell was at a hotel in Kilkeel, Co. Down, in the early Seventies. He was having a working lunch with some of his election agents. The person who introduced us wrongfully thought I was there as security for the meeting. He thanked me for coming and said he understood they were difficult times for the police. The second time I saw him in the flesh was when I entered a restaurant with a colleague in Hillsborough a few weeks later. He was sitting at a table with four or five others. Our eyes met as I passed him. He made no recognition signal. I sat down and thought, typical politician—he doesn't remember me. We had our meal. Powell and his party left shortly before us, and again no recognition as he left. When I went to settle the bill, however, my inner thoughts went into reverse gear.

'Your bill has been taken care of, sir,' said the waitress.

I realised then that Powell was a very astute man indeed.

The third time was when I received a call from a uniform police officer who had a relative working as one of Powell's election officers. I knew this officer a long time, and trusted him. He wanted me to agree to call with Powell at his house which was only a half hour drive from my own. We fixed a time and date, and I duly arrived at the appointment. He opened the door himself and showed me in. I remember there were dozens of heavy books on the table, each with a piece of white paper jutting out acting as bookmarks. He came straight to the point.

'I didn't know you were a Special Branch detective until after I saw you in the Hillsborough restaurant. One of the party knew of you.'

I smiled at him.

He went on. 'I am being bombarded with certain rumours that concern someone who assists me in my constituency, I could go to higher places but that would inevitably expose one of my staff so I have chosen a different course.'

He outlined the rumour in detail, and then he said, 'I will accept a yes or no answer if you wish.'

'That would suit me,' I replied. 'The answer is no.'

The rumour, of which I was aware, concerned a different individual. He thanked me and offered me a brandy, which I declined.

'You do a dangerous job,' he said.

'At times,' I replied. I asked him what he thought of the situation at present.

He said, 'I can see no quick fix to the present troubles here, the sides are too polarised, and you can't impose the will of a minority on a majority. Now if the IRA had a political machine or party, a fact which they will realise sooner or later, things might change. Their aim, we are told, is a 32-county socialist Republic, so they will have to organise politically North and South, but if they try to mix force with their politics then the two governments must enforce the law with great determination.'

He went on to say that the PIRA hierarchy were a rum lot, like gangsters out of a Twenties movie, and that the only one with intelligence and sensibility appeared to be David O'Connell. He got up and thanked me for coming. As we walked to the door he said a few sentences in a foreign language. I smiled and asked what he had said.

'It's ancient Greek, and translates "We are all actors in a daily play titled *History*."'

He went on. 'In ancient times you would be a soothsayer, or work for one. They always liked to forecast events, and to be proved correct for their masters. They employed a huge army of secret spies to do this.'

I laughed. 'If only.'

I only saw him in the flesh a couple of times after that and, just as in the Hillsborough restaurant, there was no recognition shown.

Chapter 22

Michael McVerry

Is it wrong for a soldier brave and true to see a mirror of himself in his enemy? When a British soldier talks of fighting for Queen and Country, does an Irish soldier fight for President and Country? What do we do when one set of people, namely the IRA, self-styling themselves as the true Irish Army, come up against the other legal Irish Army? A true citizen in Dublin or Cork would support the legal version as demanded by Dáil Éireann, but they also have a soft spot and admiration for the illegal version, as after all they state they are fighting British rule in a part of the island of Ireland. Did all justification for these actions end when the British government made clear they would end their presence when the majority decided on this course? They also have an admiration for heroes, and for those who die for Ireland, whether it be in the Congo or in a grassy field in South Armagh. There are names which linger on in the memory, people who are a bit different than the others, people who you have a sneaking admiration for, and you really wish that they had met a better fate.

I have interviewed many so-called terrorists, of many hues and colours, and I have watched the actions of many at first-hand. One name that stands out is that of Michael McVerry from Cullyhanna. He first came to our notice in the summer of 1971, when we were building a picture of the IRA in South Down/South Armagh. The bits and pieces of intelligence on him grew lengthier. IRA sources in neighbouring units would describe him in terms ranging from ruthless to a likeable rogue. I remember well the day I was introduced to him for many reasons. My PIRA source, McMahon, had phoned late the previous night wanting me to call at his house. I told him I wasn't keen on this, but he was adamant. He had already met my wife when I brought her, as I occasionally did, to a meeting with him in Ardee. A man and woman in a car look less suspicious.

'If you're worried, why don't you bring that good-looking wife with you?' he said.

I agreed to do this, and to decrease my trips across the border, I always tried to kill two birds with one stone. I phoned my Garda colleague source in Dundalk.

'Anything new?' I enquired.

'Aye, I've a few bits and pieces, do you want a meeting?'

I arranged to meet him a couple of hours before my meeting with McMahon. My wife could pass an hour going round the shops in Dundalk.

Before going home to pick up my wife, I drove into Newry. It was my intention to buy a pair of winter shoes at a shop on Hill Street, the main shopping area. There were quite a few shoppers about and I saw what appeared to be an American tourist, complete with lumberjack's tartan jacket and a cowboy hat. He had a large camera hanging from his neck, which he lifted now and then to take a photo. As I passed him at the entrance to the shop he appeared to purposely bump into me.

'Sorry,' I said.

'You bloody should be,' he drawled.

He lifted his head and I saw it was Robert Nairac. He smiled and walked on past me. I hadn't a chance to ask him what the hell he was doing there. I was in the shop about ten minutes and when I came back onto the street, Robert was about 50 yards away, still taking photographs. I wondered what the hell he was doing and had he cleared it with the local Special Branch.

I put it out of my mind and headed home, to have lunch and inform my wife she was going on a trip with me to the Republic.

We set off shortly before two o'clock and arrived in Dundalk. We went through the now permanent vehicle checkpoint entering the town. I dropped my wife off to window shop and went to meet my Garda friend. I wanted to hear the latest on the Provos around the Dundalk area and he wanted to talk about possible loyalist paramilitary incursions into the Republic. I explained again to him that I had no loyalist paramilitary activity in my area and anything I gave him would be of a general nature. We talked, I believe, about the Sunningdale Agreement, and shared our views on it. I remember he told me of a pub that the guards in Dundalk had used for years to socialise in. The owner had politely told them not to frequent the premises in future. The owner had apparently been ordered to this course of action by the Provisionals. He was very annoyed at this state of affairs.

'Can you believe it, we asked him to name who had threatened him, but we knew what his answer would be before we asked.'

'I would say you'll be carrying out covert observations of the premises,' I laughed.

'Too bloody right!' he replied.

I believe he also mentioned that day that the uniform guards in Dundalk had been instructed to cooperate fully with their Newry RUC counterparts in any urgent matters involving the border crossing at Killeen. I was pleased to hear that cooperation between the two police forces was growing. After a good productive meeting we parted, and I went to an arranged spot in the town to pick up my wife. We continued our journey through Ardee, and arrived at the house of McMahon without incident. Then my heart sank. As I stopped at the gate I saw McMahon talking to two men at the door of the house. They had all seen me so I couldn't drive on. I got out of the car, whispering to Eileen to come with me. We had to brazen it out.

As we walked up the path McMahon called out, 'Ah, Seán and Eileen, come on in, what kept you, I thought you were coming this morning.'

'Bloody roadblocks and traffic,' I replied.

McMahon turned to the two men. 'This is one of my cousins from Belfast.'

One of them smiled and said, 'You brought good weather with you.'

I looked at him and the recognition penny dropped. It was Michael McVerry, from Cullyhanna, arguably the probable OC of the South Armagh ASU which had been waging death and destruction on the security forces for nigh on two years.

'I can't shake your hand,' he said, holding up his right arm.

I could see the hand was covered with a woollen mitt.

'What happened you?' I asked, already knowing the answer.

'Oh, I put it where I shouldn't,' he replied.

McMahon put his arm around Eileen, 'Go on you two in, I'll be in shortly.'

He turned back to the two men, and my wife and I went into the house. After a couple of minutes the men left and McMahon came into the house.

'For God's sake, we'll never get fucking home.'

'You're okay, you're okay,' he repeated. 'If he suspects anything, then he's a good actor. You recognised him fairly quickly then?'

'I bloody did, didn't you point him out to me working at a wall along the road about a month ago.'

'I'd forgot about that, that's one of his safe houses.'

'Look, when you went into the house I whispered to him that you did courier to Belfast for me. He then was anxious to talk to you. I explained you weren't involved on the military side. He accepted that.'

'I hope to God he did, and he's not waiting on the road home.'

'He won't. He'll be here till bedtime, I have a couple of pistols coming up from Drogheda for him. He's got paranoid about his own safety.'

'Who is the guy with him?'

'I think he's also Michael, and I think he's from Lisburn or Lurgan. He's always with him, and you know I can't ask, it's something you don't do. You just listen and pick up the clues.'

'What was he saying?' I asked.

'Oh, he's on about the Belfast boys running about bombing businesses and stupid targets. He says he told Brian Keenan as much, and told him to get their arses down to South Armagh and help take on the British Army on the ground face to face like proper soldiers. He's saying Twoomey sent him a message he was doing a great job, to ask for any weaponry he needed.'

'Why ask you for pistols?' I asked.

'He wants small .22 calibre pistols that fit into the palm of your hand, and I know where I can get a couple of such weapons. In America they call them "Ladies' Guns", as they fit into a purse. They are being brought to me tonight and McVerry is waiting for them.'

'When you pointed McVerry out to me a few weeks back you said you hardly knew him.'

'I don't really. He's only been coming to the safe house this summer, and I knew when he waved at me on the first day I saw him that he had been briefed on who I was and the role I performed. We don't tell each other of our role, with one exception, and that is if we are on active service together.'

'He didn't tell you what his next job in South Armagh was?' I laughed.

He laughed at that question. 'I would say his own mother wouldn't know.'

'Right, what's the reason for wanting to see me?' I asked.

McMahon didn't answer. Instead he turned to Eileen. 'You must have infinite patience with this man.'

She had been reading a paper. 'Oh, he's not so bad,' she replied. 'I don't know what you pair are talking about and I don't want to. I'll just read the paper.'

Mahon got down to business—'There's turmoil in the Belfast Brigade, since Adams was arrested last month. Not only Adams, but they lost half of their senior GHQ staff. I hear Ivor Bell and Brian Keenan are now the main men. A lot of communication lines have been cut. It'll take months to get the show on the road again. There are those in Dublin who would talk to the Brits again, with a different negotiation team.'

He went on to say he didn't like Keenan. 'I've only met him a couple of times. He has an overbearing personality. He looks down on you.'

He warned me that the Provos were very worried about leaks. 'They imagine that any volunteer seen talking to a stranger is a tout. It's dangerous stuff. I've no doubt innocent men will be executed.'

'Anything else?' I enquired.

'There is. The word is that a new RPG (rocket-propelled grenade) is being developed and tested in Donegal. The range is short but it produces a massive explosion.'

'Have you anything more on it?'

'No, but unless talk of its size is exaggerated, they'll need a bloody tank to carry it. If I get anything else I'll let you know. There's always talk of new weapons, and how great everything will be, but most of it is wishful thinking.'

We had been in the house about an hour, and when I got up to go I enquired, 'I wonder where McVerry is?'

'He'll be standing up the road,' he replied.

And when we left the house, sure enough there he was, standing at the gate of the neighbour's house, only this time there were three others with him. Was he watching me, I wondered? As we drove past him he waved. We both waved back. I felt better.

'Who is that lad?' my wife asked.

'A Provo,' I replied.

A few months later Michael McVerry died from wounds sustained during an IRA attack on Newtownhamilton police/army base. A monument erected in his memory near Cullyhanna speaks of Captain Michael McVerry. I have no doubt he rose quickly through IRA ranks. He died bravely doing what he believed was his duty, but was he really fighting for his country? The legitimate government in Dublin, of that country, would reply in the negative!

Chapter 23
Further Meet of Triangle

I remember a meeting of the triangle in the autumn of 1975. Garvin and I had discussed colour television sets and compared the cost North and South of the border. He had mentioned the name of a set manufactured in Sweden—I can't remember it now—but I could buy one in the North for 40 per cent less than he could in the Republic. I agreed to get him one, and headed south with the purchase to a rendezvous near Drogheda. We met up in the car park of a hostelry as arranged and I was pleasantly surprised to see McMahon sitting in the car with him. Garvin led us in through the back door of the premises and to a small private room, where the table had been set for lunch.

'Don't worry about anything. These people are sound, we're completely safe here,' said Garvin.

I asked McMahon how things were going, and had he anything of interest for me. I remember him telling me of friction between Provo groupings in Belfast and a power struggle, and I remember Garvin laughing.

'Listen, you are, not you personally, but the IRA are the greatest bloody rag-time outfit ever.'

'What do you mean?' asked McMahon.

'I mean the whole set-up of the Provos.'

'How?' enquired McMahon, looking around.

'Well, first of all your so-called Army Council, with its grand name, is feckin' useless.'

He went on. 'These feckin' so-called leaders are only good for two reasons, to bring weapons in and to administer discipline. They don't issue orders on campaign direction or what targets to hit like a real army would. It's a target at will situation for each and every unit. If a job goes right, the Army Council take the credit. If it goes wrong then they didn't authorise it. No wonder when they offered themselves to the Germans at the start of World War II, they were soon regarded as an amateur bunch of greenhorns, and the short liaison ended as quickly as it started.'

I remember McMahon looking sort of annoyed and arguing with Garvin on the point he had made about the Germans.

'I'll tell you more,' said Garvin, winking at me. 'The Army Council do most of their business in retrospect. The real leaders out there, and there are one or two I suppose, are the young guns who take on the Brits at the border areas, or in difficult circumstances. Each Brigade area spawns at least one ruthless individual who dictates targets at will in his own domain. The feckin' Army Council know nothing of it until it happens. I'll tell you more. Some areas don't even know who is in charge. Take yourself, you train people in weaponry, they arrive to you, do their stuff and go home. At times you don't even know who they are, or where they come from. They could be anybody.'

McMahon laughed. 'That's the way it has to be,' he replied.

'Why, who taught you to play it like that?'

'No one, it's just done that way.'

'That is proving my point. There's no order or discipline. There is no great mastermind controlling things from Council level. I spoke to a source recently as to why PIRA were murdering Protestant farmers who had farms across the line of the border, in Tyrone, Armagh and Fermanagh. Were you ordered to do ethnic cleansing? No, he explained, there was just a general word out to target farmers who had joined the UDR or the RUC reserve. The ones who lived at the border were easier to hit, and we had an easier escape back to the South.'

I joined in the conversation. 'I once spoke to a volunteer, who had never been sworn in and had never joined the IRA with any official person. He just went with a mate on a couple of jobs. The first one was a hijacking and the second was firing a couple of shots at an army patrol. What I would like to know is this. If he had been shot dead would the movement have claimed him as a member?'

McMahon answered. 'I think they would leave it up to the family. If they didn't want any republican trappings at the funeral, then they would adhere to their wishes.'

'Come on, George,' said Garvin. 'You've talked to and interviewed a lot of these young so-called Provos. Do they seem to you as disjointed and rag-time?'

I laughed to McMahon. 'I'm afraid I have to agree. They can't maintain the thrust they had in '71, '72 and even '73. I think personally a lot of this is due to bad management, which in turn has led to security force successes. They have no training in many areas. I mean, by now you would have thought they would be trained in anti-interrogation methods, but this is not so.'

'Do you believe that the initial recruitment surge to the IRA after internment has waned? Have they problems in that respect?'

'I believe they have,' I replied.

'They also know they have been heavily infiltrated. It has got to the point where new recruits, who haven't had time to become tainted, are trusted more than some senior ranks.'

McMahon interrupted me. 'You can say all you like, but the systems being perfected within the active service units make it very hard to pick up any prior intelligence regarding IRA operations. You have a cell of four or five. One, the leader, decides on a target, and the others may not know what the job is, or where they're going, until they set out on the job. It's easier to hear who was involved after the event, there are sometimes nods and winks, but that's not what you guys want, you want to know before the event. I mean, I can sometimes by paying attention to movements of people, and other pointers, make a good guess that something is being planned, but I won't know where or when.'

Garvin then started to speak of loyalist paramilitaries and the threat they posed with possible further incursions into the Republic. He knew I had no UVF/UDA in my border area.

'Dublin is screaming out for any intelligence. Having said that, I believe there is communication starting now between Belfast and Dublin, but I feckin' know Dublin will only give what suits them. I know from the Branch meetings I attend, and if they knew I was talking to you I'd be sacked on the spot. The thing that worries them is that many UDR soldiers are believed to be active with the paramilitaries. We read of this regularly in the press. Is it as bad as it seems?'

'It probably is,' I replied. 'We vet all applications to join the UDR and police reserve, but except if I can make a good case otherwise, then they'll accept them if they fit in all the other criteria. If I point out an applicant has a brother or cousin involved with the UDA or UVF, they'll say, well he can't be his brother's keeper, that the vetting refers to him, not his brother. This is, of course, because they badly need to keep up recruitment.'

Garvin laughed at this. 'It's the feckin' same down here. If I point out that an applicant to the Gardaí is from an old IRA family, and has republican views, then believe it or not, they seem to have a better chance of reaching Templemore.'

McMahon, who had sat quietly for a few minutes, laughed and said, 'Sure we have sleepers in every organisation.'

We all had a laugh at this, and had a bit of banter.

Then McMahon continued, 'Look I've told you both already. This is the last IRA campaign, this one goes on until they achieve their objectives, and I quote Joe Cahill when I say that once the nationalist population in Ulster and indeed on the whole island of Ireland realise this, then their support won't only come from the lower working class, but from the middle class and professional people. Cahill believes that Sinn Féin will become a dominant party, even in the twenty-six counties. Cahill also told me they need cash and sympathy in equal doses, and that they would concentrate on the United States of America. He thinks that this is where the secret to success lies. They must organise groups there to maximise propaganda against British occupation in Ireland, and more importantly to collect money.'

'What do you feel yourself about things at present?' interrupted Garvin.

'Well, I talk to a good cross-section of all ranks in the IRA and I get the feeling they are in for the long haul. They are still recruiting heavily.'

'Do they not worry about this rise in loyalist paramilitary activity recently?' asked Garvin.

'Well, the one aspect that really worries them is associations being developed between the RUC and loyalists. They think they are becoming part of the same sword.'

'What about their attitude to the Garda Síochána?' asked Garvin.

'The guards are to be left alone. This is in general orders to all volunteers. The exception is where an operation looks like being compromised by the presence of a Garda. They are to be given fair warning that their presence is not wanted, and force should only be used against them as a last resort.'

'Surely that's a licence to kill,' I interrupted.

'If they shoot a guard, their support in the South will drop like a lead balloon,' said Garvin.

'It would certainly make it harder for those guards in the force who turn a blind eye to their activities,' I said.

'Look,' said McMahon, 'I have spoken to Séamus Twoomey and Billy McKee on this and they told me to ensure the Gardaí were left alone. During the recent ceasefire I spoke to many members of the Belfast Brigades who came down for a few days' break. They were told to steer clear of the Gardaí.'

'Is the Army Council still engaged in talks with London?' I enquired.

McMahon laughed at this. 'Sure you should know more about that than I do.'

'No, I don't really. One hears little whispers now and again. Military Intelligence seem to know more about it than Special Branch, which I suppose is understandable. I hear a lot, in Special Branch circles, that it is generally perceived that security force success made them call a ceasefire to regroup, but I'm not so sure,' I replied.

'Well, I'm told the talks are continuing at whatever level, and that it's causing a big split in the movement. The guys in the jails in Belfast are totally against it, and there are some senior men in there like Bell and Adams. I don't know how O'Connell and Brady are on the issue, but I suppose as they are the only Southerners left on the Army Council, what they think is probably immaterial.'

'Do you think the talks should continue?' asked Garvin.

'I do, I do, I would love to see an outcome, but I fear the hawks will win the argument, and the increase in activity by the loyalists in the murder of Catholics certainly isn't helping. At the moment there are too many chiefs and too few Indians. Someone will emerge as a leader and bring it all together.'

Garvin then asked McMahon to draw up an up-to-date list of all those he knew of who were involved in the Louth/South Armagh area. 'The uniform lads are having a hard time up there with these bastards, and it would certainly help if they knew the people to watch for.'

McMahon promised to do this.

'I'll have a copy too,' I suggested.

He laughed.

'Anything more on London?' I asked.

'No, nothing. I've told Hewson that the last I heard they are going to build an active service unit in London. This is to enable them to melt away rapidly after they attack. They'll have a few safe houses to go to. I've told him that unless I'm lucky I won't be able to forewarn him of any of their plans. He's crying out for names but I can't help him at present.'

'You mentioned Brady and O'Connell, just what are they up to now?' said Garvin.

'Well, I spoke to an old associate of the late Jack McCabe from Dublin, a couple of weeks ago. I met him accidentally in Drogheda. We had a good chat. According to him David O'Connell is pissed off the way things are going. He thinks the IRA are a Northern organisation now. He feels like surplus baggage, very disillusioned. I can't tell you anything about Brady. I also learned that O'Connell thinks the British are either up for a deal on Ulster or they're casting a long line. He's also unhappy about the ceasefire, and thinks we should be building up for a couple of spectaculars which would make the Brits focus on the situation more clearly.'

At that moment our conversation was interrupted by the owner entering and motioning to Garvin, who went over to him. They spoke in low tones but I heard him say, 'There's two guards just arrived in the bar.'

'In uniform?' enquired Garvin.

'No, they're in plain clothes, but I know them, and they are uniform lads. They must be off-duty.'

'Are they ordering food?'

'They have.'

'Well, let me know when they start to eat.'

He turned to me. 'Right, I think we'll call it a day. The craic's been good. Once the lads start to eat I'll leave with Séamus. Give us five minutes start, and then leave yourself. Are you okay about this?'

We shook hands, and I then remembered about the TV in the boot.

'Ah shit, we'll all go together,' he laughed.

A few minutes later the owner gave Garvin the nod and we went to the car park, transferred the TV to Garvin's car boot, and away they went. It had been an interesting meeting. I headed home fairly happy. I would go to Belfast the next day and report verbally to my colleague in charge of the Republican Desk at Special Branch Headquarters, who would disseminate it as he thought fit.

Chapter 24
Too Many Cooks

Regarding the infiltration of the IRA, my input into intelligence-gathering was more or less confined to sources in my own area about my own area, with the exception of McMahon and my Garda sources. On occasions I did receive intelligence on the campaign and I did realise that there were many others in Special Branch and Military Intelligence who, unknown to me, were doing exactly the same. Only the senior desk officer at Special Branch Headquarters receiving all the material could envisage a broad picture of IRA activity Province-wide. The thing that did worry me was that covert operators like the SAS, MRF, and indeed MI5 were acting on this intelligence and operating on the wrong side of the legal/illegal line, and that such operations were being carried out daily in my own area without my knowledge. If the senior Special Branch officer in my area knew anything about them, then he was a good liar. I realised later with hindsight that I was probably being a trifle naive in these matters, especially when I relate what happened to a young source.

I well remember a Saturday night in the spring of 1972 around 11 p.m. when I received an urgent call from a young PIRA volunteer. He sounded distressed. The IRA campaign was reaching new levels of death and destruction. We had made some arrests of suspected IRA in the Newry/Bessbrook area, and out of this I had recruited this young volunteer. His parents were in business and I couldn't understand him getting involved. I put this to him.

'Jesus, I just had to. A couple of my old school mates joined and hinted a few times, especially after internment, that I should go in with them. They took me to a guy, Liam Fegan, at Ravensdale. He talked to me for half an hour about my family and then he swore me in. I was shitting myself. He told me I would receive training and in the meantime to take any orders from my mate who brought me down. He said my OC at Newry would contact me in due course. I was really worried about my father. If he knew he would send me away to Australia or somewhere.'

When he had agreed to help me, on his release he kept to the arrangements for contact. Our first meeting was in Banbridge at his suggestion. He thought there wouldn't be any Provos there to see him. I had met him three or four times since and he showed good potential. On each occasion he gave me names of people he had seen in Dundalk with his mates, and people he had seen on a further visit to Liam Fegan's. His potential was looking good, and each time a £20 note brought a hearty thanks.

'I need to see you, I need to see you, I'm getting out.'

'Getting out of what?' I asked.

'Out of the IRA and out of working for you.'

I arranged to see him at a pre-arranged spot on the Rathfriland Road on the outskirts of Newry. He was there when I arrived and he jumped into the car.

'What the hell is wrong with you?' I asked.

'What's fuckin' right with me. You told me you would look after me if I had any trouble from the soldiers, isn't that right?'

'That's right, what's up?'

'I'll start at the beginning. What a fuckin' day!'

'What happened?'

'Well it's Saturday, so we've got into the habit of going to Dundalk on Saturday afternoons for a pint and to see what the craic is. A man in Mulligan's Pub told us to report to Liam Fegan's at Ravensdale. It must have been about three o'clock. We headed out in the mate's motor to Ravensdale and as we approached the house there was a Garda car on the road which stopped us. We could see another cop car nearer the house. The guard asked us where we were going. My mate said we were just out for a drive. "You're going to Fegan's, aren't you?" he said. My mate the driver denied this. I suppose there was fuck all else he could do. "You're telling lies, your vehicle has been at Fegan's before, hasn't it?"

'My mate denied this but the guard ordered him to park on the verge slightly and not obstruct the road. Other guards came walking from Fegan's. They got us out of the car and searched us. After noting our names and addresses, one of them said, "Right, get in the back of the police car."

'As we climbed in I could see two other men in the back of the other police car. What the fuck is going on, I thought. Did we just appear at the wrong time, or were they expecting us? Has something happened, have they found any weapons or explosives? On the way to Dundalk Garda Station my mate started to talk to me. He was immediately silenced. "No talking."

'My mate looked at me and drew his finger across his lips like a zip. When we got to the station we were split up and I was taken to a room and left on my own. About five minutes later two guards came in and sat down.'

'Were they in uniform?' I asked.

'No, they were detectives.'

'What did they say to you?'

'They told me I was in the IRA, and if I didn't answer all their questions truthfully I would be charged with IRA membership. They kept telling me I was a known IRA volunteer. I doubted this, I hadn't been in long enough or did they have a tout who told them about me when I joined? I decided I would answer their questions, and kept saying that I had only went to Dundalk for a pint with a mate, and that I didn't know Fegan's, that I was only a passenger in the car. If my mate knew Fegan I certainly didn't, I said.'

He went on to say that after half an hour they got up and left the room and that after five minutes the younger one returned with two plastic cups of coffee.

'He asked me if I was nervous. I told him I was surely. "Look, let's cut the crap. You know that I know you are involved with the Provos. I have ways of knowing," he said. I shook my head in disagreement and wondered was it time to refuse to answer any further questions. He continued about my involvement for a while. "Right, you say you're not involved. Let's imagine this is true. We know your friend is certainly involved. Do you agree with all this killing going on?" I replied that I didn't. "Do you support this killing in the search for a United Ireland?" he asked. "I believe in a United Ireland," I replied. "So do I," he replied, "but not in this way." He went on about serving the state and how they had to stand against anyone who committed serious crime. Then he popped the question.'

'What question?' I asked, already almost sure of the answer.

'Would you help us out with information to stop this murdering? Would you call us if you hear anything?'

'I'm dying to know what you replied,' I said.

'I just told him that I wasn't going to be a tout. Then he says that if I changed my mind to phone Dundalk Garda Station.'

'What did he look like?' I asked.

When he gave me the description I knew exactly who it was.

'What happened then?'

'He escorted me to the front door and told me I was free to go. When I asked about my mate they told me to go home, that he was still being questioned. I legged it into town and hitched a lift back to Newry.'

'Jesus,' I said, 'when you phoned me I thought something was wrong, seriously wrong.'

'It fuckin' well is, you haven't heard all the story yet. I've told you the easy bit about the guards.'

'You mean there's more?'

'Fuckin' right.'

I was intrigued. 'What happened then?'

'Well it was about seven o'clock when I got home. My father asked me where I had been. We usually eat at 6.30 p.m. each evening. I told him I was in Dundalk. He doesn't like me going there. I told the truth in case someone had already told someone in my family that I had been seen in Dundalk. When I had my dinner I thought of going out for a pint to calm my nerves after the happenings of the day, and to have a smoke. My parents abhorred smoking. So far I have been able to hide it from them. By ten o'clock I was dying for a fag. I said I was going to see a mate who lived nearby. I was also dying to hear what had happened to my other friend at Dundalk Garda Station. My mate's house was in darkness, and I wasn't in the mood to go looking for him in the pub, so I headed home again. I lit a fag and headed round the house to finish it in the back garden. I had both front and back door keys. It was dark, the venetian blind stopped any real light shining on the patio. Just as I was about to stub out the cigarette I was grabbed from behind. A gloved hand was clasped over my mouth. I felt that at least two men were holding me. I could smell leather and rubber. An English voice whispered in my ear. "There's a gun against your neck. If you understand nod your head."

'I fuckin' nodded I can tell you. Then the voice says, "I'm taking my hand from your mouth, if you make a noise you are dead, do you understand?"

'I fuckin' nodded my head off I can tell you.'

'What happened then?' I asked anxiously.

'They frog-marched me down to the back of the garden, where it was really dark, I could hardly make them out. I think there were four of them. I could only see white eyes briefly. Their faces were definitely black or maybe they wore hoods. I was told to look at the ground, again by an English voice. I could feel the barrel of the gun on my neck. I have never been so frightened in my life. It got worse when the English voice whispered in my ear, "We are going to ask you some questions to which we already know the answers. Do you understand?"

'At that moment my heart stopped. My mother had opened the back door to go to the bin. She went straight back into the house, banging the door. The voice said, "I see you are a smart young man, one shout and you were dead. Right, we'll start with the first question." "Who are you?" I asked.

'The next second I got a whack on the head from something, something heavy. I guessed it was a gun. "We ask the questions," whispered the voice. "Your first question is, are you a member of the IRA?"

'I didn't answer. The voice again whispered, "If you don't co-operate you will be taken to Newry canal and executed tonight, do you understand?" "I am in the IRA," I said. "When did you join?" asked the voice.

'I made up my mind there and then to tell the truth. I said that I had only joined a few weeks before and that I was an agent for Special Branch. At this two of them moved away and began whispering. I couldn't make them out. The voice then said, "What is the name of your Special Branch officer?"

'I gave them your name, and they whispered to each other. Then the voice said, "Lie on the ground and don't move."

'I did as he asked and then they whispered a while, and then there was silence. After a few minutes I realised they were gone.'

'What did you do then?' I asked.

'I lit a fag and headed straight for a phone box and called you. I was fuckin' trembling. Now you tell me what the fuck is going on?'

'I don't honestly know,' I replied. I was dumbfounded by the whole story.

'If you don't fuckin' know then it seems very strange to me. You promised you would look after me and keep me covered. I promised you that I would be truthful to you, and withhold nothing from you no matter how trivial it appeared. That was the deal. You have not kept your end of the deal. You don't fuckin' know what is going on in your own area.'

He put his hand on the back of his head—it was covered in thick blood.

'Let me look at that,' I said.

He bent his head. I parted the hair and saw a gaping wound about an inch long.

'That needs stitching,' I said.

'Drop me at Daisy Hill Hospital,' he replied.

I started the car. 'Look, I'll look into this for you, I'll meet you here, same place, same time, on Monday night.'

He was silent as we headed for the hospital, and as he got out of the car he said, 'I want out, and I'm getting out of the IRA too. I'll make some fuckin' excuse to them.'

'Meet me on Monday night.'

'It'll be the last meet, I couldn't go through that again,' he said as he closed the car door.

I headed home. What on earth was going on? Who were these people? The source was sure of the English accents. How was I going to play this? Would I ask overtly and let everyone know what had happened or would I do it covertly and hope for even a nod or a wink in the right direction. I chose the latter. I would have a long talk with the MIO. If he was unaware of the incident, then I knew he would wish to know who these men were with a greater degree of urgency than my own.

The next morning I spoke to the MIO. I told him of the events of the previous night. He listened intently.

'I know absolutely nothing. I know of no covert operation and if indeed it was the security forces involved, then you know without me saying, that I should have prior knowledge of any operation, covert or not, in my area. I will go now to army Headquarters in Lisburn and investigate.'

'I could play it another way,' I replied. 'I could go to Special Branch Headquarters and create a fuss. I'm about to lose a source of good potential. He'll not work for me anymore.'

'Give me a few hours to get on this, before you do anything, okay?'

I agreed to this and we arranged to meet in the late afternoon. I realised that in the present climate of death and destruction sweeping the Province, the British government and the intelligence services were pulling out all the stops in the quest to infiltrate the IRA, but there had to be some basic ground rules between the various agencies. I started to think about the event. How did the military patrol, whoever they were, know that the source was involved? Just who had access to my intelligence reports from the source?

That evening I met again with the MIO. He told me he had made exhaustive discreet enquiries, but had so far drawn a blank.

'So it was the SAS?' I said, smiling.

'I'm told not.'

'The MRF?'

'Denied, at present anyway.'

'Have you spoken to the colonel at Bessbrook?'

'I have. He is not a happy man.'

'Well I'm fairly happy that this was a military agency. I don't know whether to go to paper on this or not. If you can't find out, how on earth can I?'

'Leave it with me and I'll continue my enquiries, say nothing yet.'

I looked him in the eye. Did he know, and was playing for a bit of time, which is a good healer? I knew that some of those covert agencies kept little or no records, and would refuse to comment if it suited. They made their own laws as they went along in the name of national security. I agreed to leave it to the MIO.

On Monday night the source kept his appointment. I enquired as to his head wound.

'I needed five stitches, I told them I had fallen in the garden.'

He asked me about the men who had held him. I told him I was still working on it. He couldn't believe this. He reiterated his decision to leave the IRA.

'If I can get out, I will. It's fuckin' amazing you know nothing about them.'

I felt very small. I tried to persuade him to carry on as a source.

'No way, I'm through, I have had my fill. If something comes my way that might save a life I'll call you the usual way.'

He never did phone again, but I knew from intelligence reports that he did indeed sever his association with the IRA. I did see him at Sinn Féin rallies on Hill Street in Newry, and if he recognised me he didn't show it.

Chapter 25
Family Flee to London

I had been out Christmas shopping with my wife. We returned home and had a coffee, and at about 2 p.m., as I was about to leave for the office, the doorbell rang. Eileen looked out the peep-hole. I could hear her say, 'Can I help you?'

'We are friends from London,' came the reply.

I could hardly believe it. I opened the door and there stood Chief Inspector Hewson and a friend.

'Hello, George, how are you? Sorry to call unannounced, but we phoned all morning.'

'Yes, we were out shopping,' I replied, shaking his hand. 'Come in.'

Hewson introduced the detective sergeant with him and we went into the drawing room.

'George, we are going across the border to meet McMahon, and I thought I would call and see you.'

'How is he?' I enquired.

'He's fine, he's fine.'

Little did he know that I was seeing him regularly. Hewson looked at me and smiled. Did he know, I wondered? I offered them tea, which was refused, and after paying their respects to Eileen, they set off with me for the Special Branch office. Hewson had suggested he pay his respects to the local divisional commander, and the Special Branch chief inspector. An hour later we wished each other a Merry Xmas, and Hewson set off for the Republic. I wondered if McMahon had some important intelligence for London. He had told me the previous week that he had something for London, but I didn't realise Hewson was to come over to Ireland to collect it. Maybe he was bringing McMahon a Christmas present.

About 6.30 p.m., some hours after he left, Hewson arrived back in the police station. He asked me and the Special Branch chief inspector to accompany him to the divisional commander's office.

When we were all seated he said, 'I have high-grade intelligence to the effect that George here is going to be murdered by the IRA. This is imminent. The source, who is known to George, suggests that he and his family leave the house immediately.'

He turned to me. 'He said to tell you to cool it for a while, that he just got wind of the planned operation from a Dundalk ASU member last night. Somebody from South Down has fingered you.'

I sat back. I was speechless. I couldn't believe it. Hewson turned to the commander.

'I think he should get out today.'

'How the hell can I? I have a wife and family. It's bloody Christmas.'

'You'll have to consult your Special Branch ACC at Headquarters, but I think you'll have to get out. Good gracious, this is your life we're talking about!'

Phone calls were made to Headquarters and eventually it was decided that I and my family should leave for England early the next day. In the meantime a military detail had encamped at the front and rear of my house, organised by the divisional commander.

I went home and broke the news to my wife. She took the situation calmly. All she worried about was my safety and that of the children. We sat and calmly discussed the matter, knowing the military were guarding the house. We decided after a couple more telephone calls to stay over Christmas with a relative in London, until we could work things out. We told the children that they were going to spend Christmas in London. They seemed happy enough about it, probably too young to understand. Their Christmas presents, which had been purchased that very morning, were hurriedly packed into cases, together with as many clothes as we could manage. How many clothes can you pack for five people into three suitcases? Not many. How long were we going for? A week, a month, forever? I didn't realise then that I would purchase quite a few clothing items for myself and my family before I returned to Northern Ireland.

As we left the house hurriedly the next morning, Eileen exclaimed 'the turkey!' I went back inside and took the bird from the fridge where I had left it the previous day. I wrapped it up as best I could and put it in a carrier bag, all sixteen pounds of it. We were going to eat our turkey by hook or by crook. Eileen had already put all the contents of the fridge into the bin, and given all perishable food to a neighbour.

'I'm sorry, George,' she said, laughing, 'I knew you would bring it.'

That night we arrived in London. It was 23 December. We travelled to our relatives, and settled in as best we could. It was a bit of a crush, but being the festive season, nobody really noticed. I couldn't think. My brain was muddled. What on earth was happening?

Christmas spilled over into the New Year. I made no telephone calls, and received none, except those from family. This was not the way it had been planned, but no contact suited me for a week or two. I showed my children around London over this period. I had forgotten what it was like to have a long holiday. But, after a couple of weeks I started to feel annoyed that no one from my own department, or indeed HQ, had telephoned to see how I was coping living 'on the run' in London with my wife and family. We had been forced to buy clothes for the children. The owners of the bed and breakfast guest house we had moved into initially, after the New Year, were asking too many questions, so we had moved to another in Finchley. At the start of January, feeling bored, I requested to be allowed to attend one of the Home Office courses. This was quietly arranged. It was a residential course. After a couple of weeks, my wife and family were on the move again. I thought it best to keep them moving, but all this was costing money. I was using up my hard-earned savings. Living in London was expensive. Then, in the third week in January I received a call from the chief constable.

'Hello, George, how are you? I trust Eileen and the family are well.'

'Yes, thank you, sir.'

'I'm told you requested this course to put the time in.'

I was pleased to receive the call, but annoyed it had taken so long for anyone to contact me. I was just about to make my feelings known when the chief constable continued.

'Look, I've had a word with the Police Authority. They've agreed to give you £1 per day each for you and your wife, and 50p per day for each child. This type of thing is not catered for in the regulations.

They make the point that you would have to keep yourself in food etc., back home anyway. It's the best I can do. I've organised a cheque for £200 to be sent to you in advance.'

I felt stunned. I was in shock. It was on the tip of my tongue to shout about my expenses so far and that £200 wouldn't look at it. In fact, although I didn't know it then, this was all I was to receive. I thanked the chief constable for his kindness in phoning. I was devastated, and later that evening I phoned Eileen and told her that circumstances had changed. I explained the financial situation to her regarding the expenses, or lack of expenses.

'After all you've done, this is how you are treated. How could they do this to you? You risk your life every day. What about our savings?'

Eileen suggested that in the meantime she would return to her relatives. We couldn't afford any further hotel bills. In fact, after a further week, she opted to return to her mother in Belfast, with the children. I felt bad about allowing her to go back to the Province without me, but I was committed to finishing the course. I would be able to return home one or two weekends to see her before the course ended in mid-March. I tried to settle down and enjoy the course, but it was difficult, and I was more than glad when it finally ended and I returned home in the middle of March. It had been decided in my absence that I could remain in the same division, but move to another station twenty miles away. I had more or less refused to move house. I had been out too much money. I couldn't afford to move, and took pleasure in making this fact known. A couple of weeks later, my wife returned to our former house. She had decided that the children's welfare and education were a priority, and after the way we had been treated, she wasn't going to heed any other advice on safety. After a week, I myself returned to the house. I worried about my safety, and planned to examine my status and maybe move northwards to live.

I couldn't wait to see McMahon, and one of the first things I did was to make contact. A few days later we met in Drogheda. After a few minutes of conversation my heart sank. I couldn't believe my ears. McMahon explained that he had given no specific intelligence on a direct threat to me. It had been a general threat on some unknown detective in the Newry, South Down area. Hewson had tried to persuade him that it must be me. McMahon was completely unaware of the way Hewson had handled things, and had only known I had been sent to England some weeks later, when informed by Hewson.

On that visit Hewson had quizzed McMahon if he had been seeing me. He had of course denied it.

Looking back on the events, was there a plan to remove me from the scene? It was probably true, rather than possibly true. I had been warned to leave McMahon alone, and had paid the penalty. The sojourn in England had set us back over £3,000. I had to borrow money from family. My life had been routine but exciting before my enforced move, and I blamed myself for letting events overtake me like a dam bursting. I should have been more on my guard. If my removal from the scene had been planned, then the intelligence services must have known of my visits to McMahon. How? Had I been followed? I knew my phone was bugged. Was it from conversations with McMahon on the phone? I knew I would never learn the truth. It was at this time that I decided that I would no longer take chances unless absolutely necessary. I would curtail my visits to the Republic, and take events as they came. I had put my life on the line on many occasions, and had been shabbily treated by my authorities, both at local and Headquarters level. Others were prospering at my expense. I would take a different view on life and work. It was only the officers who received the congratulations and awards. The NCOS and operatives on the ground never received the recognition they surely deserved. Was I starting to think like a socialist? Surely not!

Chapter 26

Murder Trial and Sequel

Having regard to its geographical size, Northern Ireland suffered probably the most intense, vicious and bloody terrorist campaign in the world, and the government and indeed the entire population were totally unprepared. The lives of many, many people were to change forever, including my own. I had been trained as a policeman, to uphold and keep the law, but suddenly the police were thrust into the frontline of this so-called war being raged by Irish republicans to achieve their aims of a United Ireland. They called themselves the Irish Republican Army, but the legitimate government of that country also had an Irish Republican Army. The terrorist IRA did not recognise that legitimate army. To the outsider this must have all seemed rather strange. The police were ill-equipped and under-staffed to deal with the violence, and, since the cessation of the IRA campaign, we are now hearing many complaints in regard to unsolved murders. The police stand accused of not investigating the cases properly. I can't comment on every individual instance but I can, I hope, show the problems encountered by police detectives in the Seventies and in particular one episode in which I was involved.

In the past few years teams of detectives from a body called the Historical Review Team have been examining the files of unsolved murders. I have nothing against that—all murderers should be brought to justice—but these teams are able to go anywhere, and interview witnesses and others in peace and safety. This was not the case for detectives in the Seventies. Take, for example, the town of Newry where I served twice during that period. The detectives in Newry, which also covered Warrenpoint, Bessbrook, Crossmaglen, Forkhill, Rathfriland, Hilltown and other small towns, would have numbered about a dozen, seven crime ordinary and five crime special, which became CID and Special Branch respectively. We were badly understaffed. Murder was taking place on a daily basis. An investigation had only started when another murder occurred a couple of days later, and the next day after that another murder, or a couple of bombings. There were serious crimes sometimes being investigated by one detective. How could we cope with this day after day? Interviewing witnesses was nigh impossible. Many areas were no-go to the police. If they decided they eventually must visit a particular address, then they could only do so if the military first made the area safe, and then accompanied them in armoured vehicles. With regard to my input into investigations, when I obtained the names of individuals, I was in many instances prohibited from passing anything of a secret nature to CID and anyway, the terrorists had flown to Dundalk where the Irish government allowed them to claim that their activities were a 'political offence'. Extradition was not on the cards then. There was absolutely no help or assistance from the public, especially in Newry and South Armagh. Anyone seen talking to a policeman for whatever reason was immediately in big trouble, and could end up dead.

It was in this climate of fear that I became involved in a murder trial. I remember a night at the end of April 1972, during a sustained surge of terrorist activity, when I was called into Newry police station by the CID. On arrival I was told that the military had arrested three people in an ambush situation, and that when detectives started to interview them, one of them told them he would only talk to Special Branch, and that he needed to see someone as soon as possible. I visited the station and was introduced to him, and arranged to talk to him alone. I remember his first words when we were alone.

'I'm fucked. Jesus my life is fucked.'

He held his head in his hands. I got straight to the point.

'Why do you want to see me?'

'Because I want to cut my losses! I'm not a fuckin' idiot. I know what you guys want. The CID can't help me but I know you can.'

I asked him to explain himself, and was shocked when he replied, 'I worked for you guys when I was a "Stickie"' (Official IRA).

The realisation of what he had said intrigued me. This lad was from the area—was he working with one of my colleagues?

'No, the Branch man I helped doesn't work here anymore. He moved away a couple of years ago.'

He went on to name the officer. I knew him, he now worked in Belfast.

'Did he not want to hand you over to someone else when he moved?'

'I don't know. When I shifted to the Provos I kind of went on the run to Dundalk, but I don't think he tried to contact me. He could have sent me a letter like he did a couple of times before, but he didn't. I had only given him information a couple of times anyway and nothing but names.'

'How did you meet him?'

'He knew my father, and he got me off when I stole a bike.'

'Did your father know you were helping him?'

'No way.'

'Right,' I said, 'Why do you want me?'

'I'm going to give you the names of the unit which murdered the policeman at Bessbrook last night.'

'How do you know this?'

'Because I'm the fuckin' quartermaster,' he replied.

He went on to elaborate that he wasn't involved, but that he had learned of the plans when they wanted rifles for a hit.

'I'm going to give you the names of the three guys involved. I don't know if they are at home or gone to Dundalk.'

He gave me the three names and addresses, all in the Newry/South Armagh area, and I immediately gave the information to CID, who arranged to hit all these houses immediately. Unfortunately only one was at home; the other two had gone on the run to Dundalk.

I continued to talk to the informant. He described in depth how the weapons, I believe it was three rifles, were to be left in a hedge not far from the scene of the shooting an hour before the event. They were then to be returned to the same place, for collection at a later time. In answer to questions from me he gave me the names of everyone in the PIRA in his company area. He gave me an insight into the future threat, and targets that had been discussed. After an hour or so I handed him back to CID, but not before he enquired as to his future.

'What can you do for me?' he asked.

I told him that I wasn't in a position to promise, but that anyone who should know or needed to know would be told of his help. It was by now four or five in the morning, and after a talk with the CID sergeant I went home for a few hours' sleep. Around nine o'clock I was called back to the station. The prisoner had asked to speak to me again. I went to see him and he was very agitated.

'I know who has been lifted,' he said, 'and don't deny it, I saw him being taken along the corridor, and he fuckin' saw me too.'

'Didn't you finger him? What made you think he wouldn't be arrested quickly?'

'I know, I know, but it's just sinking in what I've done. They'll get me after my sentence, if they don't get my family first. I'm fucked.'

'Are you sure he saw you?'

'Yep, he'll fuckin' put two and two together.'

'What about the other two arrested with you, it could have been one of them,' I replied.

'Think again, I'm fuckin' quartermaster. Once the weapons are retrieved I'll smell like shit.'

'Does he know where the weapons are?'

'He does.'

'Do you think he'll come clean to the detectives?'

'Can't say, he's new to the game, I don't know what he's made of.'

He went on to express his worries that the detectives would put something to the prisoner which would point his way. I assured him I would talk to the detective in charge and endeavour to ensure this would not happen.

'I'll never admit to talking to you. I'm going to say that I was tortured.'

'That'll create problems for me.'

'Probably, but I fuckin' have to, this is why I called you in, to warn you.'

'At least you're honest about it.'

'It's my last small hope. It might save me in the long run. I don't know.'

'Everyone usually alleges torture anyway,' I replied.

'I know, there's boys running around Dundalk being treated as heroes who say they survived torture by the Brits. I know it's mostly shit. I don't see anybody being tortured here.'

'How did the soldiers treat you on arrest?'

'Oh, they were shouting and yelling, making us lie on the ground and they were pretty rough putting us in the Land Rover, but nothing too bad.'

I agreed I would keep an eye on his case, and handed him back to CID. The CID kept me informed of their interviews and I eventually received a call from the CID sergeant, whilst having my lunch.

'He'll not admit anything. It took me a while to even get him to speak, and a couple of times I thought he would tell us his story, but he lapsed into silence each time I got to the point.'

'You'll have to release him then?'

'Looks like it. I'm talking to him at Bessbrook, and I've about two hours of time left. You'll be wanting to speak to him before he's released. You'll have about an hour after we've finished. Why don't you come on out about two o'clock and come in with me during my last hour?'

I agreed, and eventually talked to him with the CID sergeant. After I was introduced to him, I decided to tell him my information on the murder. How it was planned. About the rifles in the hedge, and other points which I had prohibited CID from using to safeguard the informant. I asked him why he should take the rap for everyone else. That was about it. He looked at the floor continuously, silent. After five minutes I gave the CID sergeant a nod and we got up to leave the room. Just as we opened the door the prisoner spoke.

'If I tell you the truth, can you bring my mother to see me before I go to jail?'

We sat down again, and he made a full confession to the CID sergeant. He cried the whole time.

I was now involved in a murder enquiry. I had heard verbal statements from the accused. It was too late to exit and bring in another member of CID. I knew I would be exposed in open court at a future date, but it would be worth it to bring someone to justice for the murder of a policeman, one I knew and respected. The rifles were recovered after information from the prisoner given to CID.

At that time the murder of a policeman was a capital offence, with death by hanging the mandatory sentence. At the first trial at Armagh the jury failed to agree by eleven votes to one. The judge had demanded a unanimous verdict for capital murder. The re-trial was held at Belfast, in the spring of 1973 I believe. During cross-examination I was asked to what department of the RUC did I belong. When I replied it was Special Branch, I was asked why I hadn't declared this fact. I replied that I didn't know I had to, that I was a policeman and entitled to witness a statement. The judge then inferred that Special Branch didn't have to worry about their methods of interrogation as they didn't have to appear in court. Defence council then suggested that 'hoods and noises' had now entered the equation. The judge agreed, and dramatically cleared the court of everyone and asked me to remain in the witness box. He and I had a right old argument. He saying I should have declared my role, and me replying he shouldn't believe what he reads in certain newspapers, including *An Phoblacht*. He actually shouted that he was not allowing the statement of admission by the accused, and was dismissing the case. In essence he believed the accused's allegation that one SAS man told him he had done over fifty murders and was going to drop him over Carlingford Lough, and that other members of Special Branch had seen him during the previous night. This was all bunkum. I stated that I was the only Special Branch officer involved in the case, to no avail. It didn't take conviction by any judge and jury to tell me who was responsible for Sgt Morrow's murder. I knew who had committed the foul deed. It was only sad that the word of a terrorist was taken against those of two long-serving, respected police officers. It would never in my opinion have happened in London or indeed Dublin. It showed that IRA propaganda really worked, and down the years since, many IRA volunteers have received sums of money in settlement of claims for alleged brutality by Special Branch. Why did the government settle the claims? To refute them would have meant exposing half of Special Branch in court.

After the court case I remember sending a report to Headquarters stating that only when witnesses can appear in anonymity, or the jury system changes, could the government expect any success against the terrorists through the courts. I am informed that this case was a watershed, and the reason for the subsequent changes in the make-up of the courts for terrorist offences. It is a common belief that the outcome of this murder case sent a shock wave through the British government. There would have to be other ways of bringing the terrorist to justice. The courts would have to change. Juries were no longer an option.

This story has a sequel, as I was again to speak to the judge, outside the confines of the court, a couple of months later. Our contact with

Garda Special Branch was growing, and although it was still unofficially official, or the other way around, we were now meeting regularly to compare notes on terrorist activity in the border areas. On occasions we would meet under the guise of a social event. Where better to talk openly without fear of eavesdropping, mechanical or otherwise, than on a golf course? The Gardaí arranged a golf match between us, I brought three colleagues and we met at Dundalk Golf Club, and as co-operation was growing we each brought a senior uniform officer. We had an enjoyable game. It was confidence building and would do a lot of good for future relations. We adjourned to the clubhouse where our hosts had laid on a meal. We ate in an open area in the clubhouse bar, and our meal was over when I saw two men enter. They were quickly followed by another gentleman who acknowledged the senior Garda officer, who jumped to his feet to greet him, but it wasn't this I was watching. I had recognised the two other men. They were RUC drivers from the judge's escorts pool. I knew them both. I was still wondering what was going on when the senior Garda officer started to introduce this man to all around the table. I suddenly realised who it was, and when he shook my hand he looked at me and said, 'We have met before, have we?'

I smiled and replied, 'Yes we have, judge.'

'Where?'

'At a murder trial.'

I saw the penny drop and the change in his face, and as he moved away I continued, 'A certain innocent man is now unfortunately in jail. My good colleagues here arrested him in possession of a gun in the middle of Dundalk a couple of weeks back.'

There was no reply. The rest of the party looked on speechless. I received a very unfriendly look from my own senior officer. The whole episode had happened very quickly. I was shocked to see two RUC drivers in Dundalk at that time. It was the height of the campaign. On our return journey home it was decided no mention of what happened would be made. The matter was now closed.

I was to remember the night of the arrest for another reason. One of those arrested at that time did indeed try to cover himself for helping me. I was also to receive a letter from the Secretary to the European Commission of Human Rights that I was required as a witness in one of the cases they had decided to proceed with at the Court of the Council of Europe, Strasbourg. In relation to allegations under Article 3 at the European Convention on Human Rights I would be required to appear on dates at the end of June 1975, at a locality unknown. I was to be informed of travel arrangements shortly before I was required. I eventually travelled by plane with many other members of the security forces to a secret destination, the venue of the court. Most of the security at the venue was carried out by military personnel. I remember that well with amusement. The colonel in charge would socialise with us in the bar at night. He was continuously telling 'Paddy the Irishman' jokes, which made the Irish out as stupid idiots. I didn't mind but an officer in our party asked me if I could tell the colonel an anti-British Army joke to make them look thick. I told of the colonel in the desert who was requested to go and talk to the sheik in regard to certain hostilities. He was told to appear alone with his batman/driver.

'Now, Sergeant, when we arrive we must observe their customs and etiquette. You will do nothing, or say nothing, unless I give you a nod of the head.'

The sergeant agreed and they duly arrived at the sheik's tent. They were shown in and saw him sitting on cushions. He beckoned them to sit on cushions opposite him. They duly obliged. He clapped his hands and a servant arrived with three coffees, which were handed out. No word was spoken. The sheik poured his coffee into his saucer and added milk. The colonel nodded at the sergeant and they poured their coffee into their saucers. The sheik put two sugars in the saucer and proceeded to stir it with his little finger. The colonel nodded at the sergeant and they both stirred the coffee with their little fingers.'

I stopped speaking and the officer said, 'Is that it?'

'Oh, no,' I replied. 'The sheik bent down and put the saucer in front of the cats.'

The bar erupted in laughter. There were no more Paddy jokes.

We hung around, unable, unallowed, to leave the premises. We were virtual prisoners, but always on stand-by to be called instantly into the courtroom. Some cases were lasting an hour, some a lot more. Eventually I was called into the court. I was shown along a tunnel of curtains which led right into the witness box. I could see a row of judges in their finest livery, they were right beside me. They could see me and the whole well of the court. I could only see them. I heard some submissions being made and was then examined by the Crown counsel. I denied all accusations of any ill-treatment, and told that the person concerned had been more than helpful voluntarily, and had helped us in our actions against terrorism. When my examination finished, there was an awkward silence while some of the judges conversed. Then the nearest one to me asked, 'Why would this man make up these stories of ill-treatment?'

I thought quickly and decided on a course of action which I had sort of pre-planned.

'Because he has to. He is under orders from his superiors in the IRA.'

I put my hand in my pocket and produced a document stamped 'Secret'. It was a one-page order entitled 'What to do when arrested' and issued by the Army Council of the IRA. It stipulated about ten actions a volunteer must take when arrested. The first was to give your name and date of birth and refuse to answer any questions. One of the orders near the top of the list was 'you must allege serious ill-treatment after each interview', or words to that effect. I handed this towards the nearest judge, unseen by the court. It was passed slowly along the line of judges. It eventually made its way back to the first judge. I held out my hand and he surprisingly handed it back to me. I drew my finger under the word 'Secret'. The judge nodded. I felt relieved. If he had chosen to hold the document I would have been in big, big trouble. I was not to hear anything further about the case.

Chapter 27
Port Laoise Jail

In the fight to infiltrate and defeat any terrorist organisation, including the IRA, the forces of law and order must have good intelligence. This intelligence is gained in many ways, and even with the ever-increasing emphasis on eavesdropping techniques, nothing beats the verbal sort from a good apprentice positioned well within the organisation, as eavesdropping sometimes requires expert analysis and grading. These sources have, of course, what is commonly known as a shelf life. Some young volunteers recruited to work for Special Branch, have, if only because of their inexperience and impetuosity, a short shelf life. They are probably good for only one good catch. Then they are arrested, or may not be used again for some time, although on a future date, they may be very valuable by being in the right place at the right time. Some sources in the outer periphery, not in the organisation, but close enough to a member to see and hear, and then deduce what is going to happen, can prove invaluable. These non-members—casual contacts as they are called—are sometimes in a position to provide vital information with safety, and without being involved in the danger of an IRA headcount. Some sources become aware of one piece of good intelligence accidentally, in their everyday life. They may tell a friend, who tells a friend, who tells a uniform policeman. He then passes it to Special Branch. I never put a low grade on such intelligence, but passed it into the pipeline as unable to assess accuracy. This grading ensured the information was taken seriously up to the point where it was proved inaccurate. One or two good Special Branch operations were to obtain IRA sources at Brigade level. This may sound great, but really, at the end of the day, these people did not know a lot going on outside their area, and any continued security force success could spell doom to themselves. Great care had, and has, to be taken at what to act on, or otherwise. The intelligence had to be handled like fine china.

The best sources of intelligence on the activities of the IRA were the unseen godfathers of terrorism, who, on the surface, had no rank or direct involvement. Their names were known to Special Branch, but they never appeared on the current list of the Army Council. These mostly elderly old IRA organised, trained and recruited. They took no glory nor showed any emotion; they kept open lines of communication, filled urgent vacancies caused by arrests, provided safe houses and swore members in on oath. They were recognised by all in the movement as having substantive rank. Nobody questioned them. The new young eagles looked up to them. These were the men on whom Cahill, McKee, Twoomey, O'Connell etc., were very dependent. They were the pillars of the movement. If these godfathers fell, the movement fell.

McMahon could be classed in this category, although he openly acted as a training officer. Many of the Army Council visited him, and he could call a couple of them very good friends. He was therefore completely trusted, especially as he resided well into the Republic, far from any suspicion of being recruited by the British. Even so, McMahon's knowledge on PIRA operations was at times limited. He may be asked to organise a training camp for a specific mission and, having done so, see the members leave after their training exercise, without knowing the target. He couldn't ask; it wasn't the done thing, so really he had to wait his chance. Even then, being McMahon, he would think hard about the consequences of passing the information to Special Branch.

There were times when good intelligence came from the most unlikely sources, such as from within a jail. I was to receive a telephone call from D/Sgt Harry Garvin of the Garda Special Branch early one morning. It was a strange call but I was happy to carry out my friend's wishes. I was to pack an overnight bag and meet him at Slane, Co. Meath, where my car would be garaged. I was then to accompany him on a mission. I felt excited, the adrenalin was pumping as I pulled up in Slane.

Garvin greeted me. 'How are you, George, it's nice of you to come, I'll explain all in the car.'

I drove into the garage as directed, and gave my keys, as requested by Garvin, to a lady who closed up the garage and waved us off.

'She's family,' laughed Garvin. 'I can tell you're not happy.'

'Not at leaving my keys, I'm not,' I replied.

'It's only for emergencies, I can assure you,' said Garvin. 'No one will touch the car.'

We hadn't gone far when I said, 'Right, Harry, you can put me in the picture.'

Garvin laughed and explained to me that we were going to Port Laoise.

'I want you to do something for me in the North, I'll explain to you later, and in return I'm going on a mission now which may repay you in another fashion, and anyway it's time we had a long chat again.'

This all sounded Dutch to me.

'What are we going to Port Laoise for?' I enquired.

'Intelligence on a dump,' answered Garvin.

'In the North?' I asked.

'Probably, although I'm not sure,' said Garvin. 'All I know at the moment is that I must be in Port Laoise tonight. The window of opportunity may close after that.'

I didn't really understand so far what was going on, but I had complete trust in Garvin and settled down for the journey. As we drove along, Garvin tried to explain to me why we were heading for Port Laoise. A PIRA source of his had been unfortunate to be found in possession of a weapon, and was in custody awaiting trial with another member. He had, during his remand, gained valuable intelligence which he wanted to pass to Garvin at first hand. He had been at his wit's end. He could have openly asked the prison authorities to contact Garvin, but such action was fraught with danger. He might have picked the wrong prison officer, and his treachery may have been exposed to all and sundry, and anyway he needed to talk to Garvin to do a deal, before he parted with the information. In the end, he alleged to the prison authorities that he had been tortured in Garda custody and requested a member of the force to visit him when he would formally make his allegation. When the Garda officer arrived, he had an envelope squeezed into his hand addressed to D/Sgt Garvin, Special Branch, and the allegation was withdrawn. Luckily the officer knew of Garvin, and the envelope, unopened, was in Garvin's hands within hours.

'He wants me to arrange a covert meeting in the prison, can you fucking imagine it?' said Garvin, and before I could reply, he continued, 'And it had to be tonight.'

I said nothing for a while.

'How can you do it?' I eventually asked. 'Will the prison authorities cooperate?'

'I'm taking no chances,' said Garvin. 'I have a half plan worked out with a senior prison officer.'

We arrived in Port Laoise in the late afternoon. It was a cool brisk day. We had two hours to pass, so we ate in a small restaurant and then adjourned to a pub on the main street. Garvin bought me a hot whiskey, and we sat and chatted for a while. Suddenly Garvin stood up and went over to an unknown man who had entered. They shook hands and spoke for a couple of minutes. Garvin returned to me carrying a case.

'Can you wait here until I return?' he said.

With that he was gone. I ordered another whiskey and waited, and waited. About an hour and a half later, Garvin returned. He stood in front of me and opened his overcoat. He was resplendent in a prison warder's uniform.

'I've joined up,' he laughed. 'Would you look at the trousers.'

I laughed when I saw the trousers were a good three or four inches too short.

'I'll be back in half an hour,' he said.

He returned a short time later and sat down. I waited for his story.

'I have a good friend in the prison staff who was able to organise a quick meeting with the informant without raising any suspicion, although I only had five minutes with him. He wants a deal on the sentence, and more importantly, wants some cash posted through a certain letter-box in your area immediately, like tomorrow.'

'You bloody knew this,' I said.

'Not really, but I know where his wife is staying in County Armagh,' replied Garvin. He continued, 'He has given me the location of a large explosives dump, but it's not in the North as I thought, but here in the Republic.'

When he had mentioned the North it was in connection with his wife.

'The whole thing will have to be handled with kid gloves. I'll have to put the find down to some other source, and give the credit away. There are a lot of reasons why this has to be.'

'How much urgency is there?' I enquired.

'I have only a couple of days to organise the find of the explosives, and I've promised him the envelope will be delivered before the stuff is recovered, and this note enclosed.'

He showed me a note from the prisoner. It ended . . . 'Use it, say nothing to anyone.' The word 'anyone' was heavily underlined. It was signed with a nickname.

'How many pounds of explosives are in the dump?' I enquired.

'He says it'll take a lorry to shift it.'

I whistled. Garvin drove a short distance to a hotel where he had booked us in for the night.

'We'll have a good dinner and discuss your part tomorrow,' he laughed. 'And we'll return via Tullamore and I'll show you round the distillery, and buy you a bottle of Dew. Have you ever been to the distillery?' he enquired.

'No, I haven't, and if you expect me to deliver an envelope in a door letter-box in County Armagh, then I'll expect two bottles,' I replied.

We had a leisurely late dinner before retiring for the night. We discussed many things and really got to know each other. In fact, a lot of intelligence was shared. We left early next morning for Tullamore and the distillery and eventually back to where my car was garaged. A couple of hours later I was on my way home with a thick envelope to post in a door in South Armagh. I did this the next morning at 2 a.m., and quickly made my way home. It had been an eventful couple of days. My admiration for the Garda Special Branch had grown once more.

Chapter 28
Catholic Peace Association

The historic town of Newry in County Down was always mainly nationalist, and the people showed their anger at internment. For a couple of years, Newry was practically a no-go area for uniform police. They required military escort. There were protest meetings practically every day or night. The aim of the Provos was to bring life to a standstill, a shut-down of normality. Crowds would appear out of nowhere. The Provisionals had a system of instant meetings in the town centre. All the large stores and businesses would receive an early morning telephone call with the order to shut down. Initially the staff in the shops were happy. They had the day off, and woe betide any employer who made any reduction in their take-home pay. A similar situation existed in all the nationalist/republican towns in the south of the Province. However, the owners and managers of businesses and large stores soon became disillusioned with the whole situation and their huge loss of revenue, as people drove to Warrenpoint or Banbridge to shop, and things slowly returned to normal. This disillusionment was partly due to the tone and frequency of requests to close down. The morning of a close-down, and parade or meeting, businesses would receive nasty calls to close down immediately, and after a while they rebelled and refused. The names used in the telephone calls would be those of leading republicans. At the same time as this disruption campaign was taking place, the Provos were carrying out an indiscriminate bombing campaign. The public at large were hard-pressed and inwardly hoping for peace and quiet, but not prepared to admit this publicly. They needed a lifeline, and one morning they were handed one, to the anger of the Provisionals, and to the delight of the British government.

The military in South Down/South Armagh, had been hard-pressed since internment, especially in the Newry area. These disruptions days, which led to the Rent and Rates Strike, were giving them headaches, and it wasn't long before those in the Military Dirty Tricks Department spotted the potential to hurt the Civil Rights Association and the Provisional movement. I just happened to be in a military establishment one evening as the plan was being hatched, and was able to watch, first hand, the drama unfold. Firstly they talked of how they would telephone the large stores and businesses on good prospective trading days, like a Friday or Saturday, and order them to close, in the name of a leading civil rights activist, or Provisional. It was realised that the Provisionals depended on the premises closing on telephone instructions. They couldn't very well expose themselves, going round personally ordering people. So, when these added calls from the security forces entered the equation, it caused confusion, and started a feeling of extreme annoyance towards the PIRA and CRA. These were good businesses. Newry had been a thriving market town, and the money they had been losing to Banbridge and other neighbouring towns was colossal.

After a couple of weeks of these disruptive tactics, it was decided to give the townspeople a lifeline, and one that would involve the Church. In recent years, in fact since the Peace People, the word 'peace' has been used in daily talk in Ulster. In fact, the word has been hijacked by the Provisionals of all people. But, when the history of the Troubles is eventually written, this will be seen as the first time the word had been used to political advantage. This was before the Peace People in Belfast. I was present at a meeting when it was decided to form a new Peace Organisation, with a link to the Catholic Church. It would be called the CPA (Catholic Peace Association), and in a few days, this would hit the Province like a bombshell.

In the early hours of the morning, on the day the new association was made public, a pamphlet containing a short statement was posted in the letter-boxes of hundreds of houses in Newry town. The wording was to the effect that the good townspeople of Newry had decided to form a Peace Association, and that they were fed up with violence. Different signatures appeared on the letters, but they had one thing in common. They were leading figures in the Provisionals and civil rights movement. The headline read 'Catholic Peace Association'. Telephone calls were made to all the news agencies, who carried the story throughout the day. That night, the *Belfast Telegraph* carried the headline 'Catholic Peace Association formed in Newry'. The British government was happy. This was fantastic news. This was a ray of light. The intelligence agencies were inundated with calls about this new movement. Were the republican areas about to waver towards a peaceful solution? A helicopter arrived in Newry, with senior officials, to gather news on this Peace Association for the government. The new association was to be given help to establish themselves.

The Provisional IRA were mystified and angry. They ran round Newry all day questioning and investigating this new peace movement. This had to be nipped in the bud. I watched events unfold all day in amusement. I had first-hand knowledge of the whole scam. I moved around the town a couple of times during the day. It was the whole topic of conversation. I learned later that the government was not informed that it was a military trick until later that evening. My friends in Military Intelligence and myself hadn't realised or hadn't anticipated the reaction that occurred.

The Catholic Peace Association had only a one-day life, but I had no doubt that it had put a brake on the deferential attitude of the people of Newry towards the PIRA. Things were never the same again. Businesses were never asked to close again. It was a watershed. I wondered how many other tricks were being played that I had no knowledge of.

Chapter 29

Charlie Haughey and the Bugging Devices

The triangle of association between myself/Provo/Garda continued over a long period of time and I developed a good friendship with Garvin and McMahon, up until the late Seventies. We became good friends. I brought Garvin to Knock Headquarters, then Garvin brought me to Dublin. McMahon persuaded or dared me to attend the Provo Bodenstown Commemoration Ceremony in Kildare and I couldn't resist this challenge. I discussed this with Garvin, who was amused to say the least. He was already going on duty, so in fact all three of us attended the ceremony. McMahon wore his black beret and waved at me. I worried throughout that a hand would appear on my shoulder. I travelled back to Dundalk with Garvin, who had been taking photographs, as had many others there. If I had chanced a camera, it wouldn't have looked out of place. Commemorations in Ulster were different in that the Provos expected the Special Branch bogeymen to be covertly watching. In Kildare they were relaxed. I laughed when I thought of uniform Gardaí applauding Roman Catholic Provos who were speaking in commemoration of my Protestant ancestors. It felt unreal.

At times I would feel sorry for Garvin when he told me stories of the manipulation of the Garda Síochána by their political masters. He blamed senior officers who were only worried about their promotion. In Éire, the commissioner in Dublin lacked the operational independence of the chief constable of the RUC. He, and indeed all the Gardaí, had to clear anything at all radical with the Justice Minister and his officials. They held many of the aces in the promotion stakes. Garvin said it made him sick. It also made him sick the way quite a few guards had a tolerant attitude towards the IRA. Many were openly critical of Special Branch operations in the Republic. Garvin told me many times he had to watch colleagues as well as the IRA. With the Official IRA pulling the hand-brake on violence in 1973, and the emergence of the IRSP/INLA in late 1974, our task actually became easier. In the Newry, South Down/South Armagh area, historically Official IRA members just became inactive. Few, if any, moved to the new Séamus Costello organisation. Garvin told me that his seniors, under orders from their political masters, were pulling out all the stops to infiltrate this new IRSP/INLA with a sense of urgency absent in their actions against the Provisionals. Maybe it was the inherent fear of a socialist republic. Maybe they envisaged the Provo fight would end with the removal of the border and British troops, whilst the other crowd would continue towards a communist type regime for the whole country. Garvin had no time for some of his senior officers. When the Dowra Affair strained RUC/Garda relations for several years after, with no real contact between the forces, Garvin took Jack Hermon's side.

'Only God could work with our head of Special Branch,' he would say unashamedly.

He told me on several occasions that he was ashamed of their lack of effectiveness against PIRA, their lack of even basic equipment, and most importantly, their lack of will and dedication in tackling PIRA. The lads on the ground were given no direction. There was no policy thread which ran from Donegal to Cork. Each area was different. The policies of any one police area were more or less guided by the local politicians. I could understand, as the RUC were in the same boat until 1970. McMahon laughed one evening as Garvin and I discussed police methods.

'When we take over you'll both be redundant,' he said.

We all laughed.

As the Provo cell system made it very hard for an informant to be good for more than one piece of good intelligence, and informants themselves would only know of what they themselves were involved in, mechanical intelligence-gathering came more and more into the picture. But even mechanical gathering has to have a starting point, and that brings me to the informant. Surveillance teams needed to know where to go. What houses to target. What vehicles to follow. Bugging devices were more and more easily obtainable from the mid-Seventies onwards, and they were readily on sale from commercial outlets. MI5/MI6 were not the only experts in the game. I was able to loan bugs and other devices to Garvin, who used them to devastating effect against the Provos in his area in the South who were unsuspecting to say the least. Garvin had never seen or handled a bug until I brought down a simple 13-amp plug adaptor, which worked off a little FM radio. Garvin fitted the adaptor in his living room and sat outside in his car listening to his wife talking to someone on the phone. He was really excited. This was better than any Christmas toy. I left the device with him for a couple of months. Later he confessed that although he had used it to good effect, he had used it one day too often in his own office. He would not elaborate on what he had heard, but said, 'Although I needed to know what I heard, I sometimes wish to Jesus I hadn't.'

The people in surveillance unit E4, which came under the Special Branch umbrella, weren't used in South Down/South Armagh during their initial few years. It was too dangerous an area. They were used mainly in Belfast and Greater Belfast, and Mid-Ulster areas, and in parts of Londonderry. The SAS were the people used in South Armagh.

The bug that I had loaned to Garvin was never to be used again in the war against terrorism, and indeed may have found its way to the IRA, or to some household who didn't even realise that the adaptor had a dual use. It was stolen. I had been to meet Garvin in Ardee. After a chat and a coffee, I had set off towards home. I had the little radio lying on the back seat. The adaptor bug was in a plastic bag with a pair of gloves, and a box of golf balls, a gift from Garvin. It was rarely that I stopped in Dundalk, but I had remembered that it was my wedding anniversary the next day. It was late afternoon, so I pulled in and parked to look for a florist. I was away from the car about twenty minutes, and when I returned there were three or four people standing at my car. The rear passenger window was smashed. I immediately saw that the radio and the plastic bag were gone, as was my coat, which had been lying on the back seat. A woman had seen the youth run off.

'He had a hammer,' she said.

A patrolling guard appeared. 'What have you lost?' he enquired.

'Just a good coat,' I replied.

He pulled out his notebook.

I said, 'It's okay, I'm not worried about the coat. I'm heading north, forget about it.'

I thought the policeman looked relieved. How could I have given details of what had been stolen, and of course, my car was wearing false plates. I was glad to set off home.

About a month later in mid-1974 I had been invited to Scotland Yard by Hewson. I received the customary tour of London and was wined and dined royally. During our conversations we talked of bugging devices, and Hewson insisted on taking me to a business premises where they specialised in this equipment; apparently the owner was happy to loan him devices on occasions. I thought of Garvin. He would love to see the stuff obtainable here. Hewson introduced me to the owner, who took great delight in showing me the world's most up-to-date listening devices. There were devices in the form of pens, badges, belt buckles and many other everyday objects. I remember drooling over some of them.

'Believe it or not, my best customers are private detectives working on matrimonial cases, although in the months leading up to various large company takeovers, they are bought by these detectives to bug boardrooms and other key places. Why don't you get your crowd to buy some?'

I laughed at this. 'Don't MI5 and MI6 buy any?' I enquired.

He laughed. 'They have their own technical department, but they come in here and steal my ideas.' He turned to my English friend. 'These guys borrow equipment but they never bloody return it.'

As we were leaving he handed me a box. 'There are three devices there, one for a phone with a little tape, a three-point plug adaptor, and a fountain pen. You can tune your portable or car radio into the frequency, it's marked on the box. They have a range of about 75 metres. Here's my card. If you keep them send me a hundred quid, or return them after you use them for a job.'

I thanked him and left. In the weeks that followed, I used these devices with some success, and was considering keeping them and forwarding a cheque to London. After a conversation with a uniform superintendent I loaned him the adaptor for use in the station snooker room. After a week of listening to the conversations from the comfort of his own office, there were one or two transfers!

On my next visit to Garvin in Dublin, I brought the devices with me. He had put the previous devices to good use, and I took great delight in showing him the new kit. After he practised using them he requested the loan of them. I agreed of course. About three weeks later we had a meeting regarding explosives 'escaping' from the Navan mines. He told me things were being tightened up. There was to be a stronger Garda presence and systems were being devised to account for every stick of explosive used or not used, as was the case. I mentioned the listening devices. He was apologetic.

'I took them up to Dublin and showed them to a friend in Special Branch Headquarters, and about a week later I had a call from a senior officer in Special Branch. He asked if I still had them, and could I bring them up to him in Dublin. I explained I only had them on loan, but did not say where they came from, but anyway, I agreed, and brought them to him. He still has them, but I'll phone him and get them back.'

I told him I was in no hurry and not to worry. During the next couple of meetings we had, the devices weren't mentioned, and then one morning Harry phoned. We met at Dunleer. After we ordered coffee he became quite serious.

'Look, I've just had a row with Dublin on the phone. I asked for the return of the equipment, but the senior officer told me he can't concur and that he'll explain when he sees me again. I'm bloody mad.'

I told him not to worry.

'I'll pay for them, do you know what they cost?'

'Not an awful lot,' I replied. 'Actually I sent the cheque to London last week. Even if I had them in my possession I would not have had the brass neck to return them after so long a period on loan. You can consider them a gift from me.'

Harry thanked me, and that was that.

At subsequent meetings, there was no mention of the devices, and a year must have passed when, at one of our meetings, in Navan town as I recollect, Harry suddenly brought up the subject. He told me that he had pressurised his senior officer so much that he asked him to visit him at Headquarters in Dublin. There, he was told that they had been passed to a politician who had requested bugging devices and he was refusing to return them. Garvin was sworn to secrecy and told to claim expenses towards their cost.

'He's feathering his nest. Senior promotions in the Gardaí are political. Then the officer asked me from where I had obtained the equipment, and on the spur of the moment I told him they had come from a friend in London. It was left at that.'

I told Harry not to worry, that as previously promised the equipment was now his.

'I know,' he replied. 'But I would just love to know the identity of the politician.'

About a fortnight later Harry phoned. He sounded excited. 'Can we meet at Glasgow?'

This was our code for Ardee. I remember the day well, as I had been caught in a line of traffic being filtered through a Garda VCP on the bridge entering Dundalk, and who was standing with a colleague having a discreet peep at all the drivers, but one of my Dundalk Special Branch contacts. He looked at me as my driver's licence was checked by a uniform guard. He raised his eyebrows quizzically. I gave a shake of the head and moved on into town. When I met him again I would say I was visiting a Provo source. He knew nothing of my other Garda sources. It had to be that way. I parked on the main street in Ardee. Harry was already there. He got into my car. We passed pleasantries and he got down to his reason for calling me.

'I was up at the Castle in Dublin yesterday to see the boss. I had done a job for him, a friend of a friend of his was being summoned for a driving offence, and I had the uniform lads withdraw the case. He was in a benevolent mood, so there and then I asked about the devices. We were alone behind closed doors. He stared at me. "Harry," he said, "we have known each other for twenty-five years, you are the one man I have total trust in, so I'll tell you. No other living soul knows of this." He paused. "I have known Charlie Haughey well for many years and when he asked me about bugging devices I couldn't refuse him. When I met him at a Fianna Fáil function a couple of weeks ago, we had a couple of minutes together alone and I asked him about the equipment I had loaned him and he said to me, 'I trust you will never talk of these things to anyone ever.' I assured him I would keep his trust. Haughey finished the conversation with, 'These gadgets have changed the course of Irish political history and taught me a lesson—that in life, things are never as they seem. In politics, one must have a Machiavellian personality, it is crucial to know your friends.'"

'I wasn't really surprised to learn about Haughey,' Garvin continued. 'He had been on my shortlist of three, and on the spur of the moment I said to the boss, "Well next time you talk to Charlie privately, you can tell him that it was devices on loan from the RUC Special Branch that changed the course of Irish political history."

'He was taken aback. "You told me they were from London," he replied.

'I laughed at him. "Same thing," I said.'

I listened to all Garvin had to say.

'I wonder what politicians he eavesdropped on,' I replied.

Garvin gave a hearty laugh. 'I'm sure there were a brave few, because he's the sort of person you either love or hate.'

The subject was never raised again at our subsequent meetings.

Chapter 30
Visit to Chief Constable

It became obvious to me from 1972 onwards that there were an ever-increasing number of intelligence agencies at work in the Province. One of these new agencies, the MRF (Military Reconnaissance Force, a forerunner of the Force Research Unit), called on occasion at the office to see the Special Branch chief inspector, looking for work. That is, to be fed intelligence on known PIRA addresses in South Down/South Armagh, which they could observe. They were usually in a couple of unmarked cars, and only the officer in charge would enter the police station, so it was impossible to get to know many of them. I did get to know one of them, on a long day which I won't forget in a hurry. It was one of those days.

At about 8 a.m. the phone rang at home. It was my chief inspector.

'Morning, George, how would you like a game of golf?' he enquired.

'What's the catch?' I replied.

'Would you play a game of golf with someone, at Royal County Down?'

I looked out the window, the weather looked fine.

'With whom, and why Newcastle?' I asked.

'It's an officer from MRF who has a day off, I promised him someone would play with him. He has this wish to play Royal County Down.'

'Why can't he go on his own?' I asked.

'He's not allowed, one of our department must be with him as player or caddy.'

I agreed to be at the golf club at 10 a.m. After a quick breakfast I travelled to Newcastle and met the officer in the club car park, as arranged. He was late twenties, tall, short hair, clean cut, with the usual tailored suit, check shirt, yellow tie and brogue shoes. We shook hands and walked to the changing room. I changed beside the officer, who introduced himself as Tom. I couldn't fail to notice the transfer of weapons from Tom's holdall to the golf bag. There were at least two large pistols. I had come unarmed and thought to myself how heavy his golf bag would be.

At the first tee, Tom asked dryly, 'What's your handicap then, mine's ten?'

'Thirteen,' I replied.

'Level match then?' he asked, not a smile.

I was taking a dislike to this man.

'Level for £10, and if you give me two shots, it'll be £20.

'Level for £10,' he replied.

I tried to make conversation over the first few holes, and sometimes all I got were nods, so I gave up trying. This was a real dour character. Was it just his will to win the match, I wondered to myself?

'I'll not speak again until spoken to,' I decided.

And in no time it seemed we were on the 18th tee. I was one up, having won the previous hole. I drove first, into the short rough on the right, not too bad. Tom followed me. I quickly found my ball, and saw my opponent's ball a few yards away, partly covered by a tuft of grass. I saw Tom walk past it a couple of times, but said nothing to him. Eventually he elected to return to the tee and play another ball. When he left, I lifted his ball and put it in my pocket. Tom hit a good drive and finished with a six. I was bunkered, but sank an 18-foot putt to halve the hole. I had won the game. Tom opened his wallet on the green and paid the £10 wager.

'Thanks for the game,' he said, striding off.

I was amused. My thoughts of buying lunch were ended when the steward approached us in the changing room.

'Are you George Clarke?' he enquired.

'I am indeed,' I replied.

'You're to phone home as soon as possible.'

I thanked him, excused myself to Tom and headed for the call-box.

'Hello, dear, what's up?' I asked my wife.

She sounded distressed. 'You're to go and see the chief constable immediately.'

I made her repeat herself. 'He phoned at ten o'clock this morning. He had called your office and they told him you had the morning off. He thought you were at home.'

My mind was racing. What on earth was I wanted for at Headquarters?

'Right, dear, I'll head for Belfast now, I'll be in touch.'

I headed back to the locker room to tell Tom I couldn't buy him lunch or even coffee, that I had to go to Headquarters. I needn't have worried, he was gone. I was astonished. I gave the steward a £1 note and headed for Belfast. When I arrived at Headquarters in Belfast, it was three o'clock. I hadn't eaten, but headed for the chief constable's office. I introduced myself to a chief inspector staff officer, who jumped to his feet.

'Come on, he's waiting for you.'

He showed me in.

'How are you, George?' said the chief, waving me to a chair.

He was on a phone call, which ended a few minutes later.

'Did you enjoy your game?' he laughed. 'I can't take a morning off to play.'

'Well, sir, it was really a working morning. He was an officer from MRF.'

'Oh, did you hear anything?' he laughed loudly.

'Yes, sir, how to win at the last hole,' I laughed, and told him the story about the ball. He had a good laugh at this. He then turned serious. 'These will help you in your quest,' he said, handing me some papers.

'An elderly close relative is going to the States and she requires her birth certificate. She has never had one, in her memory, and she was born down in your area. I could arrange things with a phone call, but I want it played anonymously, for various reasons, apart from security. I immediately thought of you.'

'No problem, sir, I'll take Eileen with me, when do you need it?'

'This is the problem, I need it tomorrow,' he replied.

'Right, sir, I'll get weaving in the morning at 9 a.m., I could have it up here to you by lunchtime hopefully.'

'Brilliant,' he said, standing up.

'I'll see you tomorrow then.'

As I left the outer office the staff officer was on the phone.

'Hold on,' he said, and offered me the phone.

'George, it's me,' said my wife. 'Your friend has been on from across the border.'

'Which one?'

'Seán.'

It was my up-to-date code for McMahon.

'Is it urgent?'

'He said it was fairly urgent.'

'Right, dear, I'll be home for tea, hopefully.'

I set down the phone. I would have to meet McMahon that night, but I had a limited window of time. I couldn't go to Drogheda in the morning. I would be going to Headquarters to the chief constable with the document. I called at the office en route home and phoned the contact number for McMahon to be used in emergencies. He wanted me to come to the house, and although I hated the prospect, I agreed. I always worried like hell at such visits. I always thought the worst, that is, McMahon had decided to remove me from the picture. After all, I was the only one who could shop his treachery to the movement. A worse worry was that PIRA had caught up with McMahon and were forcing him to make the telephone call to lure me to the Republic. I knew I would worry, and worry, until I came home. Was it all worth it?

I arrived at McMahon's house about 9 p.m., and he met me at the door.

'Where's the car?' he asked.

'Along the road a bit,' I replied.

I entered the house, and there stood Garvin. He laughed.

'I bloody knew you'd be here,' I said.

'Pal thought I should come, he was lucky to get me in,' replied Garvin.

We sat down.

'Would either of you like tea or a drink?'

We decided we wouldn't. I turned to McMahon. 'What's up?'

'They've got a Belfast man at Hackballscross or Culloville,' he replied.

'What do you mean?' I asked.

'A Belfast Provo has been brought to South Armagh for interrogation and Court Marshall. God help him, he can only be found guilty by those bastards.'

'Any names or anything?'

'No, two of the South Armagh lads were down for training on Sunday. They told me they had heard just what I've told you.'

'Anyone missing from Belfast?' enquired McMahon.

'I've heard nothing,' I replied. 'I'll enquire when I return home.'

Garvin interrupted. 'Now tell him what you've just told me.'

McMahon carried on. 'McGuinness was down this way from Derry with a couple of boyos on Sunday. He's in bad form. He thinks Special Branch are having too much success, especially in Belfast. The active leadership are being destroyed by constant Special Branch success. He thinks the campaign has been stopped in its tracks, there has to be a re-think, a re-group.'

Garvin interrupted again. 'No matter what McGuinness says, the shooting of RUC/army has to be intensified, according to a source of one of my lads at Navan. A Belfast Brigade officer is married to a cousin of his tout who has been on the run for over a year. The young bloods in Belfast want to take over, and he also says the lads in Long Kesh are controlling things a lot, outside, from inside the jail. Billy McKee and company are powerless. They are the past. Adams, Hughes and Keenan are the present.'

I asked Garvin if he was putting any of the intelligence into his own pipeline.

'I am, but you can use it as you wish,' he replied.

Garvin gave me a couple of names of Belfast men who had appeared in lodgings at Bailieborough. He suspected they were on-the-run Provos.

McMahon again warned me of the danger of Dundalk. 'The lads are paranoid about Branch men being seen in Dundalk.'

'Aye, you tell me this after you bring me down,' I laughed.

'Do you want me to lead you up through Dundalk?' asked Garvin.

'No, no, I'm okay,' I replied.

'Do you want some Armalite ammo?' asked McMahon.

'You mean to hand in?'

'No, for yourself, don't you keep one under the bed?' he laughed.

'Sometimes I wish I had one,' I replied.

'Do you want one now? I can get you one in twenty minutes.'

'No thanks,' I replied, laughing.

'By the way,' said McMahon. 'Those two South Armagh lads I told you about who were down on Sunday, one of them was stinking with explosive mix, whatever they were doing before they came to me. I would say you'll have a big bomb somewhere in South Armagh very soon. I heard them talk of being in Whitecross and Markethill recently. I would keep the military away from those areas.'

I listened and replied, 'I'll pass it on, that's all I can do, the military do their own thing regardless. Sometimes I think they want action. A tour of duty without incident is not good for officers' mess conversations.'

Garvin laughed. 'I hear these mess dinners are the real thing, silver service and all. Do you get invited?'

'Sometimes,' I replied. 'It's usually the chief inspector who attends, he can withstand the brain-picking and bullshit.'

McMahon went to the back room and came back with a large mineral bottle filled with a clear liquid. 'Pour that into their cocktail bowl the next time and stand back and watch the craic.'

'What is it?' I asked.

Garvin laughed. 'It's the real stuff I'll bet, real poteen, I'll bet it's 200 per cent proof.'

I accepted the bottle, my brain already planning tricks. We talked on for another half hour and my hand was sore writing. I had enough for half a dozen reports. It was 10.30 p.m. I stood up and made arrangements to phone Garvin about the two men in Bailieborough.

McMahon said, 'What about us all having dinner in Dundalk some evening?'

We all laughed. That would be the day. We shook hands. I left first. I kept imagining car lights behind me were following me, and I was relieved when they drove past. I wondered who the Provos were holding in South Armagh. When I returned to base I briefed my chief inspector, and the divisional commander on those matters affecting his division. When I completed my reports, it was after 1 a.m. I headed home for tea and bed. It had been a long day—to Newcastle, to Belfast, to Newry, to Dundalk, to County Meath. I thought of the next day, and my errand for the chief constable. I set the clock for 7 a.m. and wished my heart rate would slow down.

Chapter 31

The Night I Joined the Clergy

Rumour and gossip, two fine words indeed, and two words which occur daily in the life of a Special Branch officer, and in the early Seventies I can assure you that these words were used a great deal. Let's start with Southern Irish accents and Irish vehicle registration plates. As far as the loyalist population were concerned, any person up from Dublin or Cork to visit relatives was in the IRA. The uniform lads would come to the office and tell you, 'Joe Bloggs must be involved, a car with Southern registration plates has been parked at the house regularly,' they would report.

A friendly postman would tell you of delivering letters which were posted from Dublin to a particular house regularly. Once a news item reports that it is believed arms are being brought in on fishing trawlers, then every trawler must be bringing them. If a known republican family visit the cemetery every Sunday, they must be hiding weapons in the grave. Stories abound. Stories they will tell you that come from 'the horse's mouth' and stories they would 'stake their life on'. Ninety-nine per cent of this gossip and rumour is ill-founded. The unfortunate thing is that it has to be graded F6 and investigated in some manner. This is why the grading of intelligence is so important. The grading determines the level of security force reaction to the information. If intelligence was received that six rifles were hidden under a five ton load of herrings on the way to Belfast from Kilkeel (I use the word intelligence, but it may be just rumour or gossip), and if that intelligence is not gradable or of a low grade, it would take a brave officer to order the load to be dumped somewhere to carry out a search! I always favoured downgrading intelligence slightly on the submission form. If the desk officer at Special Branch Headquarters had other collaborative intelligence from elsewhere, then he could upgrade it, and the reaction to it, accordingly.

I remember a piece of gossip that did prove to be true. It was in the summer of 1972. A lorry driver who hauled freight between Belfast and Dublin, and who lived in Newry, gave some information to a friend in the police reserve who passed it to me, and it concerned suspicious goings-on at a small town between Dundalk and Dublin. At that time all lorries were inspected by customs both North and South, and large convoys used to build up at the Irish customs clearance post situated on the Newry Road out of Dundalk. It took the drivers some time with paperwork, and they used to chat in groups and have tea. The Newry driver was some yards from a group of Southern Irish drivers who were having a banter, and overheard what he thought might be useful information. I was now in receipt of that gossip and had to decide what action to take. As the information concerned the Republic I had to decide if it was worth passing on to the Gardaí. I decided it was, and arranged a meeting with the Special Branch at County Louth. When I phoned, the guard suggested it was time again for a bit of a get-together.

'Bring a colleague with you, and I'll do the same, we'll have a meal and a few jars.'

'Where do you suggest?'

'Oh, leave that to me,' he replied.

A few days later I headed south with a colleague and we met up with our Garda friends John and Tony in the car park of the Fairways Hotel on the Dublin Road out of Dundalk, and followed them in convoy to our destination, a roadhouse which was about a fifteen-minute drive away. We entered the premises and headed for the bar, where the owner/manager exchanged greetings with the guards. It appeared he was expecting them. A drink was ordered, and we were handed some pub grub menus. I looked around the bar. There were a couple of dozen customers at tables eating and drinking. The decor was modern, the lighting subdued and I could imagine it being a cosy place when the fire was lit. After a few minutes we were shown to a corner table, and we ordered our food. With the background music and the buzz of conversation, we were able to talk freely without much risk of being heard. We talked about our problems on either side of the border. We spoke of explosive mix and nitrates. The guards told us they had found a large amount of fertiliser in an old trailer near the harbour in Dundalk.

'We couldn't find an owner, so we seized it. If it was genuine some farmer or company would have claimed it. No one did. It was without doubt to be used for explosives.'

I then told them of my information from the lorry driver. I explained it might be nothing, and may have been innocent chat misconstrued. I explained about the lorry drivers chatting in groups. One of these groups of three or four men were discussing who would reach some destination in Drogheda town first. The informant then heard this discussion.

'Don't include so and so in this, he's doing his "Collon" detour.'

'You're a bloody idiot.'

'I have to, but I've told them it's my last job.'

'If you're caught you're fucked.'

'You know who they are, don't you?'

'It's the fuckin' Provos you idiot, the fuckers with the hoods.'

'Apparently the group broke up at this and only two men were left talking,' I told them. 'The source didn't hear much after that, except the two men would see each other again at the weekend. That's more or less it, I know it all seems rather vague but you may make something out of it.'

'Actually Collon has figured in a couple of reports recently,' Tony said. 'One of them concerns an OTR Provo from Belfast who has been noted calling at a farm there. We'll have to have a closer look at Collon.'

At that moment our food arrived and we had an enjoyable meal. We talked of everything from politics to sport. I realised those two young men were intelligent, up-to-date and a credit to their force. During a meal where the craic is good and you are enjoying yourself you don't really see or hear much outside your own company. I was conscious of people entering and leaving the premises and of staff moving between tables, but that was more or less it. But it appeared that our Garda friends were more observant. John leaned over to me, and spoke in a low voice.

'Bandits at two o'clock, your time.'

I waited until a waiter passed our table and glanced at the point mentioned. There were four men, all in darkish clothes sitting at a table near the door. As I looked, a fifth man arrived and sat down, he must have been at the toilet.

'Who are they?' I enquired.

'I interviewed the two younger lads. They were part of the Sinn Féin guard of honour at the last Edentubber parade and commemoration, black beret, dark glasses and all. They said they were only in Sinn Féin. The other three are strangers.'

'How long have they been in?'

'About twenty minutes, I didn't want to spoil your meal.'

'Have you been recognised?'

'Yep, one of the young guys I interviewed lifted his hand and gave me a sort of half wave when they arrived.'

'Do you think they're all Provos?'

'No doubt at all, I only wish I knew the other three, do you know any of them?'

'No, do you think we should leave?' I asked.

'I don't think so, we'll play it out for a while.'

At that the manager arrived at the table, and handed John the bill. He studied it for a while, and handed it to me. I started to reach in my pocket for money, when I saw a message across the bill.

'The guys at the door are asking who your two friends are.'

Before I could speak John got up and went to the counter where the manager stood. I watched him pay the bill and exchange some banter with the man. Both were laughing. He returned to the table after a couple of minutes.

'You've just joined the clergy,' he said, laughing.

'I've what?' I replied.

'I've told Mícheál the manager to tell them he has found out that you are a priest, a relative of mine down from Belfast.'

'Shit, do you think that's wise?' I asked.

'I'm not sure, but it'll give them something to ponder on.'

Half an hour passed and we continued our chat. It was by now ten o'clock and the meals being over, the place was filling with drinkers. Tony had the best view of the men's table; he was in direct line of sight, and only had to move his eyes.

'They've just been served two more pints of Guinness. In fact, it appears only two are drinking alcohol. I see an orange, a Coke and a tea or coffee on the table,' he said.

'This would be a good time for us to go,' I ventured.

'It would,' replied John. 'I'll be the only one to make eye contact as we pass their table.'

We got up from the table, and as we passed the bar counter John shouted a thank you to the manager Mícheál. We passed the men and headed out the door. Tony must have turned around, as the next I heard was, 'Fuck, they're coming out behind us.'

I gripped my pistol in my pocket, but as I looked towards the car park there was the welcome sight of a Garda patrol car sitting with the engine running. The five men saw it also, and turned and re-entered the pub. John started to laugh.

'Did you see their faces?' he asked.

'Do you think they were going to confront us?' I enquired.

'I was taking no chances,' he replied. 'When I paid the bill I whispered to Mícheál the manager to phone Dundalk and tell them I wanted the patrol car in the car park from ten o'clock, to wait there for me.'

He went over to the police car and spoke to the crew. As we headed out of the car park, the patrol car remained. Thankfully, we had an uneventful journey home, and when I discussed events of the evening with John a couple of weeks later I learned that he had had a rather pleasant outcome. It transpired that when he spoke to the two uniform guards the next day he discovered that when the five men eventually left the premises, one of the guards recognised one of them. This man had been giving him information on crime in the Dundalk area for over a year, but he was unaware of his Provisional IRA connection. When he learned of this, he promptly handed him over to Special Branch.

'He has agreed to help me, apparently he had only recently joined the Sinn Féin Cumann. I'll let you know how things work out in due course,' said John happily.

The only worry for me now, of course, was that my face was now known to five people with SF/IRA connections. Five too many, I thought. I would have to be more than careful from now on. Regarding the information the lorry driver heard about Collon, the Garda Special Branch had success at a later date with the seizure of explosives in that area.

Chapter 32
Ice Skating

It was December 1971. Things had been really hectic since internment. I had by now cultivated three Garda sources. One of these, the one I had first met before internment, phoned me one evening about six o'clock wanting to see me urgently. We arranged to meet at location F, our code for the Fairways Hotel car park, on the Dublin Road out of Dundalk. It was cold but otherwise a clear moonlit night. I can remember it was a Friday and the traffic on the Newry to Dundalk Road was particularly heavy. When I reached my destination my friend was already there. He got into my car and we exchanged pleasantries.

'Look, after I phoned you I had an urgent contact from a Provo source. I have to meet him in Dunleer. It suits that we use your car.'

'Fine with me,' I replied, but wondered that he would bring me to one of his IRA sources. I needn't have worried, as when we eventually arrived in Dunleer he told me to pull into a space on the main street.

'Wait here,' he said, and jumped out of the vehicle.

I waited a fair time, probably more than twenty minutes, before he returned.

'Jesus, it's freezing,' he laughed.

I replied that the road gritter had passed a few minutes earlier. We set off northwards again towards Dundalk. He then directed me off the main road, and ten minutes later, after many left and right turns, we arrived at the Roadhouse Pub.

'You'll be okay in here,' he said.

I parked up and he led the way into a fairly busy pub. It was a Friday. He found a table towards the rear. I scanned the sea of faces, but recognised none. I felt a bit happier. He went to the bar and returned with two lagers.

'Things are looking bad up your end.'

'You ain't kiddin',' I replied.

'I was up at a meeting in Dublin yesterday, and a general question was fired at us from the boss. He wanted to know if any of us were talking to RUC Special Branch. There was silence, but we all denied it. Have you said anything up at Knock?'

'No, I haven't, I put the intelligence into the pipeline as from a casual contact or from another registered source,' I replied.

He was pensive for a moment. 'Look, George, no matter how smart we think we are, one of these days things will blow and either you or myself will be found out. I think we should each go to our IRA Desk Officers and register each other. What do you think?'

'I've been thinking along those lines myself, I think we should do that,' I replied.

Little did he know that I had already taken the steps just two days earlier, in respect of another Garda source who was providing Council level intelligence. I wasn't putting pen to paper, but would drive to Belfast and report to ACC Special Branch verbally.

'The reason I arranged this meet was to give you a piece of intelligence I obtained yesterday. It seems the Provos are in possession of a fair number of US Army rifles, called Armalites. Some of their Belfast Brigade are over in the States negotiating their purchase. This is a fantastic weapon. A semi-automatic, and if they have sufficient numbers they will be capable of causing havoc in the North.'

'How are they getting them in?' I enquired.

'In cargo ships on the Atlantic routes.'

'I had a report from a source some months ago who reported boxes of rifles coming into Drogheda Port, but he thought they were Kalashnikovs,' I replied.

'Yeah, I heard that. I think this is a different batch.'

'Another piece I have for you is that Joe Cahill and Séamus Twoomey have been seen regularly in Dublin this past few weeks. Cahill is handing out cash to OTR volunteers at Kevin Street. My source is an old age pensioner who provides Cahill with overnight accommodation on occasions. It seems he never goes to bed, but sleeps in a chair at the fire. Any time he has called with him he has taken a bus the twenty-mile trip to Dublin in the morning. Cahill trusts him implicitly. He talks little, but did say that he wouldn't be going North for a while. The source was involved many years ago and knows him since the Forties or Fifties. He has been giving us bits and pieces for a long time.'

I laughed. 'Ever since he was caught for drink driving!'

He laughed. 'I don't know actually, he was given to me to handle by a retiring member.'

'Do you think Cahill is in charge of finance now?'

'Well, that's how it would seem,' he replied.

He leaned over the table to me suddenly and whispered, 'Go to the gents toilet now, and then head for the car. The exit is along the same corridor. I'll join you outside.'

I got up and went to the toilet as instructed and then headed out the door to the car. A couple of minutes later he jumped into the car. 'Go, go, go.'

I headed out of the car park. The roads were white with frost. My friend kept watching in the mirror as we left.

'It's okay,' he said. 'There was a guy at the bar when we came in. I knew him and he knew me, but he left shortly afterwards and I was happy enough. Then fifteen minutes later he returned with a stranger. I caught them looking at us. No point in taking chances. The guy I know was seen talking to Seán Mac Stíofáin in Navan. You never know, do you?'

I agreed, but at that point I was more concerned at the state of the road. It was like a skating rink. I crawled at 5 mph. We were lucky to make the main Drogheda to Dundalk Road without meeting any oncoming traffic. Surely the main road would be salted. To my horror it wasn't. Traffic was crawling. We reached Castlebellingham, where the road snakes through the village in an S shape. I was travelling slower than walking pace. Suddenly an articulated lorry met me on the first section of the bend. He started to slide towards me. I shouted, 'Oh shit,' as he met me full on. He carried me back the way I had come for a good twenty yards. I could see a car approaching my rear. I pulled hard left on my steering wheel, spun on the road, and was facing the wrong way. The lorry somehow slithered past me, his rear end pushing me half into the ditch. The lorry travelled another fifty yards before he got stopped, narrowly missing the car which was coming behind me. We got out of the car. It was a miracle no one was hurt. The lorry driver came back to see us, and helped us pull the rear of the car from the ditch. Luckily it was front wheel drive. The car was undamaged except for a dent on the door and some scrapes. I couldn't believe our luck. The driver of the lorry started talking about giving me his insurance details. I stopped him.

'Look, I'm happy enough to forget this, if you agree.'

He was quite happy at this and we shook hands. We crawled to the Fairways Hotel car park, where I could have downed a large brandy, but decided against it. My friend was worried.

'Are you sure about driving home?' he enquired.

I told him I would take it easy. We said our goodbyes and I set off northwards. Fifteen minutes later I crossed the border, and was glad to see the roads had been gritted. I didn't mention my mishap to my wife. When she saw the scrapes a few days later I told her it must have been done in a car park.

Chapter 33
Brush with Royalty

In the early Seventies, 1974 to be precise, I was moved temporarily to a Special Branch office in a County Down town. There was a military presence at the police station for guard duties, and local patrolling with and without the police. The unit at the station was DERR, Duke of Edinburgh's Royal Regiment, and although their duties and patrols in the area would be more or less controlled by their local 10 and the MIO who dealt directly with Special Branch, the officer in charge always liked to pay courtesy calls to the Special Branch office, to see if they could assist them in any way.

I was sitting in the office one evening catching up on some paperwork, shortly after my arrival on temporary secondment, when there was a knock on the door. I shouted, 'Come in.'

The door opened and a young officer entered. He held out his hand and announced that he was Lieutenant David Bowes-Lyon in charge of the troop detachment at the station. I introduced myself and asked him to have a seat. We passed pleasantries and discussed the local threat and the general situation in the area. He seemed a pleasant, courteous and intelligent young man in his late twenties. He stayed for half an hour discussing the current threat, and when he got up to go I said, 'The only Bowes-Lyon family I have heard of is the Queen Mother's, Glamis Castle and all that.'

He smiled as he opened the door. 'Same family,' he replied.

I told him to call at the office any time he wished.

'I probably will,' he replied, 'the military accommodation is cramped to say the least.'

David called to see me at the office a few times after that. We spoke about the royal family one evening. He was quite open and didn't mind me asking questions.

'Cousin Charlie is a good lad, he speaks his mind, he's okay. I'll probably see him next weekend, I have a couple of days off,' he informed me.

'Will he be a good king?' I laughed.

'He certainly will,' he said.

A few weeks later David called at the office. 'Would you fancy taking me out of this place for a drink and a meal?'

'Would you be allowed to go?' I replied.

'You're the only one who will know,' he smiled.

'When?' I enquired.

'I could go tomorrow evening,' he said.

I thought for a moment. I realised I had someone to see the next evening near Kilkeel. I explained the situation to him.

'You mean a source, an IRA source?' he questioned.

I laughed and didn't answer. He went on. 'Now that is what I would like to do.'

'What?' I queried.

'To go see an IRA man with you.'

I laughed. 'No can do, if anything happened to you, I would end up in the Tower of London.'

He became serious. 'Come on, I'll not say a word to anyone.'

I thought for a moment. I had to meet the source in a car park in Kilkeel, and there were a couple of nice hotels nearby. I could leave David in the hotel bar, go see the source and have a meal afterwards.

'Okay,' I replied. 'Be at the office here tomorrow evening at six.'

I wondered if I was wise, as David bore a strong resemblance to the royal family. The next evening I drove David to Kilkeel and left him at the bar of the hotel nearest the car park. I went and saw the source. The meet only lasted ten minutes and concerned PIRA movement in Castlewellan, which was David's patrol area, by coincidence.

'Where are you headed now?' enquired the source.

Stupidly I replied, 'Belfast.'

I headed back to the hotel bar. David was talking to the owner. I whispered that I should introduce him.

'What name would you like?'

He laughed, 'My own!'

I did as he asked and saw the owner look at him quizzically, and as he told me later, he could see the family resemblance. We had a couple of drinks and as we passed the entrance hall I saw the source enter the bar. As we passed him he whispered, 'I thought you were going to Belfast.'

On the spur of the moment I turned to David.

'This is Seán, a friend of mine.'

David held out his hand, 'Pleased to meet you, Seán,' he said.

I explained we were eating in the dining room and we left him. We had a nice meal during which David talked of the County Down coast, Newcastle, Annalong, Kilkeel and the fishing industry. He seemed to love the area. After a pint of beer we headed back to base. When we arrived back at the police station he thanked me for the night out.

'Well, I'm glad you enjoyed it, you got your two wishes.'

'Two wishes?' he said.

'Yes,' I replied. 'You got your evening out and you met your IRA man.'

He looked at me blankly.

'You remember me introducing you to a Seán in the hallway as we went in to dinner, well that was him. You will never know who he was, and he will never know who you were.'

He smiled and shook his head in disbelief as he left the car. A couple of weeks later he returned the compliment and invited my wife and I out to dinner, and we had a lovely evening. David left the area soon afterwards. Before he left he gave me two telephone numbers. One in the north of England and the other on the south coast, but I never used them. I have only seen David once since then, when he appeared on TV sitting in a horse-drawn carriage with HM the Queen when she attended Royal Ascot races. My wife really liked him. She thought he was the nicest, most down-to-earth army officer she had met, and believe me she had met many.